FINAL ACTS
of LOVE

FINAL ACTS
of LOVE

Families, Friends, and
Assisted Dying

Stephen Jamison, Ph.D.

A JEREMY P. TARCHER/PUTNAM BOOK
published by G. P. PUTNAM'S SONS *New York*

A Jeremy P. Tarcher/Putnam Book
Published by G. P. Putnam's Sons
Publishers Since 1838
200 Madison Avenue
New York, NY 10016

http://www.putnam.com/putnam

Most Tarcher/Putnam books are available at special quantity discounts for bulk
purchases for sales promotions, premiums, fund-raising, and educational needs.
Special books or book excerpts also can be created to fit specific needs.
For details, write or telephone Special Markets, The Putnam Publishing Group,
200 Madison Avenue, New York, NY 10016; (212) 951-8891.

First Trade Paperback Edition 1996

Library of Congress Cataloging-in-Publication Data

Jamison, Stephen
    Final acts of love: families, friends, and assisted dying /
Stephen Jamison
        p.   cm.
      Includes bibliographical references and index.
      ISBN 0-87477-849-2
      1. Assisted suicide.   2. Terminal care—Moral and ethical aspects.
    3. Right to die.   I. Title.
    R726.J36   1996   95-11174 CIP
    179'.7—dc20

Book design by Lee Fukui
Cover design by Lee Fukui
Front cover photo © by Tessa Codrington / Tony Stone Worldwide

Printed in the United States of America
10 9 8 7 6 5 4 3 2 1

To

RYLAND AND IDA

ACKNOWLEDGMENTS

This book could not have been written without the support of a community of friends. I'd like to express my personal gratitude to Nancy Hills, Angelika Lizius, Mary Jamison, and Kelley Test for their love and support, and my children, Joshua and Sarah, for their patience and understanding. I'd also like to thank Derek Humphry and Sally Shute for their friendship and assistance throughout this project; John Oliver and Meredith MacArdle of the Voluntary Euthanasia Society for their help in London; my editor, Alan Rinzler, and my publisher, Jeremy Tarcher, for their vision in clearly seeing what was needed; and Ram Dass for telling me to "just be there, don't judge." In particular, I'd like to thank the many partners, family members, and friends of the dying, whose names can't be disclosed, but who agreed that there was a story that needed to be told. I hope that I've told your stories well, and have done you justice.

CONTENTS

INTRODUCTION

Final Acts is the product of my own journey over the past twenty years. It began with training in humanistic and social psychology and led me to work in family counseling, research consulting, and then to teach death and dying at the University of California. At the time, death and dying was not my primary interest. Personal experience, however, quickly interceded, and eventually impelled me to work directly with the terminally ill, their families, and others around end-of-life issues, conscious living and dying, and the topic of assisted death.

In the early 1980s, my academic approach to the topic was permanently altered as I watched my sister Patty gradually lose her fight against progressive multiple sclerosis. Over the years I'd seen my parents, well into their seventies, take my thirty-one-year-old sister into their home and then, over time, bring her to surgeons, holistic practitioners, and Mexican "cancer" clinics in an attempt to reverse the process of her illness. None of these efforts altered her own path. Patty finally died at age forty, after a nine-year struggle that—like a mean-spirited and brutally long game of strip poker—first took away her ambitions for a new career, then her ability to parent her teenage children actively, her sight, muscle control, and finally, two years before her death, all means of communication except for an almost imperceptible and, at times, questionable squeeze of the hand.

On my visits home, I watched as my father moved her in and out of her bed, wheelchair, or chaise longue on the front porch, as he and my mother took turns feeding her, placing a tray across the arms of her wheelchair, like the highchair at which I'd only recently fed my own two children. For me, the most telling moment came during my last visit, when I climbed onto my sister's bed, held her, and prayed; I was hopeful for a miracle, either for a cure or a way to break through the silent wall that had separated us for two years. After a period of quiet, I opened my eyes to see her still shaking from the illness, her head turned, staring into emptiness. As I realized the irreversibility of her fate, I cried and once more held her close. I told her for the first time in my life that I loved her. When I looked at her next, I saw that she too was crying; we had broken through the silence. Within a few seconds, however, I felt a sense of horror: If she could understand my words, she also knew that she was trapped in a body that could no longer laugh or play, but could only express itself through these rare tears.

A few months earlier, after finishing a lecture at the university on end-of-life decisions, a student had brought me an article about the formation of a new membership organization—the Hemlock Society—which would work for the right to die, for the right of terminally ill to receive physician aid-in-dying. I had shaken my head and smiled, thinking to myself that the world is full of such a strange cast of characters.

Now at my sister's bedside, I understood. I wondered if, given the chance, she too might prefer an assisted death, and if I'd be able to help if she could somehow ask. Later I was overcome with guilt for harboring the thought and for ignoring, for a moment, the depth of my parents' love for her, the gift caregiving had brought them, and what her death at that time would've done to them. However, even now I feel her pain and I wonder; I've never found the answer.

I never saw Patty again in life. Before my next visit, she was hospitalized, first by a leg broken from brittleness and then by pneumonia, from which she finally died. And I continued to teach courses in death and dying.

Less than two years later, my father and I met for the last time, and he told me his plans for stopping his medication, for "choosing" congestive heart failure instead of lingering any longer from emphysema and other failings while waiting for an inevitable rupture of his aorta. He said, "Your mother doesn't understand that I'm going to die. I've talked to your aunt about it, but your mom doesn't want to hear me talk about it. She won't believe me until I'm dead." He then smiled and added, "I guess I'm just going to have to prove it to her." He knew that he was failing, and over the previous months had done all he could to complete the business of living. He had sold the house, established a living trust for my mother, and paid bills in advance. A week after my visit he stopped taking the diuretics that had kept his lungs clear of fluid. Four days later he died, but not before an early morning 911 call and heroic efforts by my nephew, Patty's son, to keep his grandfather alive. In looking back, I've felt privileged to know my father's deliberate plans to end his treatment, but also saddened that he couldn't talk about them with others, that the family couldn't have been prepared. And I've also wondered what more might have been gained by discussing it, by facing the inevitablity of his death, together.

I continued teaching, but after yet more deaths in the family— one of them medically "managed" by withholding life-sustaining treatment—I finally left the academic environment to work directly with the dying. Perhaps in some way I needed to expiate the sins of geographic distance that had kept me from my sister during her final days. After a year facilitating community workshops and groups on issues of living and dying, I was introduced to local Hemlock Society representatives who first asked me to lecture to their members about grief, and then coaxed me to run support groups for the terminally ill. I naively agreed.

In these groups, I listened as members discussed quality of life, the inevitability of death, medical treatments and experiences, plans and aborted plans for the future, and their joys and regrets. They also talked about their families, dogs, vacations, careers, and now-dead friends. But the topic always turned back to their imminent deaths, and the group became a safety valve where they could discuss their concerns. Each week there would be other stories, other friends who had died or were physically and mentally unable to take matters into their own hands. These stories inspired comments like "I'll never wait that long," or "I'll end it while I can still think clearly." Members would talk about getting their "kits" together and also about their sadness and fear. The topic would then always shift to the dilemma of preparing for death while still enjoying life. All were concerned about knowing if and when the time would ever be right to end their lives and, if so, how they would do it, whom they would involve, whom they would warn.

Within two years, all of the original group were dead, most by natural causes, but others aided in their dying by family and friends who saw their own involvement as final acts of love. According to family and friends with whom I talked, some of these deaths were positive. Others were less so. Without informing family or friends, one group member died alone; his death was covered up by his mother who found his body but then discarded his note. Before these events, however, I had begun to hear the details of other deaths, and to feel that the desire to end suffering needed to be balanced with thoughtful reflection and dialogue. These were often missing.

I had come full circle. My earlier thoughts on my sister's bed, my secret conversations with my father, these came back to me. But now my long-term interest in death and dying focused almost entirely on issues involving assisted death. This developed even further throughout the next year.

Early that year, a support-group member with AIDS confessed that he had helped his partner die some years before and said he still bore the emotional scars. He talked of his anger toward his partner for not taking responsibility for his own death, and how this man finally pleaded with him to "do something." After providing his partner with several sleeping pills, this member explained how he then smothered him with a pillow. I began to hear similar stories from other members, deaths in which they'd participated or of which they were aware. Some stories were positive but, like this man's, others were not.

Also in January, I walked into a San Francisco church and heard Derek Humphry, founder of the Hemlock Society, talk about the right-to-die movement. Ron Adkins, the widowed husband of Janet Adkins, then spoke about his wife's death—assisted by Dr. Jack Kevorkian. Adkins described his wife's battle against Alzheimer's, and her decision to be the first person to use Kevorkian's "suicide machine," a device that he connected to her via an intravenous line, which, at the press of a button by Janet, began the flow of lethal drugs that stopped her heart. Adkins, who was not present at his wife's death, described how she died in the back of Kevorkian's Volkswagen van, which was parked in a campsite outside Detroit. After the speech, I asked Adkins, as diplomatically as I could, whether this could have been carried out in some other way. He turned to me and said, "There were no other options. Kevorkian didn't put Janet in the back of that van; society did!" Maybe. But I still felt sickened. There had to be a better way.

At the next support group, members discussed the presentations by Humphrey and Adkins the week before. Kevorkian had become a heroic figure. But I had misgivings. I felt that this pathologist, who'd spent his years working with tissues and corpses instead of caring for the needs of living patients, was not the best choice to spearhead a movement for cautious, compassionate change. One member said he hoped that he too could be helped by a Kevorkian, that he'd willingly travel to Michigan if this was necessary to achieve a peaceful death. The others agreed. Although a few members looked uneasy, I was a vocal minority of one.

By spring, at the request of Gary,* a former member and by then a friend, I agreed to be present at his death to provide emotional support to his family. Suffering intolerably, and advised by his doctor that he had but days to live, Gary alerted us of his plans and checked himself out of the hospital. That evening he took a potentially lethal dosage of drugs. Only an hour later, his father pulled a plastic bag from his jacket pocket and explained to those of us present that he needed to keep the promise that he'd made to his son. Stunned by this turn of events, I argued that he was acting too soon. He disagreed, and without further word placed the bag over Gary's head and asphyxiated him. I understood Gary's decision to die but found his father's actions premature and disturbing. As it turned out, none of us was prepared emotionally for what unfolded, and I became convinced that a different process was needed.

---

*Not his real name. I have changed the names and identifying characteristics of many when stories are told in this book, to protect their privacy and that of their family and friends.

By summer I had gone to work as the regional director for the Hemlock Society, opened a San Francisco office in preparation for the 1992 California campaign for the Death With Dignity initiative, and was taking hotline calls at the office and in my home. I began to hear stories from other survivors.

One was Gary's father, who called to say that he wasn't doing well, that his son's death and his role in it "had taken its toll." Others spoke of having similar difficulties, and a few questioned their actions. And even those with positive experiences often felt a need to share their stories.

By the end of 1991, Derek Humphrey's how-to-die manual, *Final Exit,* was at the top of bestseller lists, and Derek and I traveled to churches, bookstores, and retirement communities to speak about the topic of assisted death. I was stunned by the size of these audiences, which sometimes numbered in the hundreds. Most were elderly, and seemingly in good health. Others were obviously suffering from the ravages of AIDS and other illnesses. All seemed concerned about their limited options for dying. Many had seen their own family members suffer unnecessarily slow and agonizing deaths; they wanted another way. They wanted to be prepared, "just in case."

Listening to these experiences, hearing reasons for wanting to die or for helping, I became increasingly troubled and torn, and felt that these decisions desperately needed more guidance.

The more I learned, the more I needed to know, so I began a three-year research project throughout North America and Europe, seeking interviews with survivors. *Final Acts of Love* is the product of this effort, of calls, meetings, and conversations with hundreds of individuals, and in-depth interviews with 160 participants in some 140 assisted deaths. They came from all walks of life and included husbands and wives and unmarried partners, mothers and fathers, sons and daughters, and siblings and friends. Some were married for more than fifty years, others were but acquaintances for days.

Some of these individuals, some of whom I came to know quite well, violated laws, yet told me their stories in the hope that by so doing they could help others. This book is the result.

. . .

Final Acts of Love is not a recipe book about how to end your life or help another die. It does not advocate or promote the practice of assisted dying. On the contrary, it provides patients, their families, and physicians with the tools to work together to manage the dying process both as a physical imperative and as an end to relationships. It is grounded in the belief that that there should be no room for mistakes in matters of life and death, and that the decision to die is about more than just the freedom of choice; none of us live in a social or emotional vacuum. All of us touch and are touched by others, and our deaths, like our lives, have effects that reach beyond us. These need to be considered.

In this way, *Final Acts of Love* looks at the soul of the decision to die. I hope that it will teach the dying to explore their inner values and all end-of-life options, take responsibility for their own deaths, and include others in their decision—both in actuality and in effect. In this, it shows how the process of deciding to die can become a means to resolve relationships with those we love *and* with ourselves. It similarly aids families and friends in following their own paths. The process of deciding to help—deciding to assist another to die—can also become a way to resolve relationships, address issues around death, dying, obligation, and loss, and balance our own needs against those of one we will soon lose. Finally, I hope this book will guide physicians in untangling the request for aid-in-dying, and show how it can be utilized to identify the treatment needs of a patient and to improve the physician-patient relationship.

Final Acts of Love is also a book about managing death by making rational decisions, clarifying values, and achieving closure. By focusing on relationship, resolution, and responsibility it provides a framework for assisted dying that is an alternative to the widely publicized, quick and easy workbench approach to the assisted death of strangers by practitioners such as Dr. Jack Kevorkian. It places human relationships in the center of the dying process and sees assisted dying as a mutual accomplishment achieved over time instead of a biological end.

Final Acts of Love provides specific guidelines, questions, and step-by-step criteria with which to evaluate your particular situation. As one considering the possible option of an assisted death it helps you look at such factors as your medical status, physical and social quality of life, emotional strengths and weaknesses, potential effects of such an action on your family and other loved ones, economic considerations, personal values, and philosophical and spiritual beliefs. *Final Acts of Love* is written for those of you who are:

- Facing your own death, now or in the future, and considering all possible options and ways of dying

- Providing care for another as a partner, family member, or physician, and attempting to address their concerns and suffering while deciding for yourself the best role to take

- Serving the dying and their families as nursing professionals, social workers, counselors, and clergy, and wanting to understand the needs and feelings of those who are considering this option

Although assisted dying has become a center of controversy in medical journals and the popular press, ballot booths and the courtroom, I am less interested in how to change the law than the act of assisted dying itself and the decisions that surround it. Clearly the issues involved have legal implications as well as religious and moral dimensions. Obviously, this is a national issue that will become more heated in years to come, particularly in states where there are citizen referendums. Lost in the public debate is the fact that many of those with life threatening illnesses are already taking matters into their own hands and ending their lives—with or without help, and regardless of laws. Many are being secretly assisted by their physicians, while others are being aided by their partners, family members, and close friends. Also currently overlooked is that those taking action usually have nowhere to turn for advice. For these individuals, their own death or that of one close to them is entirely new, a wheel to be reinvented. Most have no one with whom they can safely discuss this decision or learn what to expect—either practically or emotionally. This secrecy, moreover, isolates the dying and their caregivers from the knowledge gained by others.

Final Acts was written to provide this knowledge, because I recognize from my experience with individuals from diverse backgrounds that people need practical help in these matters. It's designed to help you answer the questions that others seldom ask, to explore a way of dying for yourself, or a way of helping another, before you're faced with the need to act. It relies heavily on the words of the dying to examine their concerns and reasons for exploring this option, and on the stories of families, friends, and others who helped their own loved ones in this process.

· · ·

I believe that any assisted death should always be seen as a last option, as an extraordinary act that should be engaged in only when your physical health and quality of life have descended to a point that makes further living intolerable. It's a step to be taken only after you've thoughtfully considered all other options and are absolutely certain that your reasons are right, the timing is correct, and you've done all you can to ensure that your survivors will not be unduly burdened by the experience. Similarly, for those of you thinking about helping, it's an act to be taken only after exploring both your motives and reservations, and after considering all other options and asking what is right for you.

In this way, *Final Acts* is about taking control of your life whether you're dying, helping, or providing care. It describes the benefits of confronting the issues that can affect your decision. It argues for open dialogue, boundary setting, counseling, and the involvement of partners, families, and friends in the decision process. It shows how the transition between life and death can be a time for resolving personal issues and completing relationships; it advocates "achieving" death at the end of a process of emotional healing, instead of seeing it as just a task to be carried out.

Though I feel the act should be extraordinary, I don't believe that it's necessarily right or wrong. I believe that this is more determined by the elements that underlie the decision, and the values and motives that everyone brings to the experience.

In exploring the nature of this experience, *Final Acts* describes what can and often does go wrong. I've included these stories for a purpose: If you're considering the possibility of an assisted death, it's important that you be aware of what can happen when decisions are rushed, motives are questionable, or participants are not sufficiently prepared.

Final Acts also looks at how an assisted death can be positive when decisions are based on reasonable need, and made with thoughtful reflection, sensitivity, and right intention. Throughout this book I show that an assisted death doesn't have to be equated with either "giving up" or "killing." Nor does it have to be a cause for guilt or regret. Instead I show how some families have been brought together through the decision-making process, and even have used assisted deaths as opportunities for ritualized farewells and for achieving a sense of peace and even spiritual fulfillment.

Final Acts includes some material that you may find disturbing, especially that which focuses on preparing for an assisted death or on what goes wrong. This is a normal reaction; I too have been disturbed by such details. Nevertheless, anyone considering an assisted death should be well informed. With this intent, I've attempted to put most of this information forward in a direct and caring manner, but without emotion-filled language that might additionally obscure your ability to think clearly about these items. My own feelings will become obvious later on.

It is my hope that what I've learned over these past years will make your own decisions and process of living and dying easier, whatever option you choose.

· · ·

Final Acts of Love is organized in the following way. Chapter One looks briefly at the political debate over assisted dying and how it has been influenced by changing public attitudes about medicine. It looks at dissatisfaction with available models of dying and briefly describes what is known about the extent of assisted death. In this way, it shows the need for an approach that addresses the concerns of the dying but doesn't mimic, in cold and soulless ways, the medical intervention strategies that are the original source of public concern.

Chapter Two provides guidelines to lead you through the self-exploration process of deciding to die. It's designed to help you understand your motives by taking several key factors into consideration. These include physical and social quality of life concerns as well as emotional, economic, and spiritual and ethical issues.

Chapter Three instructs you how to open up this inner dialogue of self-exploration to others. It describes the benefits of shared communication, beginning with those closest to you, but also extending to physicians and counselors, and provides a guide to opening discussion as a critical component in the overall process of deciding to die.

Chapter Four looks at the practicalities of assisted death, and discusses where to go both for information on how to die and for securing the means to do so. It describes the experiences of others in this process and also addresses such issues as deciding the right time to die, and both involving and protecting others.

Chapter Five looks at what happens when things go wrong, when initial plans for an assisted death fail. Drawing heavily from interviews, this chapter shares the failures of drugs, circumstances, motives, and people. It describes the worst-case scenarios that are all too common when individuals make less-than-thoughtful decisions, wait too long to take personal responsibility, fail to explore all options, or choose less-than-adequate means.

Chapter Six explores the nature of the "good death" and argues that this can still be achieved through assisted dying. Again, it uses stories from survivors, but this time to describe positive experiences and to show that an assisted death does not have to be devoid of sacred and spiritual elements or have to scar those who participate. In so doing, it describes ways to overcome barriers to closure and to use the process of deciding to die as a means to achieve resolution.

Chapter Seven is for those of you who are deciding to assist another. It leads you through this decision process, by helping you clarify your values, understand your motives, and be aware of the possible effects of such an action. In this, it also furnishes practical guidelines to help ensure that you take all possible factors into consideration. It also addresses differences in levels of participation, and explores fully the process of grief, while providing practical tools to lessen its effects.

Chapter Eight is a decision-making guide for physicians and other health care providers who are considering helping a patient to die. As in the previous chapter, this one supplies you with practical guidelines for deciding if, when, and how to assist in another's death. And again, it leads you through the process of understanding your values and beliefs while assessing the needs of patients and available options.

Final Acts of Love ends with a brief Question and Response section, and a Resource Guide listing organizations and materials that can help you through this decision-making process. Above all, *Final Acts of Love* tries to provide the information I needed when I began my journey sitting with my sister a dozen years ago.

Chapter 1

Death and Discontent

Charlotte had been married to Willem for forty years when she finally helped him die. This came eight years after he developed an ultimately fatal neurological condition. From the onset he'd said that when it "got unbearable" he'd end his life. For him this would be "when he could no longer take a book from the shelf." She accepted this, but told him she "couldn't be involved."

In the last weeks, his vision and mobility became seriously affected, and he was afraid of not being able to speak or move or see. "He could scarcely sit in a chair without slipping down, and his eyes were down to a blur." When he got to where he could no longer turn over in bed, he said, "This is absolute nonsense."

It was because he was *not* imminently terminal that Willem felt he had no option. "He couldn't wait and take it day by day." This was to be a long stay in a convalescent facility, "perhaps another year, blind and unable to move."

> The thought of him of all people—a man of passion and energy—in a long-stay hospital is an obscene thought in a way that death isn't, but the doctor said, "Look, you aren't going to be able to manage."

During his final months, he kept telling Charlotte how he'd attach a hose to the car's exhaust. He repeated this until she finally confronted him: "How would you use a car when you can't turn over in bed?"

Although he never asked Charlotte to help him, his "plans" had the same effect. As she put it, "In any case you can't ask your nearest to wheel you out to a car and fix up a hose; that's impossible." He then suggested that perhaps he could use a gun he'd kept from his time in the Dutch resistance, but then thought better of it, saying, "No, I can't do that to anybody else."

At last he decided on tranquilizers and a plastic bag. Not wanting to involve Charlotte, he made a first attempt in her absence, but failed. Sleep set in as he attempted to place the plastic bag over his head. Upon recovering, he told her he would try again. It was then she realized she wanted to be involved.

> So I said to him, "I'll be there," and he said, enthusiastically, "Oh that would be marvelous, but you don't have to. I'll manage." But you can't let somebody struggle on a lonesome journey of that sort. I mean we'd been married now for forty years.

Willem warned his children that he wouldn't be around much longer and then called a few friends to say good-bye, "though not explicitly." A few came to see him. Two days later, he made his final decision, and Charlotte "was very much involved." After he took the tranquilizers and became clearly comatose, she "put the bag over his head."

The Current Debate

Cases like that of Charlotte and Willem point to the human dimension of the controversy around assisted dying. As the public debate continues to focus on whether the dying should have the right to request and receive aid-in-dying from physicians, the terminally ill—together with their families and friends—continue to take matters into their hands. In so doing they often pay little attention to the relevancy of laws and the issues that underlie the debate. Indeed, while they're often concerned about the current prohibition, they seem less interested with the philosophical issues and the illegal nature of assisted dying than in what the prohibition entails—the lack of access to assistance from physicians in the form of secure lethal prescriptions, the inability of all participants to openly share their plans with others, and the self-imposed silence which prevents survivors from grieving their loss honestly. And as their own suffering—or that of one they love—increases, they seem ready to ignore whether assisted dying violates medical principles, is an irrational act, or is considered the same as suicide or killing. Many, however, see it as a natural extension of compassionate care, as private family business, as a final act of love. But as we'll soon see, it often is a complex matter.

Opponents of assisted dying argue that the greater social good demands keeping these prohibitions in place and suggest there are alternatives, such as hospice, morphine, termination of treatment, drug-induced unconsciousness, or even self starvation. They claim that legalization of assisted dying would be tantamount to supporting an irrational act of self destruction and turn physicians from healers—bound by duty to preserve life and cause no harm—into killers.

The debate, of course, is far more elaborate. Opponents also argue that there is no reason for anyone to choose to die, as most pain is controllable and, if given the option, patients might feel an economic obligation to die, be coerced to do so, or make the decision too easily, without informing family members. Moreover, acting too quickly, some patients would be stripped of the opportunity for a later change of heart. Finally, what might begin as the patient's right to receive help upon request could be later expanded to include those who are no longer competent to make their own decisions.

Proponents reply that a change in the law is necessary based on reasons of compassion and freedom of choice in the face of intolerable suffering. They argue that no doctor would ever be forced to help a patient, that not all pain is controllable, that symptoms other than pain, like those experienced by Willem, are even more difficult to control, and suggest that loss of quality of life and "personhood" are similarly valid motives. Proponents also claim that safeguards can protect patients from choices based on quick decisions, and that laws can be designed to ensure that aid is only available to those who request it and meet all qualifications.

THE LEGAL STRUGGLE

Throughout this decade the right-to-die controversy has taken on a more public and high-profile nature. Foremost in the public eye, perhaps, have been efforts to change state laws, public actions that ignore them, and a book that provided the dying with information on how to take matters into their own hands. In terms of legal efforts, right-to-die advocates have presented three initiatives before the voters; the first two in Washington and California narrowly lost, while the third won last year in Oregon but was recently ruled unconstitutional by a federal judge in Oregon. Meanwhile, in Michigan, Dr. Jack Kevorkian has made headlines since 1990 by ignoring existing laws and using his "suicide machine" and carbon-monoxide canisters to help end the lives of nearly two dozen incurably ill patients. And in late 1991 Derek Humphry's "suicide manual" *Final Exit* reached the top of bestseller lists and has since sold nearly three-quarters of a million copies. The combination of these actions brought the topic of assisted dying to public attention.

In addition, other notable actions have also taken place. These include "confessions" of physician assistance published in medical journals and the popular press, the refusal by a New York Grand Jury to indict Dr. Timothy Quill for helping his patient "Dianne" via a lethal prescription, headline court cases and acquittals of both Kevorkian and others, and appeals in federal courts against laws from Washington State to New York. The latter cases, as well as inevitable appeals focusing on the Oregon referendum, seem likely to guarantee eventual Supreme Court action—the impact of which could either parallel *Roe* v. *Wade* in extending civil liberties to embrace the right of the terminally ill to receive aid-in-dying or lead to further civil disobedience or campaigns for change. Given all this, some form of legal assisted dying appears inevitable, especially with surveys that find some two-thirds of adult voters and more than half of all physicians support it.

Until final court action resolves the present legal impasse, however, the public debate will proceed, ensuring that lofty ideals on both sides will continue to stand in the way of a blending of caution and sensitivity. Meanwhile, as in the case of Willem and Charlotte and countless others like them, the secret practice of assisted dying continues. And terminally ill patients are helped, not just by the rare Kevorkians, but by one-quarter to one-half of physicians in the United States, Canada, Great Britain, and Australia who in certain cases see it as "just good medical practice." Moreover, like Willem, they're also being helped by their partners, family members, and friends who see no other way to relieve the suffering of one they love. This illegal assistance, however, goes on without guidelines, safeguards, psychological counseling or evaluations, required consultation with specialists, referrals to hospice, or even mandatory discussion of alternatives.

BEHIND THE SCENES

Due to its illegal nature, no one knows the extent of assisted dying. What we do know is that a large number are knowingly helped by physicians, and that as many as a third of all doctors have assisted at least one of their patients to die by providing legal prescriptions. Moreover, my own research and work with the dying has shown me that far more are aided by partners, family members, and friends—often with the unwitting help of doctors. It also has become apparent to me that assisted dying is engaged in by individuals suffering from a range of terminal and irreversible conditions, but is more likely among certain social settings and categories of patient. It appears to be far more common among those with AIDS than other groups but also is practiced in large numbers by women with metastatic breast cancer, men with advanced prostate cancer, and elderly suffering a variety of degenerative and terminal conditions. In regard to AIDS, for example, studies from New York City have found the risk of suicide to be thirty-six times higher for those with AIDS than for the general population.

Nevertheless, most assisted deaths go undiscovered and are officially determined to be due to natural causes. This is reflected in my interviews, in which I found only fifteen official suicides out of

140 assisted deaths studied, and only four official suicides among my seventy-six cases of assisted deaths involving AIDS patients. Even if we look at such figures conservatively, the actual number of assisted deaths occurring each year must be staggering.

The legal, professional, and personal implications of such involvement create the necessity for a conspiracy of silence that keeps the actual numbers of assisted deaths secret. Participation in such an event is illegal for those who either supply the means of dying or in any way help administer them. Physicians will not talk about specific cases out of fear of indictment, suspension of medical privileges, or loss of medical license. Moreover, partners, families, and friends refuse to disclose their actions also for legal reasons or to protect others from knowing the true cause of death. But usually overseeing such events are the patients, those who are dying. They often take precautions to protect physicians who have privately and willingly provided them with lethal prescriptions, or if it appears the partners, family members, or friends have to become more extensively involved. Consequently, evidence is hidden, empty prescriptions, plastic bags, and final notes are removed, physicians and funeral homes are called, death certificates are obtained, and another death from cancer, AIDS, or other cause is registered.

The rare exceptions are cases like that of Willem, whose "preterminal" condition required this to be an official suicide. This didn't sit well with Charlotte, even though all of their friends saw it as "an act of independence in keeping with Willem's personality." As a result, she eventually decided to share the truth before a nation of television viewers a few months before our interview. She saw this as the most supportive thing she could do for the British right-to-die movement. In explaining her openness, she told me, "This wasn't a suicide, and I needed to make that absolutely clear. Anyway, who's going to arrest a seventy-year-old woman and create a public circus?"

Other exceptions include those with irreversible conditions, whose deaths similarly cannot be explained away as well as those who wish to protect families and friends from any known involvement in their deaths. Therefore, in many cases, the assisted nature of these deaths must permanently be hidden to protect all involved.

To the dying, who may see no other choice but to involve others in their deaths, this decision to end their lives is rooted in a desire not to commit suicide or to die by any possible means, but to find what they see as a dignified solution—an alternative to violence—that balances their perceived need to end their own suffering with the needs of those they love to experience their death in more peaceful ways. And to partners, families, and friends who take this step and choose to help a loved one die, at the end there is usually no question about the other's decision, about the validity of their reasons, or even about their own decision to participate. This is because they too see no alternative, selflessly put aside their own needs, and, in some instances, actually give little thought to the effects of their own actions. They often see their help as the only viable way both to alleviate the other's suffering and to provide one they love with a final sense of control. Perceived as the lesser of two evils—helping to die versus allowing to suffer—the decision is seldom regretted, although the final extent of their involvement may well be. While they frequently wish there could've been a better way, after the fact they usually believe there wasn't.

Reasons Underlying the Current Crisis

In 1900, six years before my father was born at home, life expectancy in America was forty-seven years, antibiotics were unknown, medical intervention at the end of life was nonexistent, and the most common causes of death were conditions such as pneumonia, influenza, consumption (i.e., tuberculosis), and diarrhea. Other acute illnesses also took their toll, as did early childhood diseases. Although unwelcome, death was a fact of life that often took place in the presence of family, with most people dying at home.

By the time my father died in 1987, average life expectancy had risen to seventy-five years. He'd surpassed this figure by some six years, aided in his last months by diuretics and a machine that manufactured and pumped oxygen through a plastic hose that trailed behind him throughout the house. Officially, he died in a regional hospital, a "slow code" transported by a team of emergency med-

ical technicians after CPR efforts failed. The emphysema that finally took my father's life, like heart disease and cancer, the most
common causes of death today, is a chronic condition that takes its
time. Death comes slowly for most of us, with four out of every five
people who die each day doing so in institutional settings, hospitals, convalescent homes, or other extended-care facilities.

As in my father's case, one of the benefits attributed to medical
advances is increased life expectancy and victory over many acute
illnesses that formerly took many lives. Much of these gains have
resulted from the development of a wide spectrum of antibiotics,
creation of a public health service, inoculations against childhood
diseases, and improved standards for sanitation and water supplies.
Early diagnosis and treatment of several acute conditions, the development of regional hospital systems, improvements in communication and emergency medical response have also had their
impact on increased life expectancy.

Our confidence in medicine has also grown as a result of technological advances that have led to "miracles" in treatment and
surgery. This can be seen clearly in the case of dialysis and organ
transplants, but has carried over to a variety of other life-saving—
and life-sustaining—procedures. These include wide-scale use of
IV fluid treatments for hydration, nutrition, and delivery of medications, as well as in intubation and mechanical respiration. All of
these innovations have done much both to guarantee increased sur-
vivability following a number of surgical procedures and to deal effectively with several reversible conditions.

On a psychological level, however, these advances have been a
mixed blessing. As our level of confidence has increased, our expectations and hopes have been raised. The downside is that we now
live long enough to die from slow chronic killers such as cancer and
heart disease. Moreover, in the case of cancer there have been some
benefits with prevention and early diagnosis in treating varieties
normally occurring in children or young adults. But the results of
intensive research, surgical procedures, and chemotherapy "trials"
have been less than encouraging. Whether there have been real statistical gains is now subject to heated debate within the medical
community.

This dichotomy of confidence and discouragement has not been lost on those of us in the general public who continue to see our friends and family members stricken with breast, prostate, lung, or other cancers. In addition, it's especially difficult for us to understand a similar lack of success in dealing with a single virus, AIDS. After more than a century of victories over disease, it's hard to grasp that medical science has not achieved an easy cure over what is presently a certain killer.

Moreover, over the past few decades the "mechanization" of medicine, with its artificial nutrition and hydration, intubation therapy, and mechanical respiration, has been rapidly expanded for use with those in acute respiratory failure and other chronically critically ill in the ICU. Medical ethicist Dr. Thomas Raffin has said, "These interventions are provided almost as a reflex action, because the alternative—leaving the patient to die—seems morally unthinkable." The effect, for some, has been a radical transformation of the dying process that makes a death at home impossible. For others, it's led to the "creation" of a new category of patient— those in persistent vegetative states.

As a result of these medical advancements and fear over forced intervention, the right-to-die movement first concentrated its efforts on the passage of legislation allowing competent patients to specify their health-care desires in advance, or to place in the hands of another the power to make decisions for them, including the decision to withhold or withdraw life-sustaining treatment. These efforts to allow for "living wills" and "durable powers of attorney for health care" have proved most successful in the twenty years following the New Jersey Supreme Court decision concerning Karen Ann Quinlan in 1976. This held that there was a constitutional right to privacy that allowed the family of an incompetent patient with no hope for recovery to discontinue artificial life-support systems. Since then, statutes in nearly every state and in several foreign countries now allow patients to express their opposition to medical intervention.

Nevertheless, these "victories" on behalf of patients' rights to die have not answered the basic public concern over the perceived failure by medicine to control cancer and AIDS, and the perceived discomfort of the dying process. These factors have taken their toll and, at least for a time, have diminished the glow from what once was looked upon as the all-powerful promise of medicine. Witnessing others who have suffered before us, it's not easy to believe that our deaths will be any different, that ours will come gently. So we look for different approaches, investigate alternative therapies, and explore other ways of dying. We do all this, however, without abandoning medicine and without necessarily even discussing our plans with our physicians. After all, to do so would feel too much like talking to a priest about ideas for future sins.

There are other disincentives at work, however, than merely loss of faith toward medicine and fear of unwanted intervention. Perhaps none of the medical achievements that have occurred would have been possible without a transformation of the relationship between physician and patient and without what Philippe Ariès referred to as the development of the hospital as a bureaucratic system "whose power depends on discipline, organization, and anonymity . . . [which] have given rise to a new model of medicalized death." He continued to say:

> Death no longer belongs to the dying man, who is first irresponsible, later unconscious, nor to the family, who are convinced of their inadequacy. Death is regulated and organized by bureaucrats whose competence and humanity cannot prevent them from treating death as their "thing," a thing that must bother them as little as possible in the general interest.

Like many, I hold a special gratitude to medical science and the ready dissemination of its knowledge. Now in my mid-forties, I can't count the times I've been prescribed an assortment of antibiotic medications for a range of conditions over the years. And I certainly can't forget the fact that I wouldn't be writing these words without the benefits of emergency intervention as an infant, at ages eight and ten, and again three years ago. Had I been born at the time of my father, such interventions might not have been possible or had the same results. But my gratitude may not last long if the day comes when I'm suffering intolerably and feel as Sophocles did when he wrote some twenty-four centuries ago that "death is not the greatest of ills; it is worse to want to die, and not be able to."

· · ·

Until medicine can reestablish its promise, or indeed guarantee a more gentle death, one that brings back the human dimension, the dying will seek whatever alternatives are possible. It does little good for physicians to promise a good death if our experiences with friends and family suggest the contrary, if hospice is unavailable, and if we no longer can live at home and instead require final care in hospitals and convalescent facilities that we sense have little room for dignity, patient autonomy, or control over the decisions of our daily life. It's obvious that many of us desire another way of dying, which allows patients to determine the time and the place of their own death. The problem, however, is that assisted dying is new territory and we've yet to hear from its explorers.

Without guidance from physicians, shamans, or seers each of us has little to go on. We may each consider ending our life as a logical alternative, but we don't yet know how to do it in a way that makes it a positive alternative to prolonged and painful dying. If we're suffering, we don't know the criteria to use in deciding absolutely why to terminate our own life or when or whether we should involve others. And as partners, family, or friends we similarly don't know when—and when not to—become involved, when to say yes or express our reservations.

All of this requires a depth of thought unlike any other decision. If we're dying or helping another it requires that we fully explore reasons and options and what the effects might be. It means talking to those closest to us, learning their desires and deepest concerns. It means seeking help and exploring the depth of our own feelings, and it means doing our homework to know how to accomplish such a death in the most positive way possible. This entails learning about the full range of experiences that others have had and using their lessons wisely in choosing our own path. This journey begins in the next chapter.

Chapter 2

GUIDELINES FOR
SELF-EXPLORATION

It slowly dawned on me that there was another way, and that I didn't have to go to the end. I can't remember when I first considered it. It was like when I first met my husband, and we dated, and one day I realized that I was in love with him. It wasn't a single glance across the dinner table. There was no lightning.

It was kind of like that. I'd been fighting my cancer and I was full of fear because of the way my mother died. I didn't tell my husband right away, and I wasn't making any plans to do anything.

I just began to think that this made sense, and this was right for me, if things went from bad to worse. And I felt more relieved, so I forgot about it and went on with my treatments. Only after it looked like the chemo wasn't going anywhere did I decide to talk to my husband about it. Until then I kept it all inside, because I didn't want to worry him, and I really wasn't thinking seriously about it.

Annie

If you're facing a life-threatening condition, you may find yourself creating a kind of imaginary scale on which you begin weighing your reasons for living or dying. In this way, a rational decision to end your life begins with an inner conversation in which you consider—perhaps for the first time—quality-of-life issues, spiritual concerns, obligations to family and friends, benefits of continued medical treatment, and the full range of end-of-life options, including the option for a self-enacted or assisted death.

As we can see in Annie's case, it's not uncommon for many people to reflect privately in the option of ending their lives even as they continue to engage in treatment alternatives and seek out ways to continue living. Nevertheless, like others facing the concerns of living and dying, there may be periods when you become more aware of the quality of your health or experience situations you find physically and emotionally difficult. At such times you may come to see such challenging changes and situations as valid reasons for ending your life. Similarly, other events may occur that nullify these earlier conclusions. In this way, the scale can swing back and forth many times during your journey. One man told me:

> I felt like doing it the other day when the pain was so bad. Then my brother visited, and we had a good visit, and I'm glad I didn't. Now, yesterday was bad again and I got more bad news, and here I am and it makes me wonder when I'll say "enough is enough." But I think I'll know.

The decision to die is complex, and several key issues may come into focus. These often include *physical, social, emotional,* and *economic* factors, as well as those that are related to *spiritual* and *ethical* issues. Together, they form the basis by which you may eventually decide either to end your life or continue living until death takes you in its own time. Although these various issues often are interrelated, I'll be addressing each separately to help you break down into manageable categories many issues that in actual fact are not distinct. I'm doing so, however, to help you view each element in detail until you can put them all together. For example, physical and social factors are interconnected and each has emotional meaning, just as psychological concerns are often mind-body issues. Although we cannot always keep things separate in life, we can in our analysis, and that's what I will be helping you understand throughout this chapter.

To assist you in your analysis, I strongly encourage you to

begin keeping a personal daily journal, in which you clearly note your physical symptoms and any changes, your treatment regimen, and any variations in your appetite, sleep patterns, and ability to engage in daily activities. These can be especially helpful if you should need to talk to your physician about specific symptoms or treatment issues. In addition, you would also do well to track your dominant emotions, attitudes about living and dying, thoughts about assisted dying, and any special concerns that might be influencing your thoughts about ending your life. Know that it's similarly important for you to note any special social situations that have arisen or events with family and friends that may be affecting you emotionally. The various factors to note will become obvious as you read through this chapter.

Physical Quality of Life

The most important consideration in making a decision to end your life is the quality of your physical health. This includes the level of pain you experience and the discomfort you have from other physical symptoms or from the side effects of medical treatment.

Other physical symptoms may be those that affect your level of energy and concentration or your ability to engage in and enjoy what you previously considered as normal behaviors, such as physical mobility or sexually activity. You may also develop symptoms that affect simple activities such as eating, sleeping, or breathing without difficulty, as well as those activities that provide you with a basis for "dignity of life." These include your ability to feed yourself and provide for your own basic care.

I always advise people to take several specific steps as they begin to consider such a decision. Based on how you define your current physical quality of life, you should first:

• Explain clearly to your physician the pain and discomfort and possible side effects of treatment you're experiencing

- Assess whether you're satisfied with the measures that are currently being used to control your pain and other physical discomforts

- Satisfy yourself with absolute certainty that your physician understands your concerns about the physical quality of your life

- Obtain a clear idea of the future course of your condition and whether the pain and discomfort you're experiencing will lessen or whether these conditions are most likely irreversible

- Understand the possible side effects of all available measures for pain and symptom management

- Obtain a second medical opinion, preferably from a physician who specializes in your disease or condition, and, if necessary, seek a referral to another specialist or, if necessary, to a pain-control center

Even before you begin actively considering the option of an assisted death, it's critical that you assess your concerns in light of complete information about the current and likely future status of your physical quality of life and all reasonable, available options.

PAIN AND ITS CONTROL

Your primary motivation for ending your life may well be the degree of "intolerable" pain you experience and your dissatisfaction with attempts you've taken to provide a level of comfort. Know that you should not have to choose between pain and death. If pain is a primary factor driving your decision, learn as much as you can about its causes, discuss with your physician the possible use of other medications or options for its control, and assess the possibility that your physician is underprescribing appropriate amounts of medication. If you're still dissatisfied with your treatment, you would do well to seek a second opinion or a referral to a pain-control center or specialist. In the case of a terminal illness, at some time you should also explore the options of a hospice, if it's available in your area. Hospice medical directors and nursing staff are effectively trained in cancer-pain management and other measures designed to enhance comfort care.

I'm reminded regularly of the problem of inadequate pain control. Opponents to legalized physician-aid-in-dying argue that "all pain can be controlled," and that terminally ill patients seek aid-in-dying only because of inadequate pain management. There's a degree of truth in this argument. It's become obvious to me that not all callers to the Hemlock Society who complain of "uncontrollable pain" have expressed the seriousness of their complaints to their physicians, have worked with them to explore all the options, or have received the best medical care. Recent research supports this and shows, for example, that "cancer pain is widely undertreated," even though "it can be effectively controlled in up to 90 percent of all patients." In addition, a 1994 report in *The New England Journal of Medicine,* found that 42 percent of cancer patients with moderate to severe pain failed to receive adequate pain-killing treatment from their doctors. A large part of this problem is that many physicians are unwilling to write prescriptions for controlled drugs, like morphine or other opioids, out of fear that it might cause addiction or lead to investigation by drug-enforcement agencies. This report also found that not all physicians are adequately trained in terminal pain relief.

Another problem for such patients is that their physicians may not consider their pain to be real. For example, one terminal cancer patient told me that his doctor dismissed his complaints, saying that his form of cancer "was not associated with pain." Feeling like a statistic instead of a person, he "didn't know how to respond." Instead of arguing further with his physician he called Hemlock.

Regardless of arguments to the contrary, however, not all terminal pain can be controlled. Even the above quoted study found 10 percent of cancer pain to be in this category. This fact was witnessed up close by Patty Rosen, a former nurse practitioner who cared for her twenty-four-year-old daughter, Jody, who was dying of metastasized thyroid cancer. Patty told me how Jody experienced uncontrollable pain, even though Patty, a health professional, was able to fight on her behalf to receive the best care available. Toward the end, no amount of opioids worked. She told me:

> All they did was create constipation so bad it resulted in fecal impaction that, on three occasions, failed to respond to enemas, massive doses of laxatives, and other medications. I remember approaching her with a syringe of morphine to help relieve her pain, and Jody would say "Mother, how many times do I have to tell you, it's like water; it doesn't work." What a horrible lesson Jody had to teach me.
>
> Seeing her in this degree of pain I could only take so much, and as she continued to plead with me to help her die, I realized I had to do it, because I knew this was the only way I could relieve her suffering.

Jody's case points out another major issue, that medical treatment for pain or other conditions can cause intolerable side effects. Even those who receive the best quality pain management can still experience unwanted symptoms from treatment, such as nausea, vomiting, sleeplessness, constipation, dizziness, inability to concentrate, and dryness of mouth.

Although each of these side effects can usually be controlled, the "same" degree of pain, pain management, and side effects are not always viewed as tolerable by every patient. A woman in Scotland told me:

> My husband lived by, and in, his mind. When the pain could only be controlled with medications that hampered his ability to think quickly and clearly, he first chose the pain, then he chose death. The doctors could never find the right balance. They kept promising us that he would adjust, but he never regained that sharpness of intellect he had all his life. This became too much for him.

Even though discomfort upon discomfort may drive you to consider assisted dying, remember that the initial side effects of some medications diminish after time. Also know that certain symptoms can be avoided by using different medications.

Although there may come a time when the "cure" becomes worse than the disease, think deeply about how much is too much, and whether you're choosing to die only because you haven't obtained the appropriate response from your physician, possibly because he has not adequately researched other treatment possibilities, or because you're tired of complaining.

Moreover, if your illness has progressed beyond your physician's ability to resolve, you might do well to consider hospice care. If you haven't yet explored this possibility, be aware that hospice physicians and nursing staff are often better trained than other in managing the range of terminal symptoms. Nevertheless, comfort can never be guaranteed, and the natural process of dying cannot always be made tolerable. So think deeply about your own limits.

OTHER PHYSICAL SYMPTOMS

Pain is only one of many physical conditions you may be taking into consideration in determining your physical quality of life. You may also be experiencing fatigue, overwhelming weakness, sleeplessness, dizziness and severe nausea, inability to eat or swallow, shortness of breath and trouble breathing, or stomach cramps and uncontrollable diarrhea. You may find these physical symptoms as difficult to tolerate as pain.

This can clearly be seen in the 1992 Dutch "Remmelink report," which analyzed euthanasia in the Netherlands. After conducting nationwide interviews with physicians (general practitioners and specialists), researchers found that "pain" alone was cited in only 9.4 percent of cases as the sole reason that patients requested aid-in-dying. By contrast, "loss of dignity" alone or with other factors, including pain, was cited 57 percent of the time.

These findings suggest that a variety of physical factors in combination can become serious motives for an assisted death. Moreover, given the range of terminal symptoms, the need for extensive broad-based medical treatment can add to physical discomfort. This poses a dilemma. At some time you may begin to question the value of treatments that keep you alive but reduce what *you* define as the physical quality of your life and "dignity."

This can especially be seen when experiencing some of the common side effects of traditional treatments for cancer—radiation and chemotherapy. As one patient told me:

> I can't stand another blood work up, another chemo or radiation treatment, another bout of nausea, vomiting, and hair loss, another emergency transfusion, or another day of either being drugged or not being able to control the pain.

This combination of physical quality-of-life issues can most clearly be seen in the impact of AIDS, with its vast litany of physical symptoms and side effects. AIDS, which causes the breakdown of the body's immune system, can affect nearly every organ, including the eyes, brain, lungs, digestive and nervous systems, as well as both external and internal skin surfaces. It often can also lead to weight loss or "wasting syndrome" and to blindness and dementia. As a result, treatment for AIDS is usually condition-specific and can vary with each patient. More conditions mean more treatment and more medication. One AIDS patient explained to me how he was reaching the end of his rope:

> I have no quality of life. I can't walk or even stand, I'm in pain, I'm going blind, and I can't hold any food down. The only time I get out of the house is to go to my doc, and now I'm told I've got toxoplasmosis [a virus] and I'll probably get dementia. But you have to understand, it's not my fear [of dementia], but my body that's making the decision for me. I've got so many conditions, and they've got them under symptomatic control—that's what my nurse practitioner calls it—that I'm like the beast that wouldn't die. Believe me, it's time to die!

This attitude was also expressed by David Lewis, when he left his position with the Vancouver Persons With AIDS Society. He too had been diagnosed with toxoplasmosis, an often quickly fatal AIDS brain disease. In a press release issued by the Society only days before his own assisted death, Lewis gave the reasons for his "retirement."

> I am taking forty-six pills a day that I was not taking two weeks ago. Each pill seems to be causing side effects, which are treated by more pills, which also cause side effects. It's the merry-go-round getting worse.

FEAR OF FUTURE PHYSICAL CONDITIONS

Fear of dementia, uncontrollable pain, or other potential conditions may also become a powerful incentive for you to consider assisted dying even though such a situation may never actually occur. If you have such fears, first explore the facts. Be certain that other irreversible and intolerable conditions are also present before you let fear guide your final decision.

Look deeply into yourself to determine what you're truly afraid of, and whether concern about dementia, future pain, dependency, loss of control, or burdening others is the real problem. Next, try to assess what other factors may be involved. For example, you may find that your fear of dependency is secondary to your fear of abandonment, of being alone, or of being a burden to others. If this is the case, then share your concerns. You may find that others are more than willing to be with you, to share your dying, but you and others have been mutually hesitant to talk in plain terms about the possibility of your death. Ultimately, you need to ask yourself whether this hesitancy might also be tied to fear of the dying process, or if you see an assisted death as an escape from your fears instead of a release from actual suffering. If so, you might explore the possibility of talking with a counselor or hospice volunteer or joining a support group comprised of others facing a similar life-threatening illness.

Fear of future conditions is not at all uncommon. I've seen this frequently with AIDS, where concern about dementia can be overwhelming. One man told me:

I've seen it in my friends and my partner. I saw him go through hell. I couldn't stand being like that. If I begin to lose it, I'll do it. I mean, it's my mind that makes me human, and if it looks like it'll happen, I'll have to act before it gets bad. I'll have to make a preemptive strike. I don't want to miss the chance. What if I lose my mind and they put me away? Then I can't do it, because I won't have access to my drugs.

Social Quality of Life

Many have found that diminished physical functioning together with increased discomfort can seriously constrain their abilities to participate in the social world or engage in activities that formerly brought them pleasure. Like them, you may perceive these losses as having forced lifestyle changes upon you that you find impossible to tolerate.

At the heart of this problem is how you define your quality of life, and whether you can learn to accept the changes in your living that often come from experiencing a life-threatening condition. Know that change is normal throughout our lives and, though difficult, there are often ways for us to grieve our losses, to accept some changes, and find ways to achieve a sense of joy. Before you allow your perception of decreased quality of life to become a primary motive for ending your life, you might do well to:

- Reflect on *all* elements of your life that have given you a sense of quality and, up to now, have made your life worth living

- Consider which of these former elements, activities, or abilities have been lost to you as a result of changes in your physical condition

- Ask yourself honestly whether those features that are now missing have always been absolutely vital for you to enjoy your life

- Determine, with input from your physician or other health professionals, whether these features are lost to you permanently or only temporarily

- Share with your physician or with other professionals the importance of these former abilities and seek their help in exploring alternatives or modified ways in which you can still find some enjoyment

- Assess, realistically, the importance of these former abilities that are now permanently lost, and obtain help from a therapist or support group to find ways to accept these changes as much as possible and grieve their loss

- Reflect on what other elements, activities, or abilities of your life—yet unaffected by your physical condition—also have given your life value

- Make an attempt to utilize some of these unaffected abilities or engage in activities that are still available to you

Loss of Former Abilities

You may find yourself especially saddened by the loss of abilities you once took for granted. You also may regret and grieve the perceived end to activities that are now constrained or threatened by your diminishing health. Barry, for example, told me about how his terminal illness had changed his life.

> I was an athlete, I was a runner and a dancer. Terry and I even met dancing. Now we haven't danced in four years. We used to enjoy going to movies, but now with all the meds I take I fall asleep almost instantly at the show. We used to go on long drives or away for the weekend, but now I get too sick. And the one time we recently traveled, to Hawaii, I ended up in the hospital.

Like Barry, you may find yourself beginning to measure your current abilities against what you formerly took for granted, those previously "normal" social endeavors in which you're no longer able to take pleasure. My friend Joy explained:

> We used to like drives in the country or to the beach. Now I need to be nearly lying down in the car to do it without getting sick, and I still usually get sick no matter what we do. And the twists and turns on the road are too painful with my bone cancer, and to really get comfortable I have to recline, which puts my head below the window sill where I can't see a thing anyway.

When Gary, a man with AIDS, told me several years ago about his desire to end his life, he talked of the importance that simple acts such as cooking and eating played in his life. With their loss, he actively began to consider the possibility of an assisted death.

> I'm a gourmet cook, or at least I *was* a gourmet cook. I love food, but I can't eat any more. The KS [Kaposi's sarcoma] has spread down my esophagus and into my stomach, and to eat anything I have to take morphine. Now the doctor says the only way for me to get food down without pain is to surgically implant a feeding tube. That would mean never tasting anything again. Never tasting chocolate or the things I've loved to cook. It was bad enough giving up my glass of wine with dinner. Now they want me to give up dinner!

These disappointments can be constant reminders of your special health status and your inability to participate in the full—or even partial—round of daily activities you once enjoyed. In this regard, I'm reminded of Melissa, who in her final months, was forced to cancel first her birthday dinner and then her anniversary celebration with her husband, David. He later explained:

> Just once, we wanted to go out and be a couple again. To have a romantic dinner. To look across the table at each other without constantly being reminded of the cancer that was taking her away. But it wasn't meant to be.

In their case, Melissa and David invented reasonable alternatives in the form of special dinners at home, or they went out, spontaneously, when her health allowed it. In this way they worked around her health issues to take advantage of all opportunities to keep a semblance of normalcy as long as possible. Like Melissa and David, you might explore the possibility of adapting your abilities or altering your activities to meet the constraints of your health. When this is no longer feasible, consider talking with your health-care and other professionals about developing those abilities you still possess and exploring other interests. These might not be as satisfying as other activities but, nonetheless, they provide a way for you to continue to live well for as long as possible.

LOVE AND SEX

Your decreasing physical health can also severely impact the sexual and romantic aspects of your life. These changes can begin either with decreased feelings of sexual attractiveness or diminished sexual desire and functioning due to physical pain, discomfort, weakness, or the side effects of medications.

In the beginning of a life-threatening illness, even before major changes occur in your physical health, a direct relationship can develop between your diminished feelings of self-worth and loss of sexual desire and ability. This can especially be the case if you formerly defined your sense of self-worth, at least in part, by your sexual persona. If you begin to perceive yourself as less attractive, you may experience reduced sexual desire or ability, and this in turn can result in lowered feelings of self-worth. For example, Janet told me that her sexual desire ended when "the ravages" of her cancer began.

> At first I felt bad emotionally. After all, I had cancer. I couldn't feel sexy. I couldn't pretend that everything was normal. Then I changed physically and I could see it in the mirror, and I thought how could anybody want to make love with me? That depressed me and I began to feel as if my life was over.

You might even perceive this loss of physical attractiveness, though still early in the course of your illness, as a good reason for thinking seriously about ending your life. The question to ask yourself is whether this change, by itself, is enough of a reason to die, or whether it's possible to find creative ways to adapt. One woman, for example, told me that she "was always attractive and could flirt successfully," but that her breast cancer had taken away "that pleasure," and she had a hard time learning "new ways" of acting in the world. In her case she was helped by a therapist who specialized in counseling women after breast cancer surgery.

Similarly, John, a support-group member and former model, once said, "I've told my partner to kill me when I get ugly." In this way, John equated his physical attractiveness—the one thing he always valued and used—with his quality of life. When I pushed John on this point, however, he finally admitted that he feared his increasing "unattractiveness" might result in eventually being abandoned by his partner. Unfortunately, until he either discussed his concerns with his partner—or actually did lose his looks—he'd have no way of knowing whether his fears were grounded. Instead, he'd live in fear and continue to distrust any affirmation of love. As John added: "He says he loves me, but what about later?"

A terminal illness will inevitably mean changes in the physical and social quality of life. At some point it may mean weakness, pain and, indeed, loss of sexual desire and ability. Although the importance of sexual desire and ability cannot be ignored, communication between you and your partner can do much to alleviate the sense of aloneness you might feel as a result of perceptions of inadequacy and lessened self-worth. Communicating about your concerns can also help reduce these feelings, which, in themselves, often create barriers that prevent emotional intimacy. This especially can be a problem if a couple hasn't developed non-sexual techniques to achieve intimacy or to express emotional closeness.

Communication is not an end-all solution. The importance of this came home, for example, when Barbara, a young woman with bone cancer, wistfully told me:

What I really want is for my pain to go away long enough to be able to make love with my husband one last time, if he wants to. If not, then to be able to really hug him and be hugged without it hurting so bad.

She explained that while they had become "truly intimate on other levels" during her illness, "the loss of this kind of sharing" was hard for her to bear and made it difficult to go on. She said that her husband never complained and was always there for her, but that the end of their physical lovemaking had been a major loss, "another type of death" for her. Later, Barbara told me that "talking about it" with her husband didn't solve the problem, but at least "took the edge off" the loss and enabled them to discuss other ways of being together both emotionally and sexually.

At some point, you may need to place these changes in your sexual desire and ability into perspective. This is not easy. It involves looking at the likely course of your illness and facing your losses head on. In this regard, both individual therapy as well as grief counseling may be of help to you and your partner. You also may find that these changes may not seem so critical to you later on in the dying process, when other physical and social quality-of-life concerns may begin to take precedence. John, diagnosed with prostate cancer, explained this well.

After I was first diagnosed I thought I'd kill myself when I lost sexual functioning. Well, that came and went. Fortunately, my sexual desire left the same time my functioning did. Now I've moved on to other things of importance. Now I think I'll be out of here if I ever get too miserable to meditate and find peace.

In addition to diminishing abilities for physical love, you may also feel varying degrees of loss if you've yet to attain your desire for romantic love, intimacy, or family. Jennifer, for example, told me how she had "met this absolutely wonderful man" just before she received her diagnosis of ovarian cancer, and "the time and possibilities just melted away" as every day got filled with more medical necessities to save her life.

When they first told me I'd need a hysterectomy I was sad as I'd fantasized that maybe he was the one with whom I'd have a baby. Then came the surgery and the end of my hopes for someday being a mother, then came all the treatments and the uncertainty about the cancer, then came the news about the cancer. And what hit me the most was the thought of never being able to love again. And I thought, Hey, I'm too young, I've waited all my life for a love that now can never be.

Emotional Concerns

In addition to the physical and social quality of your life, there are various *emotional quality-of-life* concerns that can also affect your decision. These may include the anticipated loss of important relationships and your own membership in a partnership, family, and community of friends. You also may feel the loss of your independence, feelings of helplessness, and even a raw fear of death itself. Also, at times you may be overwhelmed by feelings of depression or intense sadness, or feel that you are becoming a physical, economical, or emotional burden on your partner, family, or friends.

As a result of these feelings, you may come to view an assisted death as a means to shorten the duration of these psychological or emotional hardships or as a way to eliminate fears about how and when your death will occur. What's important here is for you to at least make the attempt to look at these concerns individually, to see whether you can address and resolve any of them in isolation and, therefore, eliminate the sense of being overwhelmed by them. If you do feel overwhelmed, you also need to look at the possible presence of depression, which can be quite common during treatment for a life-threatening or terminal condition.

But if you're considering ending your life at least in part because of emotional reasons, take a closer look at these concerns, and make the attempt to resolve those still under your control. By doing so, you can reduce both the size of the emotional burden you face and the potential for ending your life for the wrong reasons or at the wrong time. A practical way to start would be for you to use your journal and, over a predetermined period of time, such as a week, begin taking more extensive notes. During this period, you can:

- Catalog those feelings that you most often experience, identify those times of day when they occur, and describe what other thoughts accompany them

- Note what you're feeling physically as well as what you're doing and who you're with at the time

- Track the times of your meals, periods for taking medication, and your sleeping patterns

- Determine how your physical condition or social factors in your life might trigger particular emotions

- Assess whether there are times when other—more positive—feelings are present, and again note what you're doing or who you're with during these periods

- Check to see if either your negative or positive emotions follow a logical pattern, occur during particular times of day, before or after meals or particular medications, or are more or less present while you're engaged in certain activities or with certain people

- Explore using your findings as a means to change those circumstances that might well trigger some of these negative emotions

- Talk to your physician about the possible link between your emotions and medications you're taking, and obtain information about the possible "mood altering" effects of these medications

- Consider avoiding those activities and personal contacts that seem to trigger negative emotions, while increasing those that seem to be linked to more positive feelings

By closely following your emotions and related thoughts you may obtain clues that can help you find ways to combat some of the more negative emotions you experience. For example, you might find that a feeling of hopelessness toward your condition is linked to pain that prevented you from seeing a friend and getting away from home. This linkage might well be resolved by successfully confronting your physician about inadequate pain control, and receiving stronger medication. This can have several effects. It can improve your physical quality of life, reduce feelings of hopelessness, and increase an attitude of independence through assertiveness.

One woman I knew experienced bouts of overwhelming sadness over dying. This was linked with feeling unimportant in people's lives, in particular, her disappointment over not receiving a promised phone call. An inquiry about the forgotten phone call enabled her to express her disappointment while reestablishing contact. It further allowed her to vent her feelings *as they occurred.* By similarly tracking your emotions and doing something about the cause, you can reclaim a sense of control over your life that a life-threatening illness can take away.

In both these cases, the secret is to ask yourself how you'd respond in a similar situation if you *weren't* experiencing a terminal or life-threatening condition. To respond in a way that is either more or less aggressive is to place yourself in a category that reinforces your special health status. If you respond less aggressively than you would have when you were healthy, this might be a sign of resignation, showing that you feel that you've moved from the status of living to that of dying. Does it mean that you're giving up? Or that you feel unworthy to complain? If so, you might like to explore this in more detail and think about what it means.

DEPRESSION

One of the most important emotional factors for you to consider is the possible presence of depression. It can be triggered by chronic pain, hormonal or biochemical changes, or from side effects of medication. In this way, it can be a common element of a life-threatening or terminal condition. But it also can be brought on by loneliness or isolation, chronic stress or worrying, a reduction in meaningful and enjoyable activities, and loss of lifestyle or of significant others in your life.

There are several symptoms of depression you can experience in mild or severe forms. When professionals refer to what they term "clinical" or "major" depression, they usually mean the presence of a number of the following symptoms in varying intensity over a period of time. These include:

- Increased feelings of sadness, lifelessness, powerlessness, irritability, a sense of guilt, and discouragement

- Lowered energy and reduced frequency of participation in—and enthusiasm for—previously enjoyable activities

- Changes in appetite or weight

- Difficulty making decisions, decreased memory and concentration, and inability to cope with even small demands

- Sleep disturbances, decreased sexual drive

- Preoccupation with thoughts of death or suicide

The more severe symptoms you have and the longer they're present, the more likely it is that you're experiencing depression.

Some of these symptoms are perfectly normal during a life-threatening or terminal condition. Thoughts of death, for example, make perfect sense so long as you don't become preoccupied with them. After all, you might well be dying and, as a result, lose many of the ambitions and hopes that you had for your life. You may also have economic concerns and feel guilty that you haven't done your best for those you're leaving behind. Similarly, the loss of your physical abilities and the unresolved loss of a spouse or partner can also significantly affect your feelings.

The key here is to know that many of these feelings and concerns can become more manageable with a combination of psychological counseling and antidepressant medication. The former can provide you with a means to vent your feelings while learning strategies to cope better with your illness. The latter can help bring your biochemistry back to normal. The use of antidepressants, in some instances, can also reduce pain and anxiety, and improve sleep. Since there are several of these medications, however, each with their own side effects, it may take you a while to adjust and feel the optimal results.

Though your circumstances may not change, your attitude toward them might be improved with increased knowledge of the physiological, social, and medical causes of depression. Before you make any decision about an assisted death, talk to your physician about your physical and emotional symptoms, be open to the possible use of antidepressant medications, seek counseling for unresolved emotional concerns, look into joining a support group, and increase your awareness of other services that might be available in your area. Numerous organizations ranging from suicide-prevention centers to local churches provide emotional support services. It can only help to talk. If you're depressed, thinking about an assisted death is *not* an appropriate response: only after you've made an active attempt to resolve your emotional concerns should you begin to assess this possibility.

This linkage between depression and the decision to die is often difficult to separate. You may ask yourself where your illness ends and where depression begins, especially if you believe that your feelings of hopelessness are realistic, that you are indeed dying and see little reason to live only a while longer. This feeling can especially be seen among terminal AIDS sufferers who may have already witnessed the death of their partners and many of their friends. One man who helped his partner die told me:

> I'm the only one left. I've buried my lover and all my dearest friends. I lack the intimacy that I thrived on for my entire life, a truly good friend, someone to share my concerns with. To make matters worse, I'm in pain most of the time, I can't eat, I'm going blind, and I'm nearly bedridden. Why should I be forced to go on in this shell of a body?

In his case no one was forcing him to continue living. Although he had the drugs to end his life, it was obvious to me that he'd not yet reached a point where he was ready to make this decision. If he had, he wouldn't be asking the question that he did. In response, I told him that I believed he had reasons for still being alive. I pointed out that counseling couldn't hurt, that perhaps he still needed to achieve closure with existing family members, and that, if he did make the decision to end his life, he should be absolutely certain that he did so with the best of intentions.

INDEPENDENCE

If you're incurably ill, you may find that being able to retain at least a semblance of an independent lifestyle can play a major role in preventing you from moving closer to a final decision to die. For example, as long as you can maintain your own residence or at least engage in some simple individual pursuits, such as shopping, walking, cooking, or bathing, you may be willing to keep facing whatever other conditions your illness places in your path. Nevertheless, as things get worse, and as you face the likelihood of increased dependency, you may begin to define these changes as a motivation for thinking about a self-enacted or assisted death.

If becoming dependent is such an incentive, you would do well to look at how you define your independence, and then determine if there might be other ways to grasp some sense of control over your life—even as you face the difficulties of your illness. Taking control over your health decisions is one way. Similarly, knowing that you always have control over the final decision to end your life can also provide a feeling of power when you can no longer dictate all aspects of your daily life. But you need to resist the urge to end your life as a way to "prove" your independence, autonomy, or control.

The concept of independence can have varied meanings during the dying process, and carries the potential for constant redefinition. For Ruth, a woman whose breast cancer had metastasized into her bones and brain, independence at first meant being able to work at home and continue the career that she'd built for herself over thirty years. When this was no longer possible, the meaning changed to overseeing the transfer of her business to her daughter, and then changed to mean "staying out of a wheelchair." Finally, after this was no longer possible, she came to define independence as being able to think clearly and make general household decisions. Only after she began to lose this ability, did she finally end her life.

Another woman, Louise, had lung and colon cancer as well as emphysema. She defined independence as being able to continue living alone instead of entering a retirement—and eventually a skilled-nursing—facility. To do this, she accepted in-home hospice care until a final move became inevitable. For her, this became the final straw. And for Bill, who was a well-known professional chef, independence first meant cooking his own meals then developing easy recipes for others to use. When he finally lost his appetite, he worked with his friends to ready his recipes for eventual publication.

Nevertheless, even the end of partial independence can be a difficult challenge. If at one time you hiked or ran alone, it can be a significant loss to engage no longer in these activities or even in simple solitary pursuits such as driving, shopping, or even making your own way through your home. One man, for example, described his feelings about shopping in the following way:

> I used to live for shopping, nothing extravagant, just bargain hunting. Mail order didn't do it. My idea of pleasure was going out for the day. Now I can't leave home. Even if I could, I don't like people looking at me. I keep imagining them saying, "He's going to scare off my customers" or "I hope he doesn't want to try on anything" or "Why is he shopping?" or "What's he need that for, he'll soon be dead anyway." And at some place inside, I think they're right. Now, when I'm not home I spend all my time hanging out in hospitals and doctors' offices and with other dying people. This is really much too hard to take.

Loss of independence may also include feelings of vulnerability, which can magnify your sense of loss. Another man told me how what would have previously been a "normal" encounter with a panhandler became too much for him emotionally.

> Last week, during a rare moment of feeling good, I drove my car to Safeway at night for the first time in months. What happened? I got accosted by a panhandler, a street person, who wouldn't leave me alone. I felt threatened, and scared, and no one would help. This isn't living if I can't live the life I love, if I can't leave my house.

FEAR OF BEING A BURDEN

The pressure of being cared for and the lack of resources within your home can, at times, make you feel that your presence is burdensome to others. This feeling can be further intensified if you or your caregiver are experiencing emotional stress or if harsh words are exchanged between you. This can happen when you feel a mixture of anger over your loss of independence and guilt over putting others out, or when your caregivers are not able to take the respite they need for themselves to avoid burnout.

Whether you are in your own home or another's, you may begin to feel that it might be better for you to be "out of the way" or to die quickly so others can get back to the lives they had before. If you "feel like a burden" and indeed may actually *be* a burden, this is no reason to consider ending your life. Realize that in some ways we all are both burdens and blessings to others, and instead of seeing your death as the best solution, another answer is needed, one that only requires that all involved parties adjust their expectations and learn better ways to choreograph their lifestyles and behaviors while they're together.

Maintaining schedules and specifying roles can do much to create a sense of normalcy. In this way, everyone knows what's expected and when. This can reduce stress and keep disruption of daily life to a minimum. As you and others begin to adjust to more balanced care-giving and care-receiving roles, the time you spend together can begin to become more enjoyable and start to look a lot less like a "death watch."

If you have fears of being a burden, the best approach is not to think about dying, but to share your concerns. As I'll describe in the next chapter, an open dialogue between all parties and a regularly scheduled time for everyone to discuss their concerns can reduce stress and also provide you with the validation that others still care. However, if your concerns are in any way upheld, then an open dialogue can similarly be useful for exploring alternatives, such as locating additional nursing support or respite care for your partner, family members, or friends who may be involved in helping you. Though you may not feel the need for in-home health services or hospice care, others may. Confronting the issue through discussion can do much to alleviate the feeling of being a burden, if you're willing to strike a compromise.

Fear of Nursing Homes

The thought of entering a convalescent care facility and being "bedridden and warehoused" during your remaining weeks or months of life is not at all appealing. You may equate this possibility with the end of your independence and the loss of all dignity and quality in your life.

If this is one of your basic fears and a primary reason for your thinking about ending your life, gather the facts about extended care and assess possible alternatives. Talk with your physician about the likely course of your illness, and whether you might be able to maintain your present housing arrangement until your death. In terms of alternatives, assess the range of skilled nursing facilities in your region, and also look into other options. These might include shared living arrangements, an exchange of care for room and board, a mixture of professional and voluntary nursing care provided by family or friends, or in-home hospice care where skilled nursing assistance is combined with daily visits from a nurse.

When you are in doubt, information is your most powerful tool. It can be helpful to share your concerns with your partner, family, or even your friends. You may find, for example, that your family members may be willing to take shifts and learn basic nursing skills to allow you to remain at home during your dying process. Moreover, once you check your medical insurance bene-fits, you also may find that a variety of in-home alternatives are paid for or reimbursed. By talking with your hospital social worker or calling your local hospice program, you may similarly discover that opportunities exist for residential hospice care, where physical and emotional support are provided.

For some people, the fear of convalescent care can become the final driving force that leads them to take their own lives. Unfortu-nately, these are not always "rational" decisions. This was the case with Ellen, a seventy-five-year-old woman, who was not terminally ill but had had a recent stroke, difficulty walking without pain, and was suffering from a chronic heart condition. Her son called me to say that his mother had told him she was planning to end her life, and he wanted me to talk with her. Ellen was stranded with few re-sources in her apartment in a small California town. Her son ex-plained that she had "run off" all her attendants even though she was becoming increasingly dependent. He said that she also was "cantankerous and condemning," and he went on to explain that she had no friends and no prospect for getting any, and that her neighbors wanted nothing to do with her. Nevertheless, due to her personality, behavior, and local reputation among nursing services, it was unlikely that she'd ever again receive at-home nursing assis-tance. According to her son, her independence had become a type of dependence. Instead of adapting to her changing physical con-dition, she placed increased responsibility on her family to care for her, while rejecting any help that might allow her to live independently.

He explained, "I would do anything for my mother but have her live with me." He said that his wife would "pack up and leave as they've never gotten along."

At her son's request I talked with Ellen, who told me she wanted to be left alone and was doing fine where she lived. She de-nied that she was planning to take her life at any time in the near future, even though her body was "giving out" and she was "tired of fighting a losing battle against physical decline and dependence." About her plans to end her life, Ellen explained that she was exag-gerating. "I have to blow off steam, to talk to someone about how miserable I feel." When I asked her if she had any drugs at home as her son believed, she admitted to having only a small amount of pain medication, "hardly enough to do anything," let alone kill her. When I asked her about her housing options, she told me that she "would never go to any retirement or nursing home" and "wouldn't even give it a try." She vetoed my suggestions for local counseling services but agreed to meet with me the following Friday.

Late Friday morning, as I was preparing to leave, I received a call from the county coroner. He told me that Ellen had just been found dead. She had left a suicide note in which she listed my name and phone number and asked whoever found her to call me to "cancel our appointment." Obviously shaken, the coroner, who was new on the job, explained that Ellen had been found on the floor with an empty bottle of pills near an empty bottle of bleach. He said there was a lot of blood around and he had no idea yet how she died. I called her son, who had just been told. He was upset, but even in the face of her death he was convinced that he did all that he could.

> She made her choice and, based on wanting to live alone, I guess it was a rational decision. It's not one I wanted, and I'll miss her very very much. I think I was the only one who loved her. My wife is devastated, but my mom wanted out, and she didn't want to talk about it with anyone. I guess this was her way of canceling all of her appointments.

I can only think that had she not been so set in her ways, had she been open to counseling and been able to compromise about in-home nursing care, she might still be alive. Instead, she left a grief-stricken son, and a daughter-in-law filled with a mixture of guilt for not giving in and anger that Ellen had "punished" her in this way for taking a stand.

Economic Considerations

No one should ever be forced to end their life for economic reasons. Nevertheless, I understand that lack of adequate medical insurance or financial reserves lead a small number of people to begin thinking about an assisted death as a way out of a feared or actual economic problem. Like them, you may feel that it's better for you to die early than to "spend down" your savings in order to qualify for Medicare or Medicaid benefits, in this way saving some of your resources for others for whom you'd like to leave something behind. In addition to feeling like an emotional or caregiving burden for your partner, family, or friends, you may also believe that you've become a financial drain on your partner or your family. This can lead to feelings of "guilt" or of "being in the way" or to the belief that you are using family resources that might better be spent on others.

If you have these thoughts, I'd advise you to use your journal and catalog your feelings as they occur. This may help you to locate the source of these feelings, obtain a clearer idea of how they arise, and eventually work with others to identify possible solutions. In terms of solutions, you might:

- Obtain a realistic understanding of your financial status and the current and likely future costs of your health care

- Talk to a hospital social worker and your insurance agent about your medical insurance benefits and other programs for which you may qualify

- Discuss your economic concerns with a financial planner who is knowledgeable about your assets, expenditures, likely health-care costs, and possible benefit programs

- Determine the real economic impact of your health care on those whom you feel that you are burdening

- Place yourself in the role of others whom you perceive are bearing this economic burden, and ask yourself whether your concerns are realistic and whether you would do the same for them

- Consider all the various expenditures you've made during your life, and ask yourself honestly whether your life is really less important—to you and those who love you—than these other expenditures

- Discuss your economic fears with those whom you believe you're affecting and who are more knowledgeable of the actual economic impact of your care on their lives

- Make certain that others are not pressuring you in any way, making you feel worse for being in a dependent role or making you believe that your economic impact on them is worse than it actually is

- Determine whether your economic concerns are influencing your decision more strongly than other factors, such as your *physical* and *social quality of life*

Information is a tool not only for determining whether you're an economic "drain" but also for finding creative ways to resolve any dilemma. Economic concerns are no exception, as information can help you separate facts from emotion. If you're worried about how you'll be cared for, or where you'll live later on until you die, information on benefits and programs can be useful. You might also contact cancer support groups or AIDS service organizations in your area. These types of organizations can also be effective places to learn strategies for obtaining additional benefits.

Similarly, there are a number of books with such information that are available at your local bookstore or library. I've listed a few of these in the Resources section at the end of this book. You may find, for example, that you can qualify for a number of hours of in-home health service or that you might be able to hire a caregiver, thereby providing a needed respite for your partner or family members. In addition, if you're terminally ill, there are a number of life insurance companies that allow you to cash in your policy for a portion of its face value, in this way freeing up assets and perhaps reducing your feeling of being an economic burden.

Moreover, if your feelings of being an economic burden are motivating you to consider assisted dying, you might also begin to look at your life as a balance sheet. In this way, instead of focusing solely on yourself as a current economic burden, you also need to see what you've already given to those caring for you. These might include economic support earlier in your life as well as those "gifts" that carry no price tag, such as your advice, emotional support, nurturance, or even your ability to provide peace or humor.

Open discussion is the best way to determine whether your feelings are real. What's critical here is for you to share your concerns and receive honest feedback. Only in this way can you obtain the information you need to make practical decisions and find alternatives. Ultimately, if you decide to proceed further toward deciding to die, you need to be certain that this action is based on the presence of other intolerable conditions, instead of unshared, and therefore unresolvable, emotional and economic concerns.

Some people eventually come to include economic concerns as one factor in their decision to end their lives. They do so based on their philosophy of family economics and desire to ensure the financial well-being of those they're leaving behind. This sentiment is not uncommon. One woman whom I interviewed, for example, told me that before her mother died the two of them had talked about her father. She said, "Mom decided that she wanted to leave something behind for him." The daughter explained:

> He would've spent it all on Mom, but she wouldn't let him. This was her way of giving him a more comfortable old age. Given what was not covered by insurance, the alternative would've been a fairly meager future for him. She knew this. She said to me, "Your dad's a neat guy, let's leave some for him." I agreed.

Similarly, a man with AIDS told me: "My medication is costing several hundred dollars a week, and I'm not covered." In talking about his partner, he explained: "He's taken out a second mortgage on the house to keep me going, but this is a fatal disease, and I know that if I live much longer, it's going to wipe him out. I just don't see that as fair." And a man with cancer told me that he was planning to die early because he wanted to give his niece "a head start in college." In all three cases, however, these individuals were also experiencing terminal conditions they defined as intolerable.

These decisions are seldom easy and can be motivated by either guilt or altruism. In looking at your own feelings, you need to assess which emotion is motivating you the most. Also beware of subtle manipulation by others, and ensure that your reasons for considering assisted death are always your own. It is for this reason that you need to continue exploring all possible reasons for ending your life as well as all available options for resolving your concerns. You should only proceed further toward a final decision when you find your conditions of living to be intolerable and you've begun to exhaust all reasonable efforts for staying alive. For the time being, this inner dialogue is yours alone.

Considering the Effects on Others

In facing this decision, there comes a time when you must begin thinking seriously about how the act of ending your life may affect others. You need to take a hard look and realize that your death—regardless of how it is brought about—will affect those whose lives you've touched. Knowing this, you especially need to ask yourself whether your death will be even more damaging emotionally to those you love if it's brought about by your own hand. To begin:

- Ask yourself whether others who will be affected by your death would fully support the reasons behind your decision

- Consider whether your partner, family, or friends would support your decision only because they believe this is what you want

- Determine, from past conversations, the ethical, moral, and religious beliefs of your partner, family, or friends regarding suicide and assisted suicide in the case of terminal and incurable illness

- Discuss the possibility of your death with your partner, family, or friends as a way to introduce the topic of loss and to judge how they might react to your death, regardless of how it occurs

- Use what you know about the behavior and feelings of your partner, family, or friends to judge whether such an action might in any way lead to feelings of guilt, anger, or intensified grief on their part

- Consider the psychological effects of your actions on others close to you, who may later discover the actual cause of your death, such as your children, siblings, or grandchildren

- Reflect on whether you've provided others with opportunities either to discuss how your death may affect them or to begin the dialogue they might require to discuss unresolved issues or achieve a sense of closure

If you are preparing to end your life, you need to be aware of the much larger social and psychological dimensions and consequences of your actions. This requires understanding the "web of connectedness" of which you are a part and knowing that your death is about severing these connections. It means that you need to be sensitive to the effects that your death can have on those who have been close to you over the years, even though, at times, you may feel very alone in your dying. Although this is your life and your death, you're a part of this web, and your life and death are in some ways greater than you. You are not only an individual, but also a son or a daughter, a mother or a father, a sister or a brother, a spouse or a partner, a friend or a neighbor, and part of a larger community.

Although you may believe that you have the *right* to end your life, you also have the *responsibility* to ensure that, if you do, this action is as positive as it can be, especially when others are involved or affected. In this way it needs to be an action that can release you from suffering while minimizing harm to others. As such, this decision is best arrived at slowly and thoughtfully, only after you assess and discuss the alternatives, seriously reflect on all your motives and feelings, fully consider all consequences, and consciously work to minimize any harm.

Much of this issue has to do with communication and with the need to open a dialogue with others on this topic. Only if you can discuss your thoughts with others can you make a definitive assessment as to how your actions might affect them. Until you know for sure, you shouldn't proceed further. This type of dialogue is complicated, emotionally laden, and needs to take place in several steps. I'll be describing these in detail in the next chapter. For now I'll just say that, in most instances, people don't know how to talk about this issue. I've heard many say, "My wife just wouldn't understand" or "My partner wouldn't be able to listen." One woman expressed this concern to me by saying, "How do I tell my husband that I'm thinking about checking out early rather than spending every possible moment with him?"

In some instances, you may very well have a clear idea of how others will respond. For example, one man, in sharing his thoughts about ending his life, told me, "I could only do this if it could be covered up; otherwise it would just kill my mom." Raised a Catholic, he felt that the religious considerations, which no longer bothered him, would "emotionally destroy" his mother. As he said, "She'd consider it suicide, and think I'd go to hell for it." Although Catholic theologians have softened their stand and now link suicide more with "irrationality" than sin, this man wasn't ready to use this argument to calm his mother's concerns. He then added, "Why add to her grief? I'll just have to find a way to let her think I died of natural causes." In this case, his concerns led him to create an elaborate plan to achieve his death while protecting his mother's religious sensibilities.

Others who have contemplated an assisted death have still thoughtfully reflected on the effects of such an action even at the last possible moments. For example, my friend Joy, a fifty-two-year-old woman dying from breast cancer, rhetorically asked:

> If I do this, how will it affect my grandchildren, knowing that grandma gave up, didn't keep fighting, but took her life? What message would this give them?

When she died two weeks later, it was a natural death at her home, in a hospital bed in the center of the living room, where she was surrounded by her husband, brother, sister-in-law, three children, and two granddaughters, both under five years of age. For Joy, there was no room for secrets, and no room for doubt about how others might be affected by her actions. Even so, some three days before she died she told her husband and me that she was "still reserving the option" for an assisted death, if her suffering made it necessary. Ultimately, however, her desire for a "physically peaceful death" became less important than holding on until the end so as not to harm her granddaughters by her actions.

Ethical and Spiritual Concerns

This inner dialogue, this consideration of your *physical* and *social quality of life* as well as your *emotional* and *economic* concerns, usually comes to a point where *ethical* and *spiritual beliefs* take precedence. Ultimately, you must decide whether ending your own life—with or without assistance from others—is ethically right for you, regardless of how you feel physically, socially, or emotionally. These ethical and spiritual concerns reside at the very center of the process of deciding to die. They may be either your starting or ending point. They may keep some from ever proceeding on this inner journey, and they may keep others from ever completing the final act.

At some point in your journey, therefore, you may well need to find your own answer to whether ending your life could ever be right. Before you continue any further, before you discuss with others the possibility of a self-enacted or assisted death, and before you begin actively planning a final course of action:

- Ask yourself whether you have the right to be in control of these decisions or believe that only God can give and take life

- Resolve whether it's ever right or wrong for a person to end his or her life if they're terminally ill and suffering intolerably from conditions that are irreversible

- Consider whether such a death under these circumstances is the same as an act of suicide, and if you view all suicide to be wrong

- Assess your ideas about death and whether you believe in an afterlife or reincarnation, which may be affected by a self-enacted or assisted death

- Decide whether it is right for others to assist you in your death, and if their afterlife or reincarnation could be affected by helping you in this manner

- Determine your attitude about the sacredness of life, and consider whether you might still be able to end your life in a way that respects this sanctity

These are not idle concerns, especially if you've lived your life within a religious and cultural support system that has provided you with a sense of purpose and meaningful answers. Like many, you may find comfort in looking for the deeper spiritual meaning of illness and death and for answers that help you determine whether an assisted death is right for you.

Chapter 3

TALKING TO OTHERS

David and his wife, Melissa, were driving home after seeing her doctor when she said, "Maybe we should do it early." These were the first words spoken since they heard the mixed message from her oncologist minutes earlier. He'd told them there were "still a few things" they could do, but she'd "probably continue to get worse." David told me how they were stunned by his comments as "she was feeling better." Instead, "the tumor markers were up." These test results indicated that the latest round of chemotherapy hadn't been successful. Like these findings, Melissa's statement about "doing it early" came as a shock.

> I was unprepared. She'd never even hinted how she felt about the right-to-die. And now she was saying this. It came out of the blue, and I pretended I didn't understand, so I asked, "Do what early?" And she looked over at me and said, "Get it over with."
>
> I didn't want to lose her any sooner than I had to, not even a day earlier, but in a way I was relieved she brought it up. I never would've, though I didn't want her to suffer. All I could do was ask, "How long have you been thinking about this?" And she said, "Just now."

Melissa's inner journey apparently began shortly before she voiced her thoughts. David said, "Perhaps she put it together after the exam, or in the elevator, or maybe she thought it out the same moment she told me." After fifteen years together they had "a close relationship where not much was censored."

Soon after their long drive home, they began a dialogue and over time talked in more detail about their feelings. Eventually, David undertook the task of finding out what they would need "to do it right." At first neither knew where to turn. David rhetorically asked, "I mean, how would we do this? What would we use? And where would we get it?" Gradually they found the information they needed and, after two in-depth conversations with Melissa's oncologist, finally secured his agreement to help "when the time was right."

Melissa's actual decision to die came months later, only after she joined a cancer support group, attended numerous meetings, and then finally began experiencing an irreversible deterioration she found to be intolerable. Her doctor provided a prescription that was filled over time, and the final day came a month after she began receiving home hospice care.

Opening up to Partners and Family

There may come a time when you, like Melissa, decide to take the next step and share with those close to you your innermost concerns about an assisted death. Facing a life-threatening illness is lonely and difficult enough without keeping thoughts such as these inside. To be silent only separates you from others and creates a barrier to the intimacy you especially need during this period. Opening a dialogue can provide you the opportunity to discuss your concerns about the dying process, hear the responses of others, and perhaps receive their support to resolve emotional issues. And if you ultimately decide to proceed further toward an assisted death, sharing these thoughts early on enables all of you to consider what this might entail, when this might occur, and what the consequences might be.

When Melissa told her husband, "Maybe we should do it early," she not only opened the dialogue, but alerted him that they would be jointly participating in all aspects of any final decision.

David told me, "She never asked me to help, but it had the same effect because we were always a team." He "instantly knew" they were on a "new path together" that would include a significant amount of discussion. As a result, David's help became something she just assumed. "There was never any question. This was going to be a loving act, and it was going to take place at the right time—not too soon and not too late."

THE BENEFITS OF TALKING

Sharing your thoughts with a partner, family, or friends can provide you with numerous benefits. Opening the dialogue can remove barriers to communication and enable you to:

- Express your innermost feelings and fears
- Move beyond the isolation that can accompany a terminal condition
- Reinforce the intimacy that exists in your personal relationships
- Obtain feedback and vital information from others that may lead you to postpone or reassess your decision
- Achieve emotional closure for yourself and others

Without understanding these benefits, you may feel that the aim of talking is solely to warn others of your intended action or to find someone to help you die. In this regard, you may find yourself questioning the value of such a warning. As one woman told me, "No, I could never tell my husband what I'm thinking." And a man referring to his family said, "I guess they'll find out when I do it." Unfortunately, both failed to see that lack of sharing not only makes an assisted death impossible but forever eliminates the potential for closure and emotional healing.

The purpose of talking goes beyond warning others. It enables you to take control of your dying in a way that provides both you and others the opportunity to resolve the unfinished business of living.

WHEN TO TALK

One of the problems you may face is determining *when* to discuss a subject that carries such finality. Talking about death doesn't come easy, and it may be difficult for you to bring up the topic of ending your life early, while there still might be hope for recovery. For this reason, you must find a time that's right for you. And you also need to find a way to introduce the subject that fits your style of communicating. The subject of assisted dying is special. During the course of your illness you'll need someone to talk with about your feelings. Find a balance between talking too soon and waiting too long. Consider whether sharing your feelings too soon—while there is still hope—might emotionally exhaust those close to you, or whether the consequences of waiting might be worse.

One way to find this balance is to look over the journal exercises in Chapter Two, and then separate your emotional concerns into two categories: those that involve others and should be shared with them; and those that are better discussed in a counseling session. For example, it can be valuable to both you and others to be direct in expressing your general feelings about dying. At the same time—because of their emotional complexity—your specific feelings of guilt about dying might best be dealt with in a therapeutic setting, first alone and then with those close to you. Then, when you finally determine that the time is right to discuss the possibility of an assisted death, look at the discussion guide at the end of this chapter, and select the approach that's right for you. Think about the time and the setting for this discussion and be thoughtful as to how others might be affected by the way you introduce this topic. Orchestration can be vital. In sharing your concerns with another, give yourselves the privacy that's needed and the time required to do this right.

For example, one woman told me how, like Melissa, her husband made a sudden statement regarding his death. The difference was one of location and circumstance. She and her husband were in a hospital room where he was receiving chemotherapy. They had not yet been told any news by his doctor. As a result, the statement by her husband filled her with shock and confusion.

> He was receiving chemotherapy. One minute he seemed hopeful. The next he turned to me and said, "This isn't going to work." He hesitated a second and then said, "It's okay." He said he felt a sensation of certainty washing over him that this was not the way for him. We looked at each other and for a moment I couldn't tell what he was going to do. I actually thought perhaps he was going to remove his IV and walk out of there, but he didn't. He was so calm. He smiled and then told me that we needed to "pick up that book on how to do it." Since he was smiling, at first I thought he meant something sexual, but then it dawned on me, because *Final Exit* was getting all this publicity.
>
> His smile kept me from losing it. I would've screamed right there, but he looked so calm, so certain, that I knew it was okay. At that moment I knew that treatments were out, he was really going to die, and we were going to do this ourselves. I say *we* because we never did anything without the other. If he was going to die, I was going to be there. That's the way we were. And that's what finally happened.

Although she was stunned by the abruptness of her husband's comments, she had no way to respond adequately. There was minimal privacy, and no way to not be overheard or to control access to his room. Looking back she seemed philosophical and explained that there may have been more serious problems had he waited much longer. "While Dick's statement shocked me at the time, at least it gave us a head start." As it turned out, his doctor gave them the news within a few weeks that the chemo wasn't working. Excuses aside, Dick could've waited until they got home.

Waiting too long, on the other hand, has its own problems. It may seem easier to delay until it's obvious that you're suffering or there's no hope for your recovery, but this approach increases the risk of failure. By waiting too long you may find that you've moved too far along a path toward dependency or death or that you no longer have the time required to obtain the support of your physician. As a result, it can place others in a reactive role, take away their power to make decisions for their own best interest, and can sweep them up in a rush to help. Such delays can hinder you from making reasoned and thoughtful decisions each step along the way, reduce the time for quality discussion or emotional closure and, therefore, create the potential for a more difficult grieving process for those you'll be leaving behind.

The Wrong Reasons for Waiting

You may intend to protect others for as long as possible. One man asked me, "How do I tell my mother that the only way to end my suffering is for me to end my life?" A woman with the same problem told me, "Why make them worry. Let them enjoy themselves a while longer." And another man said:

> I know my family would be there for me. They'd be concerned and sad. They're working so hard to keep me alive, I just don't have the guts to hurt them. They have to be more ready. They need to come to a place where they see that more treatment won't work. Then I'll talk to them. Not before.

In using "protection of others" as an excuse to wait, you might well ask yourself whom you're really protecting. For example, in talking about her parents, one woman with cancer told me, "I'll hold off for as long as I can, because I really don't have the strength to deal with their browbeating; they'd jump all over me and I can't handle that right now." And a man with AIDS said, "I'll just wait to discuss this until they *can't* argue with me, until I'm so close to death they won't say anything." This delay may temporarily protect both of you from dealing with the likely reality of your death, but it also prevents others from adjusting to this knowledge and from having time to say "good-bye." Additionally, it prevents both you and others from basing your decisions on everyone's personal needs.

Waiting can especially become a problem if you'll eventually want the help of another in dying. If you wait too long, the only ones left to help may be inappropriate, either because of their feelings for you or because of how such an action may affect them. Nearly all of my interviewees who participated in an assisted death expressed a strong preference for a more gradual process that would have included them earlier on. This could have provided them more time to adapt to the idea, share their concerns, accept their role, and consider the consequences more fully. A widower who helped his wife die told me:

> It was so quick from the time she talked about it until she actually died I had this picture in my head of a wife telling her husband that she was dissatisfied with the marriage at the same time she was walking out the door with her suitcase. I was shocked, totally taken by surprise. I needed more of a warning; more time to mull it over.

In some instances, more time to "mull it over" might've resulted in a very different scenario. One former support group member told me of the anger he still felt five years later, because his partner asked for his help "only at the last moment when it was too late for him to take control over his own death." He said he wished he'd said no. Similarly, another man told me how he'd felt manipulated, but added, "How could I say no when it was too late for any other solution?" And finally, after complaining about "being hurried," a woman explained, "If I had to do it all over again, and had more time to think about it, I probably would've done the same thing, but I just needed time. I didn't like being rushed."

AVOIDANCE BY OTHERS

Nevertheless, the successful creation of a dialogue doesn't rest solely in your hands. It's not uncommon for family and friends to refuse to discuss such an issue, believing that they can't talk about this *and* keep a positive focus on thoughts of your healing, recovery, or remission. This prevents them from having to cross, too soon, the bridge that leads to the inevitability of your death. In the most serious scenario, they also may not wish to deal with other important topics such as your need for a living will or a durable power of attorney for health care.

If you find that your partner or family members are in this category, consider that this avoidance may be based on fear that they may give the wrong impression if they do anything that supports the belief that you indeed are dying. They may worry that you'll misinterpret their willingness to talk as their belief that your condition is hopeless or that you have their permission to quit fighting. This isn't a message most partners, family members, or friends want to provide.

As a result, you may come to feel that you have "no one to talk to," or that no one is willing to discuss this issue. The problem may have more to do with the pattern of communication in your relationship. Though it's not your sole responsibility to break this pattern, it may be up to you to say, "Stop, I need to talk about my life and death." To do this most effectively, you might need to seek the advice of a therapist or find an outside facilitator who can help your partner or family find a balance that allows them to be both positive and supportive as well as open to your need for honest dialogue.

An Added Benefit of Talk

One of the added benefits of open communication is that it sometimes can delay or reverse a decision to die. This especially can be seen in instances where one's motives for dying might be less than appropriate or where others have reasonable doubts they can finally express. In this way, talking about this option may bring in new information as to the feelings of others, or provide you a "safety valve" that can relieve any immediate pressure to act. It allows you to share with significant others their innermost fears and, in many cases, receive in return the assurance of love and support that can keep you alive for longer. This is exemplified in the case of Rivka.

I was called by a friend to facilitate a discussion between Rivka and her private support group, which was comprised of Rivka's partner, my friend, and four others. Rivka's lung cancer had metastasized to her liver and brain and the chemotherapy was no longer working. She had told the group about her desire to die, but expressed her willingness to talk about it. I agreed to attend the session, and came with an associate.

The session began with Rivka explaining again her desire to "die now" instead of waiting for the cancer to take her through a winding course of pain, dementia, and finally death.

The group dissented and, though no one wanted her in pain, they all felt she needed to wait. To all of us, it seemed that something else, an underlying sadness, was prompting her hurried desire to die. When I questioned her on this point she admitted to an intense loneliness. In response, one of the group members talked of "a sacred moment" they all had shared a few weeks before in the courtyard of a local restaurant, before she became bedridden. One by one, the members described a "timeless moment of one mind, one soul" they'd all experienced. Rivka agreed that it was something she'd never experienced before, and then added that one reason she wanted to die was because "that moment had ended," and what they'd all shared was gone. She then said how she was reminded of this event a few days later when she saw a pottery sculpture of a "healing circle" in a store window. Emotionally moved, she bought it.

In response, her partner left the room and returned moments later with the sculpture. About a foot in diameter, it showed eight human figures holding hands, gathered in a circle around another figure in the center. Rivka said that looking at it filled her with sadness because she now felt "so alone, isolated, like the figure in the center." She'd failed to see the love and support that surrounded this figure.

To provide her a different perspective, I pointed out that the sculpture was one piece and all figures shared a common ground. My associate then told how redwoods often grow from common roots, and only look separate from the surface. As the image hit home, the group surrounded her, and Rivka smiled and began to cry.

As the session ended, Rivka said that she'd wait longer before she made her final decision. When the group met again the following week, Rivka was heavily sedated and her hospice nurse said she'd taken a turn for the worse. She was now close to dying from the brain tumor. She lasted five more days before she finally died, unconscious, free of pain, medicated with morphine, and surrounded by her friends and family.

Rivka's desire to talk about an assisted death enabled her to share her feelings of loneliness. Her statement, expressing her desire to die, opened the dialogue that allowed her to receive the feedback that changed her outlook. Instead of ending her life, Rivka and the group achieved an emotional breakthrough and final resolution.

Opening up to Your Physician

At some time you must begin to talk with your physician about *all* of your health-care concerns, including your thoughts about assisted dying. This means that you need to establish the kind of relationship with your doctor that allows you to discuss issues of pain and other discomfort as well as any quality-of-life and emotional concerns you may have. This is critical for receiving both the best quality health care possible and any eventual assistance in dying. The former may be more timely, but you'll never obtain the latter without establishing a thoughtful dialogue. These two needs go hand-in-hand. Remember that the primary goal of medicine is the alleviation of suffering, and this cannot be achieved without full knowledge of your condition and open discussion of all issues.

I believe that the ideal physician-patient relationship is one that is based on an open exchange of information, where you're able to talk comfortably about all of your concerns, and your physician is able to listen and then to respond by providing the facts needed for you to make the best health-care decisions. You have problems you need resolved and your physician has a range of possible solutions. Although it's ultimately up to you to determine what's best in regard to the type and level of intervention you desire, your physician needs to make recommendations that are based on his training and experience. What this means is that you and your physician must effectively learn to meet as equals.

Benefits of Talking to Doctors

Informing your physician about *all* of your concerns in a thoughtful manner might result in improved medical care through increased attention to your quality-of-life issues. In this way, you may be able to receive treatment that increases your overall quality of life for a longer period of time. I say this because I've often seen patients better served when they can convince their physicians that they're still not satisfied with their quality of care and are considering the possibility of an assisted death sometime in the future.

At the very least, communication can provide the information you need to make a more informed decision. Only then can you bring your thoughts and feelings to the attention of your partner, family, or friends. Beyond this, the rapport created by a more open relationship with your physician may eventually mean easier access to a lethal prescription. This can reduce the possibility of failure in any attempt you might make to end your life, and it can eliminate the need for others to become more involved in this final act than they desire. In addition, an open dialogue can provide the means to:

- Discuss your most important health-care concerns

- Reinforce the seriousness of your physical complaints

- Receive answers that can alleviate uncertainties about your health status

- Establish the possible presence of depression and obtain treatment or counseling referrals to resolve it

- Identify a range of health-care alternatives from which you can make decisions that are best for you

- Improve your chances for obtaining the best pain control and symptom management, either directly or through referral to specialists

- Learn strategies to combat difficult physical symptoms

- Obtain referrals and resource information to address a range of social quality-of-life issues

No physician can meet your needs without knowing what they are. And no thoughtful and professional physician will eventually provide you aid-in-dying without knowing that she has all the necessary information about your health-care issues and has at least attempted to address them. Because this takes time, you should establish an open dialogue with your doctor and discuss all of your concerns as soon as possible. This is especially important because some of your health-care needs may be more critical than others as potential motives for ending your life.

Moreover, since some of your concerns may be rooted more in emotional responses to your quality of life or tied to social circumstances, by discussing all of your issues your physician will be better able to respond to those that are most troublesome. For example:

> When my friend, Barry, told me that he was pushing up the time for his death, one reason he gave was that his doctor no longer cared. To him, the first sign was his physician's inability to treat his AIDS effectively. Barry had been told that he would "probably die within six months." The second sign came when, for a two week period, none of his "emergency" after-hours calls to his doctor were returned. The third and final sign was when he overheard an answering service operator exclaim, "Oh it's him again, the troublemaker." This provided him the certainty that he'd been "blacklisted" and abandoned by his physician.

I doubted this scenario, even though I could imagine that Barry wasn't the easiest patient; he was intelligent, demanding, and at times could be confrontational. I also saw this in his relationship with his partner. In fact, I believed his feelings of being abandoned by his physician had carried over from his recent feelings of neglect at home. Nothing had changed there, except his partner was working longer hours on a project and had finally taken a few days away to recuperate from work and caregiving. This vacation, though suggested by Barry, reinforced his loneliness, as his partner was "out having fun" while he was "at home dying."

It was obvious to me that Barry and his partner needed to talk about this and share their feelings. This was arranged with a counselor and proved successful. It was also apparent that Barry needed to take his concerns about being "black-listed" directly to his physician. I explained that this seemed a more reasonable solution than ending his life. He agreed.

When Barry and his partner informed his physician about what he'd experienced, his doctor became so concerned he gave Barry his home number, bypassing the answering service. By convincing him as to his availability, his doctor eliminated one of Barry's reasons for wanting to die early. And by standing up for him, his partner eliminated a related motive. Both of these issues were linked and carried the potential to affect his life-and-death decisions. Both were resolved by communication.

DISCOURAGEMENT = SILENCE

Unlike Barry, some people I've known, who faced a similar reluctance to confront their physicians, chose death. This response was driven, in part, because of their discouragement over past medical treatment and by their continued physical decline. Sadly, some might have lived longer with increased quality of life had they been able to discuss their feelings and dissatisfaction with unresolved symptoms. In talking with many such individuals, I've come away at times feeling that this person's pain and that person's discomfort might be controllable, if only patients can learn to tell their physicians the extent of their concerns and stop taking "We're doing all we can for you" as an answer. And after talking with interviewees about the deaths of their partners, family members, or friends, I again felt that their discomfort might've been better alleviated— and they might've been able to choose life a bit longer—if only their physician knew of their concerns as well as the seriousness of their interest in an assisted death; and if only their doctor was better trained in terminal care or in listening to what these patients were really saying.

Physicians and patients both share this responsibility. One doctor told me:

> Unlike animals, humans are able to describe their symptoms. But at times I often feel like I'm a veterinarian. I can't be close to a patient who doesn't let me in, or who makes it impossible for me to draw out, and create a relationship.

WHEN AND HOW TO TALK

The best time to begin to talk is as soon as possible, preferably at your next appointment. However, if you only see your doctor for a short while during these visits, call to set up an extended appointment. This ensures that there'll be adequate time to begin the dialogue.

Prepare for this meeting by developing an idea of what you want to accomplish in terms of both your short- and long-term objectives, and what you want to discuss. Using your journal, make a list of these objectives and itemize your health-care concerns in terms of their level of importance. For example, if your long-term goal is to stay alive for as long as possible with the highest quality of life, but your short-term objective is to attend a special event that requires travel, talk to your doctor about how a proposed long-term treatment might affect your ability to travel or enjoy this event.

And if your ultimate long-term objective is to receive your physician's help in dying, know that this requires that you establish a relationship. The way to do so is to hold these types of discussions and to begin working together to find a variety of solutions to your health-care problems. Only then will a thoughtful physician even begin to consider the possibility of helping.

One way to assess whether your physician will ever agree to help you die is to talk about your health-care desires in light of your condition. If you've completed whatever advance directives are available in your state or country, such as a Living Will or Durable Power of Attorney for Health Care, share these. This not only provides an opportunity to discuss a range of issues related to end-of-life care but can also protect you from receiving unwanted treatment in the future. If you haven't yet completed such documents, tell your physician you'd like to discuss your health-care desires for this purpose. In both cases, the topic of these documents can be used to open a dialogue about both practical and philosophical issues, and help you identify possible points of disagreement the two of you may have. And if he will not fully support your general health-care desires, perhaps it's time to look for another doctor.

If your physician will support your desires, however, you might then consider discussing other end-of-life choices, including an assisted death. A calm and reasoned discussion on this topic, with full disclosure of your symptoms and concerns, might have the added benefits of better pain control and symptom management—even if your doctor refuses to assist you in dying. Also remember that you're taking no risk here; you're only obtaining the information you need for determining the likelihood that your doctor will help you.

You may fear that any discussion of assisted death is tantamount to a suicide threat, which might result in a forced intervention and psychiatric assessment. Although doctors are usually required to intervene to stop suicides, they often ignore the rule when discussion is calm, it involves a terminal illness, and there's no threat of immediate action. If you phrase your statements in the right way, there's seldom any risk. One way to find out how your physician feels about the topic is to make the following type of statement:

Ultimately, doctor, I'd like to live with as much quality as I can for as long as I can. If I'm no longer able to enjoy life after trying all other reasonable options, I'd like a more humane way out, if worse comes to worse and my family agrees.

I support the right of terminally ill who are suffering intolerably to choose to end their lives with the assistance of their physicians. If I find myself in this situation, and I first try other reasonable options and talk with my family, I'd like this choice for myself.

Whether or not you receive a supportive response to such statements, realize that talking has another purpose: to obtain the information you need to separate fact from fear. This means asking for as much information as you can on your condition, prognosis, and all reasonable treatment options that might be available. Only in this way can you proceed forward in the process of deciding to die. Unless your health has deteriorated to an irreversible or terminal point, however, your physician may not feel comfortable talking about your prognosis or about assisted death. Talk of prognosis is almost always a judgment call that places too much of a burden on your doctor who may instead be willing only to discuss treatment options. Similarly, talk of assisted dying is difficult and risky, unless you and your doctor have established a relationship based on mutual trust. Also, since the decision by a physician to assist a patient usually depends on the facts of each case, your physician may be unwilling to discuss this possibility before she has all the facts.

Avoiding False Promises

Several patients and their families, as well as those who've assisted in the death of another, have told me of being "let down" by physicians, even though they thought they'd received the assurance that the doctors would "be there to help." In some instances this promise was only interpreted as such through words like "Your death will be easy" or "Don't worry, I won't let you suffer." In other cases, however, they saw promises in more explicit phrases like "When the time comes, you'll get what you need."

Statements like these can leave you wondering what is really being said. But instead of continuing to probe to obtain an explicit guarantee, you may feel as if you've talked enough. This could be a mistake, since words like these might also mean, "I work closely with hospice and I'll make sure you're not in pain" or "If worse comes to worse, I'll keep you sedated." Instead of ending here, you need to ask specifically:

Does this mean that you'll help me die? And if so, how?

or

Does this mean that, when the time is right, you'll provide me the right drugs to help me end my life?

and

Can we decide now what the "right time" might look like?

You may feel you have no one to talk to about such thoughts. Your partner, family, or close friends may be uncomfortable or unwilling to discuss this topic, or you may be separated from former friends and not on the best of terms with family members. Nevertheless, instead of growing more isolated in your thoughts and silencing your voice, it would be better for you to reach out to someone who can listen to your concerns and provide you the tools to think more clearly about your decision.

If you're alone or feel uncomfortable in sharing your thoughts with your partner or family, you might start this dialogue with a therapist or pastoral counselor or in a support group. In this way you can work around your broader emotional issues, vent your frustrations, learn how to communicate more effectively with your physician, and establish greater intimacy with those close to you.

Many who proceed toward an assisted death don't take advantage of these resources. Some are uncomfortable with the idea of sharing something so deeply personal. Others imagine a stigma to therapy, thinking that it somehow implies mental illness. Still others fear they might be "turned in" to authorities if they openly express a desire to end their life.

Indeed, there are laws to protect you if you're considered to be "at-risk" for suicide but, as I'll discuss shortly, there are ways you can talk safely with counselors and other mental health professionals or discuss your concerns in support groups. Opportunities exist in most communities for you to share your feelings about death and dying, loss of quality of life, sadness over leaving friends and family, and your difficulty communicating with your partner, family, or friends. And you may even be able to discuss your philosophy and thoughts about an eventual assisted death, if you choose well, establish rapport, and are cautious in phrasing your statements.

Sadly, however, until the laws on physician aid-in-dying are changed, specific details of an imminent act are best *not* discussed, even though this probably is the time when counseling intervention is most needed. How else can your motives for wanting to die, and the motives of others who are willing to help you, be properly understood?

The Benefits of Counseling

Although there may be risks in talking, these can be outweighed by the numerous benefits you may obtain from a counseling setting. Describing your concerns with your counselor and carefully discussing your thoughts about assisted death can allow you to:

- Explore your feelings about dying, loss of future goals, and unresolved physical and social quality-of-life issues

- Provide your therapist with a means to identify the symptoms of a possible depression and explore the options for its treatment

- Locate other sources of emotional pain such as unresolved loss or the lack of emotional support within your relationships

- Learn new strategies for combating both your emotional and physical symptoms

- Obtain practical tools to communicate with others and improve your personal relationships

- Work on interpersonal issues directly with your partner or family within the setting of a family or couples counseling session

- Acquire the attitude and means to talk more effectively with your physician to resolve your symptomatic concerns

- Assess your own needs and the needs of others for emotional closure

- Develop a plan to work with your partner, family, or friends around all of your end-of-life decisions

- Share your reasons for wanting to die, and receive feedback on your motives

- Determine the possible effects of an assisted death on those you love

- Evaluate your decision to end your life in light of other options and from a more emotionally balanced perspective

The benefits you experience will vary according to your specific needs, the ability of your counselor, and what you put into the session. The latter is critical, as therapists are not mind readers and can't help you explore your issues unless you are willing to talk from the very beginning.

One additional advantage of counseling I've witnessed on several occasions, as I described earlier in the case of Rivka, is the connection between "talking" and "deciding to die." If you address emotional concerns, it's possible to postpone or delay the final decision to die until the most appropriate moment. This is not uncommon. Elaine, a support group member, told me:

> Whenever I bring up the topic to my friends, they tell me how I "shouldn't talk like that," or that "everything will be wonderful." When I no longer had this option, I began to feel more and more isolated, as if I were living behind a mask that wasn't me. Inside I began to plot ways to end my life. Now that I can talk about it with people who don't think I'm crazy, I feel that the pressure's off.

Others have expressed to me that being able to open up is "like a safety valve." Adding to this metaphor, another person once said, "If I have to keep myself closed up, I'll explode, and there's no telling what I'll do."

THE FEAR OF THERAPY

In many instances, talk about wanting to die can be risky. Unless you structure your statements in the right manner, there's always a slight possibility that an over-zealous therapist or support-group leader might "turn you in." Indeed, there are some groups, therapists, and physicians who rigorously follow laws that require them to intervene if a patient or client appears to be at-risk of harm to themselves or others. In such a case, police could be called to take you to a community psychiatric facility for short-term observation and mental-health evaluation.

One man told me how, in another group, he'd been picked up by authorities for just this reason. He explained, "I need to be able to talk about it, but this doesn't mean I'll ever do it." Unfortunately, this member hadn't learned how to share his feelings discreetly.

A similar situation can exist for family members and others who share too much. One woman called to tell me her story of being picked up by the police after she told her therapist that she'd just helped her father "find the drugs" he would need to end his life. When she was questioned by the police, she denied the conversation. However, she worried that his future death—whether self-enacted or assisted—might result in a criminal investigation. Although she wanted to be present at his death, she no longer believed that this would be possible. Sadly, she felt that her father would now have to die alone. This fear also carries over to talking after a partner or family member has assisted in a death. One woman, who helped her husband die, explained:

> When my first husband and I broke up, at least I could tell my friends, and a few of them were really there for me. But when Jim was dying, I didn't have anyone to talk to about it. I

couldn't tell anyone what we were planning or what finally happened. My therapist was the last person I would trust.

Similarly, Ruth explained to me how she used Valium to "shut down" her feelings for two years after she assisted in the death of her husband. She never shared with her psychiatrist what she called "the real reasons" behind her grief and anxiety. "I couldn't tell anyone what I'd done. I was eighty years old, I couldn't risk arrest, and I couldn't bring this worry to my children."

This suggests a gap in mental-health service that reinforces secrecy and therefore reduces opportunities for the dying and their significant others to reach out, defuse the emotional turmoil inside, and receive the professional feedback that can help them make the most thoughtful decisions.

This situation is changing. A small though growing number of therapists are beginning to allow their terminally ill clients to talk about "rational suicide." In this regard the most significant change has come from the National Association of Social Workers. At their 1993 annual meeting, NASW's ethics and policy committee voted to change the code of ethics for association members to allow its members to be present at suicides *or assisted suicides* of their terminally ill clients as long as they don't directly assist in the death or provide them the means for dying. This step is likely to be followed soon by other professional associations. The result will mean more freedom to talk and, hopefully, more opportunities to consider thoughtfully all options and everyone's needs.

Selecting a Counselor

The relationship between a therapist and a client can resemble a marriage. A session can include a personal confrontation with some of the most painful aspects of your life, and it can bring up aspects of yourself you may find difficult to face. Since it's not always easy, absolute rapport is vital.

Like physicians, counselors can differ in terms of specialty and approach. Some are generalists while others focus only on couples or marriage counseling. When you make your selection, think about your primary concerns (as discussed in Chapter Two) and then ask for referrals from others such as your hospital or hospice social worker, minister, physician, and friends. If possible, see more than one counselor before you decide which one is best for you.

How to Talk

The secret in talking with a counselor about assisted dying is to begin by establishing rapport then focusing on the emotions and special concerns that may be linked to your reasons for wanting to die. Work on these issues separately. Only explore your thoughts about assisted dying after it's obvious to your therapist that any possibility of clinical depression has been dealt with or dismissed.

Then, if you feel the need to talk about it:

- Bring up the topic of assisted death only as one of several options you're thinking about

- Discuss this option in a calm manner, while you're in a more rational—and less emotional—frame of mind

- Avoid connecting the topic of assisted death with any discussion of strong emotions, such as sadness, depression, anger, or feelings of being a burden

- Link the topic of assisted death only to concerns about your physical quality of life or your fear that your quality of life will deteriorate too far to enjoy

- Concentrate your discussion around ways to achieve the most out of your life for as long as possible, how to include others in your decision, or how to identify rationally the point at which enough is enough

If you use this approach, any fears you might have in talking about this issue should dissolve. No therapist should find cause to complain if you make the following type of statement:

I have few options. I can continue my treatment, but even my doctor agrees that this will probably be of little value. Ultimately, I don't want to suffer, and I want to be able to maintain some quality of life to the end. If this becomes impossible it would be nice to have the option of an assisted death. I haven't yet talked with my doctor about this, but my wife agrees that if worse comes to worse, we should probably approach him together.

Before then, I'd like to be certain that I'm doing the right thing, and for the right reasons. And I'd like to talk with you about this, and eventually bring my wife in so we could talk about it together.

I hope it never comes to this and if it does it's still a ways off. But I'd prefer thinking about it now so I can get it out of the way and get back to the business of living. Does this make sense to you? Do you think you could work with us on this?

This approach—direct, rational, and practical—cannot be faulted. It makes much more sense than the following types of statements:

This illness has taken so much from me, I don't think I can handle it anymore. It's destroying what's left of my marriage, and I really feel enough is enough. I'm going to get the drugs I need and just do it!

I've become such a burden on my family, and I feel so useless, I know there's really no reason for me to go on any longer.

These concerns—the impact of your health on relationships, the feeling of being a burden—can still be dealt with safely. To do so, avoid linking them with the topic of assisted dying. Instead, connect them with your search for possible solutions.

This illness has taken so much. Now I feel it's destroying what's left of my marriage. I'd like to talk about what it's doing to me, and bring my wife in so we can work on this, and maybe put our marriage back together while we still can.

Lately, I sense I've become a burden on my family and feel useless. I'd like to learn how to deal with this and find ways to take some pressure off my family.

SUPPORT GROUPS AS AN OPTION

In addition to private counseling, there's much to be gained by joining a support or discussion group. In such groups, the most important criteria to look for is mutual support and openness. You need to feel that you can safely share both your feelings about your death and dying and your issues around your social and physical quality of life. Although it might also be helpful to be able to discuss, without judgment, your thoughts about assisted death, the primary aim of a group is to let you address the emotional issues that may underlie your decision to die. These may include: sadness and anger at your fate, your physical and social quality of life, and loss of future goals; your regret over lost opportunities or past "mistakes"; your feelings of neglect by others; or any shame or guilt you may feel for leaving those close to you. These and other concerns around dying are universal, and the right group may allow you the opportunity to deal with them in varying degrees.

Find a group where you can share such feelings openly and talk about the very real fact that you're going to die. The latter can be done in positive ways, and does not have to be morbid or negative. Beyond the seriousness of the topic, you may find that there can also be a time for laughter. (The aim of my own groups and workshops, for example, is for participants to discover the more positive effects they can achieve by confronting their deaths. I'll be exploring some of these in more detail in Chapter Six.)

For these reasons I recommend that, if you don't know where to start, begin by making a list of some of the more general issues you'd like to address. Obviously, it's difficult to know what exactly will be important until you're in a group and hear others talk, but think about what's most important to you now. Then use the same approach I just outlined for finding a therapist. In addition, you might also ask other patients with whom you have contact or find out what special organizations exist in your area that may have their own groups, such as the Cancer Society, MS Society, AIDS organizations, or even local chapters of the Hemlock Society.

Not all groups that serve those with life-threatening conditions have the same "culture," so shop around. Attend a meeting and see how it feels, and at least use this as an opportunity to get information regarding other resources that might exist. Some groups have their own ideology or are more open than others. For instance, one man with AIDS explained his complaints about one group he attended: "I could talk about my fear of dying, but I couldn't say the 's' words—suicide or self-deliverance." He continued, "I couldn't really get support, because I felt I had to censor everything." The need for nonjudgmental openness is especially crucial for discussing assisted death. As a caller once stated:

> I can't be open if I'm afraid of being judged. I need to express who I am *as I am*, and while I don't want to offend anyone who doesn't agree with me, if I need to say something, then I'll just have to say it even if it hurts someone's dogma.

OTHER RESOURCES

If you're faced with an emotional crisis and an immediate need to talk about any of the concerns I have covered, do not hesitate to call suicide prevention, a crisis hotline, or community mental health services in your local area. You'll usually find a supportive ear and can often receive referrals for counseling or lists of resources and community services to help you deal with your specific concerns. Contacts for crisis intervention can be found in your telephone directory, and a few are provided in the Resources section of this book.

In addition to private therapists and support groups, there are several Hemlock Society affiliates across the country with white-page phone listings who provide callers the opportunity "to talk." In the San Francisco office, for example, there are days when nearly a dozen calls come in from either those with life threatening conditions or their significant others. This doesn't include calls from others who are interested in finding information on how to die, where to buy "the book," or where to get a doctor to help, or where to get the drugs to die.

Upon probing these callers, it's not uncommon to hear them admit that they've not yet shared their concerns or desires with their partners, family, or friends. Although Hemlock hotlines typically don't provide any specific information, they often let callers express their feelings. Those on Hemlock phones often find that the real reason people call is to talk safely with someone who, as one man once said, "won't put a trace on my phone." Callers aren't necessarily interested in ending their lives or in being prevented from doing so. Most just want to discuss the idea.

In addition to the phones, Hemlock Society affiliates in a few locales across the country also run discussion and support groups. Affiliates in San Diego and San Francisco, for example, have been offering groups for several years.

A Guide for Opening Discussion

In reaching out to others, you should decide what you really want from such communication and, of course, what you really need. Are you looking for final approval, someone to listen, compassion, a supportive friend, or help in dying? Remember that you can reach out and talk about dying or about your desire for your suffering to end even if you have no intention of "speeding up the process." You may just feel the need to complain, to express your sadness about dying, or disappointment over not being able to live your life as completely as you'd wished. In knowing this, decide what you want your words to achieve.

In opening up the dialogue, in bringing up the topic of a self-enacted death, know that others may read your talk as asking for "permission to die," or as "a request for help." Depending upon your relationship and prior conversations with this person or persons, be aware that they may respond accordingly. Under all circumstances, be clear what it is you're expressing, and avoid setting into motion a situation you never intended. Be aware that only full communication can prevent such misinterpretation.

Although the process of reaching out is intimately tied to the decision to end your life, it has a greater potential to provide the opportunity to discuss all of your concerns regarding both dying *and* living. It is this sharing of concerns, working with others to reach closure, exploring what such a death is all about, that conceptually differentiates such an act from "suicide." It moves it from being an isolated event to one that can potentially be supported and assisted as an act of love by others. Seen in this way, reaching out should never be a "cry for help" or a plea to intervene. Instead, it should be a demand to talk and, ideally, allow you and others to open your hearts and minds to explore *all* options, including this option to die at your own time.

There are various ways you can discuss the option of an assisted death with those close to you. I'll describe three. The first involves conversations over time within the context of an intimate relationship. The second is gradually to open the dialogue to include others with whom you'd also like to share your concerns. This could occur during a series of informal family or group meetings, with the more critical meetings being structured and possibly involving someone who could act as a facilitator. The third approach is to use the format of a family counseling session, with your therapist acting as a mediator. The approach you finally choose will depend on:

- Your own preferences and skills in communication

- The level of intimacy you share with those with whom you'd like to talk

- The emotional comfort you feel with those present

- The number of individuals you wish to include in this dialogue

- The status of your physical health and your mobility

Each approach has its own features. An informal series of intimate discussions or family meetings work well if you have a close relationship and rapport with the person or persons involved. This approach, however, requires intimacy and the respect for all opinions. Without the latter, there is a potential for a shared outlook to develop that reflects the strongest opinion, regardless of what each individual wants. This can be avoided with facilitation and thoughtful dialogue.

In other instances, where emotional comfort is lacking, you

might prefer to use the more structured setting of a family or couples counseling session. The benefit is that you have a built-in facilitator who can help you introduce topics and both guide and mediate the dialogue. This approach can also be helpful if there are other subjects to discuss or if there are strong emotions involved or unresolved issues within the group. The problem with this approach is that the perceived need for secrecy may constrain openness. For example, if you've come to the point of making your decision and need to discuss final plans and levels of involvement by others in your death, such a session can create ethical issues for your therapist. She may feel bound to intervene because of conscience and legal requirements. For this reason, counseling sessions should begin earlier rather than later in your decision-making process and focus only on the general issues of assisted death. They should *not* focus on topics of "exactly when and where." Nevertheless, these sessions should be seen as valuable ways to introduce the topic, to discuss your reasons for considering it, to address related emotional concerns, and to facilitate dialogue to help resolve interpersonal issues that stand in the way of closure.

The third approach is to hold a series of family or group meetings. This works well if more than a few people are to be included in the dialogue, you're comfortable with this method for problem-solving, or if your health prevents you from leaving your home. If you don't feel at ease in leading the discussion yourself, consider having a facilitator present. Such a person—a close friend, minister, or counselor—can help lead the discussion and provide you and others with emotional support. I've been present at several such sessions and have seen the benefits up close.

The Planning

Given the importance of what is to be discussed, create a rationale for determining both who you want and don't want to attend, and take into account the feelings of the latter. If your therapist is to be involved, discuss your rationale for these meetings and receive feedback before you set them up. Select the location based on your goals for the particular meeting and your needs for both physical and emotional comfort. The key here is for *you* to be able to communicate openly and share your concerns.

Arrange a time in advance with your therapist, counselor, or minister, and inform all others who are to be present. If you're planning on leading the meeting yourself and would like several others to attend, you might have someone else arrange this for you. Have this person tell all concerned that you'd like to discuss your health status and special concerns.

If you've decided to use the format of a family or group meeting, it might be advisable to establish a firm starting and ending time, or a minimum amount of work you'd like to accomplish. If at any time during the meeting you find yourself lacking the energy to continue, stop at a convenient point and set a time for a follow-up meeting.

BEGINNING THE DISCUSSION

Everyone should be told at the outset that you want to talk about your illness, and that you're interested in open and honest discussion. Depending on how you've structured the event, it might also be explained that:

- You see this as perhaps the first of many similar discussions

- You'd like to begin by giving an official status report on your condition

- You'd then like to provide a personal assessment of your health concerns

- You plan to keep everyone informed of any changes in your condition

- You'd like to use the meeting as an opportunity to talk about a range of topics

Think about how you'd like the event to evolve and what you want to accomplish. Depending on who's present you may feel the need for "ground rules." For example, you might begin by explaining that while you appreciate support, prayers, and positive feelings about your eventual recovery, you're more interested in honest discussion. You then might feel like saying that this is a meeting to share information and feelings, that everyone's opinion will be respected, but interruptions or arguing will not be tolerated. Explain that you hope everyone is comfortable with the rules, and you might add that if anyone feels too embarrassed to share in the group, they can talk with you privately.

If you believe that your death is inevitable, you might also bring this to the attention of those present, after you discuss the basics of your condition, and explain that you want them to begin thinking about this.

> *Although I probably have looked the same to you over the past few months, I'm not feeling the same. And I want to talk about this a bit.*
>
> *The treatments I've been receiving have worked well and kept things in check, until recently. Now things are beginning to change, and I'd like to talk about it.*
>
> *Although I'm planning to continue my treatments for as long as I can, things are not looking as positive as they once did.*

If you have particular concerns about being an emotional or economic burden on others, you might take the time to share your thoughts gently and explain that you're especially interested in working together to find ways to resolve any problems.

> *You've all been doing the best you can, and I appreciate this, but lately I've been feeling that things are becoming more difficult around here and I want to talk about it and see if we might find some ways to make things easier.*
>
> *Part of the problem with being sick is that health care costs so much. I've been worried about this, looked into it, and want to share what I've learned. Then I want to talk about how it makes us feel and see if we can resolve this problem.*

You might then move on to other specific concerns or news you'd like to discuss. For example, if you haven't established a durable power of attorney for health care or living will, you might describe your own thoughts on the matter and state that you're interested in hearing other opinions. If you already have such a document, and have selected a proxy (surrogate decision-maker), inform your group of this fact. Moreover, if you've specified your preferences about end-of-life intervention, share these as well. Then ask if anyone has any comments about your preferences.

This might naturally lead to a discussion about end-of-life intervention and the ethics of a range of life-and-death decisions. You might use the comments of others to judge their openness to the topic of an assisted death. If there might be serious ethical objections or a lack of openness to this topic, you might do well to hold off further discussion of the issue until a later meeting. This is a judgment call on your part. Remember, end-of-life decisions might not be easy topics for others to discuss, especially in light of your physical condition and the special nature of the meeting.

If you decide to continue with the topic, you might begin by specifying your hope and preference for an easy death in the distant future. You might then say:

> I certainly wouldn't want a long, hard, painful dying process. Although this might not happen in my case, if it did begin to happen, I'd certainly like to have a variety of options available to me, including an assisted death.

If you meet serious opposition to such a statement, you might state that you're just sharing your thoughts, and that you haven't reached a decision or begun any planning, but you wanted everyone to discuss their feelings. In response to concerned comments, you might say:

> We've all been hopeful, and I'm still holding on for as long as I can. After all, we're a family and we're in this together. But I think it's okay to start talking about other possibilities, just in case things get bad. It doesn't mean I'm going to do anything, but I need to talk.

You might then explain that you'd never want to do anything that would hurt your family or friends, but that if you were suffering you'd have to take a long hard look at how much more you could take. You might then strongly point out that you'd never engage in such an act just because others support it or feel it's the right thing to do in your case.

These statements might inevitably lead to further sharing of ideas about the ethics of self-determination in end-of-life decisions, and religious or spiritual views about life, death, and afterlife. In this regard, a number of questions might come up for discussion, such as:

Do you believe anyone has the right to consider an assisted death?

What conditions or level of suffering should a person have before they have the right to make such a decision?

Do you believe someone in my condition has the right to consider this?

When and under what conditions might such an action be appropriate?

Do you believe it's ever right for someone to assist in another's death?

Use the knowledge you gain from this discussion to help you shape your own ideas, to determine if further discussions are necessary, and to decide whether anyone should be excluded from future meetings on this topic in order to protect them emotionally. And if you later decide to proceed further on this course of action, you might use this knowledge to exclude such a person from knowing about your plans. This is something to which you need to give very serious thought.

If it feels right, you might end the meeting with a ritual that reinforces the fact that all of you are linked, all of your thoughts and feelings are appreciated, and that it's important to continue working together to resolve what you believe are family concerns. This ritual might be in the form of words to this effect or some mutually accepted act like gathering in a circle, holding hands, or sharing a prayer or moment of silence.

You also might take this time to say that you understand that some might not feel "complete" with you, and that you're willing to meet with anyone individually to discuss their concerns. Once the opportunity for communication has been established, it's likely that several additional topics and issues will emerge. Although these may or may not have anything to do with the topic of assisted death, further meetings provide the structure to discuss such issues.

· · ·

Opening a dialogue with others is a critical component of the process of deciding to die. This component, however, should not be seen as a single event or conversation, but an ongoing pattern of interaction with others that can ensure that whatever decision you finally make is based on feelings and facts, not fears, and that it's a result of a careful balance of both your physical and emotional needs on the one hand, and the concerns of those closest to you on the other. Such a dialogue is more than a forum where you "publicly" declare your desires or demand help in dying from your physician or others; it is a conversational means by which you can share your concerns and receive feedback from others. It is a structured opportunity in which you can hear voices other than your own and express your feelings about dying. In this way, it can serve as a tool to achieve resolution, a starting point for the process of closure, and a warning to others about your inevitable death.

In addition, such a dialogue sets the stage for the practical preparations necessary for the final decision, which I'll discuss in more detail in the next chapter. Bringing the topic of assisted death into the open allows you to discuss possible ways you might die and how you might achieve the means to do so. It enables all of you to discuss practical problems, explore solutions, and trade information.

This is the last decision you'll ever make. It should be made thoughtfully and with the right motives, best intentions, concern for others, *and* planning. You don't want those you leave behind to face a legacy of regret, guilt, and grief, but to achieve resolution and find as much joy as possible regardless of how you eventually die. This dialogue, therefore, has the potential to transform your final decision from an emotionally painful experience into an act of love for everyone involved.

Chapter 4

PREPARING FOR
THE FINAL DECISION

Edie told me that when her husband, Jim, first shared his desire to end his life he also asked her to find out what he might need to "die at home, comfortably." She reflected, "I'll never forget. He said, 'I really can't go on becoming less and less each day; I want to go while I still know how to smile.' Then he said, 'Could you look into this a bit?' And the way he put it made so much sense, so I agreed."

In failing health from terminal prostate cancer, Jim was now confined to a world that included his bed and wheelchair. "On good days he'd sit for a time on the patio and read, but most of the time he'd stay in bed or lie on the sofa." What he enjoyed most was feeling well enough to eat with his family when his sons came to visit after they got off work.

After Jim made his request to Edie, she talked to her closest friend who told her about the book *Final Exit*. Edie and Jim read it, discussed it with their children, then talked to Jim's doctor, who agreed to provide the drugs. Edie said, "When Jim reached a place of pointless suffering, we followed the instructions in the book." She made pudding, their two grown sons added the drugs, and Jim ate the mixture. "This was the boys' idea; we were all to be involved," Edie explained. "Then we said good-bye—even though we'd all been saying good-bye for a solid month—and four hours later he was gone." Jim's doctor helped in one final detail; he signed the death certificate, stating that Jim died from complications resulting from prostate cancer.

As can be seen in Jim's case, opening a dialogue with others can be critical to creating the opportunity for resolution and the option for an assisted death. By sharing his thoughts with Edie, Jim set the stage for further talk and also created the possibility for an assisted death. Only by asking for her help did Jim begin the process that finally enabled him to secure the drugs he needed from his doctor. In this way, without advance preparations, the decision to die remains but a concept. While these steps don't have to lead to a final act, you may be tempted to wait and postpone even beginning the process until you're nearly ready to end your life. By then, however, it may be too late. This almost happened in Jim's case. Although he finally opened the dialogue with his family and physician and secured the right drugs, he'd waited too long to take on the task of exploration personally. Instead, he had to involve others. Moreover, he'd failed to provide himself the margin of time to find backup sources for the drugs he needed. Jim was fortunate as his physician could've refused to help. Others haven't been so lucky. A caller dying from AIDS, once told me:

> I'm too sick now to find out what I need or get on the streets to look for drugs. Maybe one day I could've done it, but not now. I need help. I know I blew it. I screwed up, but I didn't want to die before. Now I do.

This is a far too common situation. As a consequence, if you delay you may need more than just information on how to die; you may need direct help in obtaining what you need. And this may well mean involving others without giving them the time to talk and think it over. In this way, what might otherwise have been a mutually explored and planned final act of love can become an act of desperate obligation.

Beginning the Search

If you're contemplating an assisted death, you would be wise to consider the final steps early enough to prevent a rush to less thoughtful action. Soon after you initiate a dialogue with others about your thoughts and their concerns, you might consider:

- Discussing with them the possibility of moving a step farther in the decision process by gathering information on how to die

- Explaining that this does not mean that you've begun planning for an assisted death, but that you want to know more about what such an act might entail

- Obtaining feedback from them about this next step, and whether they feel comfortable with this process of exploration

- Sharing with your therapist your desire to explore this option more fully

This approach has the potential of bringing you closer to those who care for you by eliminating the secrecy that can otherwise surround this exploration. It also can enable you and others to replace illusions with facts by learning what an assisted death might entail.

If you decide to move forward, the next step is to obtain information on ways to die that are peaceful and humane and won't tragically scar those you'll leave behind. This information will most likely pertain to the use of prescription drugs and dosages that do not accentuate suffering, but bring on rapid unconsciousness followed by death in a predictable period of time. If assisted death is the path you choose, any other method—especially violent means—should be avoided. After all, what we're talking about is an act that brings death as peacefully as possible, eliminates the need for further involvement by others, and enables others to be present to provide you support during this ultimate rite of passage.

Although opponents of assisted dying have argued that decriminalization is unnecessary since "we all have the right to kill ourselves," the current legal situation leaves few options available if you have a life-threatening condition. Without resorting to violence, you must either follow the course of your illness to its natural end or identify and secure the proper drugs for a peaceful end. The latter takes planning and time. A close friend, suffering severely from AIDS, once told me, "The only way for me to kill this disease is to kill the host." But he then added, "I won't do it violently; I'll get the right stash, and take my time until I can't stand it any longer." He continued, "Violence would feel too much like suicide, and this act is *not* suicide." Remember, violence leaves a shocking visual and public legacy with even the most supportive partner, family members, and friends, and it prevents any possibility for their being with you at the end of your life to share their last words and final good-byes. While this may not be important to you, it may be critical to others and especially helpful in easing their grief.

THE ULTIMATE WINDOW SHOPPING

Although exploration is a key part of the final process of deciding to die, it might be best if you consider this step as not irreversible, but merely providing added information. The great majority of explorers I've talked with continued no farther, but treated this as a serious form of window shopping. It provided them the opportunity to see if this path was right for them. It wasn't, but they needed to find out for themselves.

Like them, this exploration can help you decide either to continue forward or accept the path toward a natural death. Ultimately, it can give you the knowledge to decide if this is the best alternative for you and your loved ones. To reach this point you need to learn what's involved, what works and what doesn't, and which method—if any—is right for you.

After you've discussed this next step with your partner, family, or close friends, assess what sources of information exist. Where you finally go depends on your preferences, abilities, personal contacts, and amount of special knowledge you may possess. For instance, if you can express yourself comfortably in talking with your doctor, you may decide to begin your search there. Or if you want to take a slower and more "private" approach, you might peruse written materials on the topic. You might also use personal contacts with medical training or even reflect on your own experiences as a medical professional or patient, as a part of the cancer or AIDS "communities," or even as a former law-enforcement officer, substance-abuse counselor, or drug user. Any past experience may have relevance.

One night, in the summer of 1991, discussion in a Hemlock support group turned to the book *Final Exit*, which had just been published. One member explained his recent purchase by saying, "I love reading *Road and Track* and *Car and Driver* too, even though I'll never buy another car." Another member equated it to a travel guide or ads for vacation getaways.

> It's not like I've decided where I'm going or even *if* I'm going. I haven't bought a ticket yet. I'm just window shopping. Like they say, knowledge is power, and as sick as I am, right now I have too little power. Maybe this will give me a little more.

As in the case of these two men, many others—healthy or not—buy books like *Final Exit* for both information *and* insurance. These books often stay on their shelves until much later, until changes in their quality of life prompt them finally to begin reading. "Security for the future" is the only way to explain why *Final Exit* reached the top of *The New York Times* bestseller list, and also why many Hemlock Society members keep old copies of the *Hemlock Quarterly* in their files or buy other books the Society offers. Author Anne Fadiman claims to be in this category, explaining in one article that she'll keep her collection on hand just in case she might need the information they contain.

Whatever amount of special knowledge you possess, always remember that more is better. It provides you the opportunity to double-check and cross reference what one source says against another. If you eventually proceed to the end of this path, knowledge reduces the possibility of failure and the likelihood that others will become inadvertently involved.

SOURCES FOR INFORMATION

If you decide on a more private approach, you might begin your study with a trip to your library or local bookstore to pick up any readily available books on the topic. The most obvious choice is the above mentioned *Final Exit* by Derek Humphry, which contains chapters on "self-deliverance" as well as a chart of drugs and lethal dosages. It has now sold nearly three-quarter of a million copies and has been translated into several languages. An earlier book on the same topic, also by Humphry, is *Let Me Die Before I Wake.* First published in 1981, this book, initially available only by mail order to members of the Hemlock Society, was labeled "the Bible of euthanasia" by *60 Minutes.* This first "how to" guide has been updated and presents case histories of how several terminally and incurably ill ended their lives.

The original source for "how to" information in America was the Hemlock Society and its many local chapters or affiliates. Founded by Derek Humphry in 1980 as the nation's first modern pro-euthanasia organization, its emphasis has changed. While callers still ask for information about drugs, seek counseling, and request books and materials on lethal dosages, the Society no longer provides drug information or phone counseling services. Nor does it make available the *Drug Dosage Table,* an oversize fold-out reprint that originally appeared in 1984 in *The Hemlock Quarterly,* the Society's former newsletter. The *Drug Dosage Table,* with revisions, served as the centerpiece around which Humphry crafted *Final Exit.* The Society does continue to sell *Final Exit, Let Me Die Before I Wake,* and other volumes on the right-to-die. Some limited phone "counseling" is available from ERGO!—the Euthanasia Research and Guidance Organization, and from Compassion in Dying. (The phone numbers and addresses for these and other sources of information are all listed in the Resources section at the end of this book.)

Most callers to the Hemlock Society and its chapters are unaware that nearly all materials can be found in local bookstores and libraries. Some are aware that books such as these exist, but don't know the titles or assume that any "how to" information must only be available from Hemlock. This is far from being true. Still others contact the Society because they're unwilling to go to their library or local bookstore out of fear that someone will assume they're planning a suicide. In fact, some callers to Hemlock and its chapters request materials be sent in "plain envelopes" to not alert others as to their thoughts. Such requests are seldom met.

In addition, many believe that the Hemlock Society—because of the aura of mystery that some attach to it—has "secret knowledge" that's unavailable from other sources. In this regard, callers (and some members) often think that, after they join, they'll be sent lists of "special" easily obtained drugs. On the contrary, the organization does *not* possess any secrets. Instead, almost all "how to die" information (except that which I'll describe in the following pages), has been available in the above listed publications or in articles and letters published over the years in the old *Hemlock Quarterly.* Since Humphry's retirement, Hemlock has taken a conservative turn away from providing "how to" information, in favor of public and medical education about the need for legal reform. Even the *Hemlock Quarterly* has been renamed *Time Lines* and "sanitized," according to author Anne Fadiman, as "part of Hemlock's conservative repositioning."

Another source for "how to" information is ERGO!—the Euthanasia Research and Guidance Organization. ERGO! was founded by Humphry after his departure from Hemlock to fill a larger educational need in the right-to-die movement. It has now taken over both the "how to" and "how *not* to" banners. By mail order, it makes available updated copies of *Final Exit* and also markets some of my own cautionary work along with a fold-out brochure Humphry has written entitled *Self-deliverance from an End-Stage Terminal Illness by Use of the Plastic Bag.* In this brochure he details how an individual can end his or her life without the help of another and without needing potent sleep medications.

You might also consider ordering a copy of *Departing Drugs,* written by a team of right-to-die activists from America and Great

Britain. This new "how to" booklet lists several of the same drugs found in *Final Exit,* as well as other more easily obtainable medications that the authors claim are just as effective. Whether these other drugs work both easily and humanely, however, is open to question. I remain very cautious of any approach that's unsupported by either scientific evidence or a strong body of anecdotal reports. But I'm also cautious about every other published "how to" guide and brochure. For this reason, I would suggest checking several sources.

To obtain *Departing Drugs* you must be a member of a right-to-die organization for a minimum of three months. This has nothing to do with any "secrets" it contains but is a result of an agreement made by co-sponsoring organizations in North America and Great Britain. This means that, in America, you need to be either a contributor to ERGO! or a member of the Hemlock Society or of one of Hemlock's many chapters. You have several other choices in various other countries. You need to contact American author Cheryl Smith or the Right to Die Society of Canada or the Voluntary Euthanasia Society of Scotland. For a German-language version you should contact the Deutsche Gesellschaft für Humanes Sterben (DGHS)—the German Association for Humane Dying. (Again, see the Resources section for further details.)

MEDICAL CONNECTIONS

You may also decide to begin your exploration by contacting trusted friends or close family members who are medical professionals. This individual may be able to provide you with information on drugs and dosages. But this may not be forthcoming. A physician once told me, "When members of my family have asked me, 'What works?' they assume that, because we may know what heals, we also know what kills. But we don't."

There can be several advantages to having a dialogue with a medical professional. First, by alerting this individual that you're considering an assisted death, she may be able to talk with you about your condition and even provide you with the names of specialists who can help you deal with some of your medical concerns.

Also, if your condition deteriorates further, this person may serve as a sounding board for you before you make any final decision. And finally, she may also be able to furnish you the means to end your life eventually, should this become necessary. This, of course, is only a possibility. Never expect any such connection to take a personal and professional risk, especially if you aren't their patient.

This use of close family ties to the medical profession can be seen in the following case. Rochelle, who had metastasized breast cancer, asked her daughter—a dentist—to find the "how to" information she might need if she decided to end her life. Her daughter knew about *Final Exit,* bought a copy, read it, made a list of possible lethal drugs to which her mother already had access, and then compared these with the information provided in her own copy of the *Physician's Desk Reference.*

Instead of using her medical authority to write a lethal prescription, Rochelle's daughter used her medical knowledge to interpret existing information, ask the right questions, and read between the lines. She then called the local Hemlock chapter to get more precise information about a drug in her mother's possession. The person taking the call refused to discuss the drug, but advised her that, if the drug were used, the family "might be forced to intervene in a less than pleasant task of direct assistance." Adequately forewarned, Rochelle's daughter went back to *Final Exit,* and read the section on using the plastic bag. She later told me, "As a result, we were all better prepared emotionally for what finally became necessary."

In addition to such personal contacts, you might also approach your own physician for information, that is, if you've established a comfortable relationship with her and have already shared your general thoughts about assisted dying. This has the added benefit of setting the stage for requesting assistance at some later time. My own preference is for a more straightforward approach but, depending on your own communication style, you might find out the information you need by saying:

> *We've talked about all this, and you know how I feel. Though I'm still a long way from making any final decision, I believe it does no harm*

to look into this a bit more. Do you have any idea what I might use if worse comes to worse?

This testing the waters was useful to Elizabeth, who was dying of breast cancer and who, together with her friend Jayne, shared the same internist. Elizabeth wanted to die, and Jayne wanted to help in whatever way she could. After explaining her desire to their doctor, and asking him about names of possible drugs, he said that he knew "what they needed," and told them. A month later they came back and discussed their difficulty securing the means. Only then did he agree to help, by providing each with their own prescriptions that, combined, would be enough to "do the trick."

Others are often not so lucky, telling me quite different stories about being refused outright. In a much smaller number of cases, they're informed by their doctors that they "don't know" what they could use, or they are instructed to call Hemlock.

The latter occurred in the case of "Diane" as described by Dr. Timothy Quill in *The New England Journal of Medicine*. His patient for many years, "Diane" was suffering from a form of leukemia that had, at best, a cure rate of 25 percent. Without treatment, there would be "certain death." Diane opted for no treatment, but told him that when the time came, "she wanted to take her life in the least painful way possible."

Knowing her desire for control, Quill thought her decision made sense. It became clear to him that "fear of a lingering death" would prevent her from "getting the most out of the time she had left." He told her that the Hemlock Society might have the information she needed.

A week later she phoned with "a request for barbiturates for sleep." Knowing these were "essential ingredients in a Hemlock Society suicide," he asked her to come to his office to "talk things over." He made sure she knew how to use them for sleep *and* for a self-enacted death. They met regularly, and "she promised to meet" with him before she took her life to ensure that "all other avenues had been exhausted."

UNDERGROUND CONDUITS

Another source you may be considering are acquaintances and other patients you've met along the path of your illness and treatment. In AIDS circles, for example, the impact of this disease has created an array of support groups, services, and buying clubs for both non-FDA-approved AIDS drugs and marijuana (to relieve nausea). This shared experience of death and dying has also led to a steadily evolving sophistication about methods for assisted death and an oral history of anecdotal tales of successes and failures. In larger cities with more centralized AIDS populations and support groups and services, most everyone knows others who either took their lives, were assisted, or were present at such deaths. Questions get asked, such as "What did Robert use?" and "How did he get hold of it?"

I've seen the same sharing of information albeit to a lesser degree, among some groups of women with breast cancer. It's not unusual for such women to share a common "culture" in terms of treatment and palliative (comfort) care, to belong to the same support groups, and even to see the same oncologists. As in certain segments of the AIDS community, some groups of women have also become knowledgeable of the methods of assisted dying, and after a "suspicious" death within their friendship group, ask the same types of questions about what drugs a member used.

There are individuals who often serve as conduits for knowledge and who, given the right circumstances, will make such information available to others. As the stigma of talking about rational suicide has begun to lessen a bit in some areas, these information conduits have become more visible. However, unless you'd trust someone with your life, don't trust them with your death. Many people talk as if they're knowledgeable, but too few actually are.

When you do find a knowledgeable person, she may also be able to provide you with names of specialists or information about the latest treatment alternatives or community services. In addition, you may also learn the names of doctors who, under the right condition, might assist in your death. Additionally, these conduits may eventually provide you with access to the needed drugs, should you finally decide to take this next step.

DEALING WITH PERSONAL REVULSION

Regardless of what information you acquire, none of it is easy to accept. Books like *Final Exit,* and brochures like the *Drug Dosage Table* or *Self-Deliverance . . . by Use of the Plastic Bag* are not pleasurable reading. Like many, you may find these quite disturbing: I too am often disturbed by what I read. But I'm more sickened when family members share with me the horror of being unprepared and tell me stories of gentle deaths gone wrong, of drugs that failed to work, and of having to use nearly any means available to "complete" the act.

Herein lies the catch-22. If you want to find an easy and sure way to die, and you can't obtain guaranteed help from your physician, you need to know the intricacies that can prevent failure and unnecessary involvement by others. Not everyone sees it this way. One man explained to me, "If I need a heart bypass, I don't want to know how to do it, just that it'll work." The point he missed is that to end your life without direct help from others—which is not always available—often requires that you become both patient *and* surgeon.

Knowledge of ways of dying and access to the means may not become relevant to you until treatment options fail and the course of an illness becomes obvious and irreversible. Although you may begin your search soon after being informed of a potentially life-threatening illness, you may decide only to glance through publications like *Final Exit,* be "turned off" after reading the author's recommendations for using a plastic bag, or assume that securing the drugs listed in the book might be an easy task.

This is not uncommon. For example, Pierre Luddington, a panelist at a *Preparing to Die* workshop in San Francisco, told me that he was "physically sickened by the thought of a plastic bag demonstration," and left the stage before it began. He did this even though he'd publicly acknowledged his own involvement in the death of two of his friends, and that he was thinking about ending his own life when the time came. He explained the apparent discrepancy by saying: "What I did in helping was humane and loving; I merely provided the drugs and was there when they died." He then added, "This is different; it was more than I could bear." This of course was the whole point of the demonstration. It brought home the seriousness of what it often means for a person to end her life. Lonny Shavelson said during the event, "The plastic bag is to assisted suicide as the coat hanger was to abortion." Lonny meant that under the current prohibition, unless one prepares well and secures the right drugs, she may be forced to choose seemingly desperate and less than aesthetic ways to die.

If you're considering an assisted death, you need to take complete responsibility for knowing what works and what doesn't, and you can't ignore this away. If you do, you may select the wrong means and, therefore, place an extraordinary burden on others who might be present.

I don't believe it's ever easy to begin the quest to find the means to die. Nor should it be. After all, we're talking about human life and ways you can end it. From what I've seen, however, reading is easier either when your quality of life remains fairly good and there is still hope for recovery or when your health has depreciated to a point where the desire to die replaces hopefulness as a driving force. In the former case, the possibility of death is distant; it's not your own death you're studying. In the latter case, death as the end of suffering may sound a siren's call. What's most difficult is the place in the middle. But this is also the place where you often need to begin.

Securing the Means to Die

If you eventually decide to move forward with your process, it's critical for you to obtain the means to do so. Unless you begin early or have a concerted plan, help from others may be needed in this task. It's easier to move forward if you're a patient with conditions that require large amounts of opioids or sleep medications, have a compassionate physician with whom you can converse, or have access to other connections. If you don't fit these categories, this may appear to be an insurmountable problem. Nevertheless, by understanding how others have met this challenge, you should have a clearer idea of how to proceed.

Securing the means to die is typically the second part of the exploration process. The questions "What do I need?" and "Where do I get it?" and "Can you help me get it?" are often asked at almost the same time. More than one caller has said, "I'm tired of dying like this. I'd like another way out, but I don't know what I need or how to get it." With only the slightest hesitation they then ask, "Can you help me?" At times like these, I suffer small deaths, feeling their vulnerability, need, and confusion. I have great difficulty ignoring their pleading requests for a humane death. Each time I'm forced to repeat my refrain that "I have nothing to give, sell, or make available," that "I have no secret sources, knowledge, or names," and that "the only thing I can do is give my emotional support" and, in some instances, provide some tough questions they can ask themselves to assess if such an act is the right one for them.

One thing I often recommend: Begin your search early, while you're still healthy enough to explore your connections, and before you're faced with the absolute medical need to do so. This requires a move from a purely philosophical view of assisted dying to actively planning your death. This doesn't mean, however, that such a day always comes. Many have told me that the sooner they took this step, the more time they had to reflect on their decision and ultimately discover that it wasn't right for them.

To secure the means, people reach out to many of the same places they went to learn how to die. Like the rings that spread from a stone thrown in a pond, most begin close to home, with their doctors, partners, family, or friends. If these resources fail, some gradually move farther out to the next ring of acquaintances and to the next.

If you find yourself wanting to take this next step, are early enough in the dying process, and well enough to take the time required, begin by continuing the dialogue that you've established with others. You should:

- Discuss with your partner, family, or friends your desire to proceed further toward a decision by having the necessary means available, just in case

- Elicit feedback from those close to you about this next step and take their needs into consideration before proceeding any further

- Continue your dialogue with your therapist or counselor about your desire to move further ahead, eliciting her opinion about the possibility of seeking the means to die from your physician or with the help of others

This level of discussion is critical to prevent secrecy regarding your intentions to separate you further from those you need the most at this critical time. This openness is also important because you may require the help of your family or friends later on to complete this task. If your discussions provide you the support to continue in your search for the means to die, you should then make a decision about where to begin.

How Physicians Help

The most obvious starting place is with your physician. In most instances, she can write the prescription you need for a potentially lethal drug. Although the number of physicians who help their patients die is not fully known, a study in the San Francisco Bay Area found that 23 percent "were likely to grant the patient's initial request for a lethal dose of drugs to aid in a planned suicide." More surprising were results from a survey of all physicians in a part of England, which found that nearly half had been asked by a patient to take active measures to hasten their death, and that 32 percent had complied at some time. Several physicians I've talked with have told me that rates are far higher among oncologists, who treat cancer patients, and internists with large numbers of AIDS patients among their caseload.

These numbers obviously show that your own doctor is your

best bet as a first stop on your search for the means to die. Nevertheless, you should be aware that while physicians frequently help, they often do so only when a patient is experiencing irreversible suffering or is near death. In this way, you may receive help, but only when your doctor feels the time is "right."

Assistance also requires the right combination of doctor and patient. Physicians have told me that the "right" patient is emotionally stable, mature, and terminally ill with a mutually recognized level of discomfort. One doctor simply said, "If a patient is calm and seems rational and trustworthy, he's far more likely to [get] what he needs." This patient should also have a supportive partner or family who won't cause problems later on. All of this translates into reduced risk. In addition, though physicians claim to be universalistic in their approach and treat all patients with the same conditions in the same way, a doctor who helps one patient may not help another. In some cases, low risk must also combine with what one doctor calls "a special empathy." She explained, "I've only helped twice and each time I was especially moved."

By comparison, the right physician is one who isn't morally opposed to assisted death in all cases, who feels that a patient with a terminal condition should be able to determine the time and means for her own death, and that this method of dying—under the right conditions—can be a natural extension of compassionate medical care.

Between you and your physician may lie another chasm; both of you need to share the same goals. Your physician's goal to heal and relieve suffering must match your own. When healing is no longer possible, then both of your definitions of suffering must match. Also, to help you, your physician should be able to note on your chart a condition or symptom that supports the prescription.

Doctors typically help their patients die in three ways: by increasing amounts of IV morphine to lethal levels, by "innocently" providing patients with prescriptions for oral pain medication in large doses they can take at home, and by deliberately prescribing potentially lethal medications.

The first two are easily disguised. Hospitalized patients, in pain and near the end their lives, are often provided with increasingly higher amounts of IV morphine until death occurs from depression of respiration. This is termed *double effect*, and requires the guise of pain control. A poll of doctors in Wisconsin, for example, found 65 percent had given a drug to a terminally ill patient "to improve quality of life . . . knowing that it would expedite death." An article about this survey quotes a Milwaukee nurse who said that at her hospital "the majority of cancer patients die of morphine overdose." I've also talked with nurses who've worked with doctors to ensure "managed deaths" in this way, and a few doctors have even admitted deliberately "pushing the dose" themselves for the purpose of ending a patient's life.

Although this form of help is common, it often requires hospitalization and pain so severe as to demand use of IV morphine. This precludes the possibility of dying at an earlier time or in the absence of pain. This type of death can and does also occur under home hospice care with the use of an IV morphine pump. Though these devices are computerized, as I'll describe later, at times these controls are deliberately overridden.

The second way physicians help is by providing patients with prescriptions for oral pain medication in potentially lethal doses, all the while avoiding any real discussion of assisted dying. According to Derek Humphry, a physician who talks around the issue is more likely to avoid criminal charges, since prosecution would require evidence of "deliberate intention to help a patient die." This provision of potentially lethal self-administered drugs occurs both with cancer and AIDS patients, who are commonly provided with extra-large amounts of oral morphine. Without physicians openly discussing their intent, however, a patient doesn't know if he is deliberately being "helped." In this way, a doctor may leave it up to a patient to use these substances for either pain control or for an assisted death. A critical problem, however, is that such oral medications may *not* work if the patient has developed a tolerance for morphine. Each patient is different, and very few substances actually work.

Without explicit disclosure, patients can be confused. For instance, Lonny Shavelson, a physician-photojournalist, visited a friend dying of lung cancer who complained that she didn't know what to do about securing drugs. But when Lonny opened her re-frigerator, he was stunned to find a large bottle of liquid morphine. This had been prescribed by her doctor and placed there by the hospice nurse. Lonny's friend was shocked to discover that she po-tentially had what she needed, but a few steps away. Lonny told me that she had no way of knowing if her doctor deliberately or inad-vertently provided her with the possible means to die.

The problem here is that without explicit discussion between you and your doctor, the possibility for failure is too high. For ex-ample, had Lonny's friend taken the morphine by itself, it's likely that it wouldn't have ended her life. Again, this is why materials like *Final Exit, Departing Drugs,* and the *Drug Dosage Table* are so valu-able. They can serve as an additional resource, even if your physi-cian's intention to help is clear, and even if he is certain that the drugs provided will "do the trick." When in doubt, double check.

The third way doctors assist is by explicitly and deliberately providing potentially lethal prescriptions to patients, hopefully after discussing it in detail and attempting all reasonable treatment alternatives. This is what occurred in the cited case of Elizabeth and her friend Jayne, who shared the same internist and who each received prescriptions for Seconals. This also took place in the story of Dr. Timothy Quill and his patient "Diane." Only after he referred her to Hemlock for information did he provide a pre-scription that allowed her to end her life at her own time and by her own hand. As it turned out, "Diane" held on to these drugs for sev-eral months before she finally used them.

ASKING FOR HELP

With these thoughts in mind, prepare yourself for your next meet-ing with your physician by more clearly defining your reasons for wanting to take this further step. During this preparation, you should:

- Use your journal to determine, in writing, your current physical and social quality of life and level of irreversible suffering

- Assess how your condition has worsened or failed to improve even with aggressive treatment measures, palliative care, and counseling

- Reflect on your overall demeanor, and calm yourself to where you can thoughtfully describe your level of suffering, philosophy of living and dying, and reasons for wanting to take this next step.

After you've prepared in this manner, make certain to give yourself enough time at your next scheduled appointment to discuss your thoughts even though you may not accomplish your task upon the first request. Depending on the depth of the relationship you've established, you may choose either to discuss your needs directly, making an honest request for help, or take a more indirect approach by using physical symptoms like "pain or sleeplessness" as a ploy. I'm opposed to the latter because it cuts off discussion of your reasons for wanting to die and diminishes the possibility of working more closely with your physician to resolve your symptomatic and pain-control issues. Nevertheless, in regard to this indirect approach, Derek Humphry has written, "Doctors close to Hemlock advise the indirect, slow approach" to receive medication for feigned sleep disorders. He suggests going back a second and third time, complaining that the prescribed drugs failed to help, until you finally receive the heavy dose of barbiturates needed to end your life.

This approach may work well if you're *not* terminally ill, but I have reservations against any method not grounded in honesty. As I've stated several times, you have much to gain by establishing an honest dialogue with your physician. You have much to lose if you don't. I would strongly suggest that you:

- Continue the dialogue you've previously established with your physician

- Discuss openly your current condition, quality-of-life issues, irremediable suffering, and likely prognosis

- Introduce the topic of assistance with your physician by disclosing your needs and by describing what drugs and dosages you've identified

- Explain that you have no immediate intention of ending your life, but would like a prescription as insurance in case worse comes to worse

- Describe your attitudes about living and dying and what you'd still like to accomplish before you die, stressing your desire to continue living for as long as you can enjoy a measure of quality

- Reassure your physician that you have the full support of your partner or family, and that you're working with a therapist on these issues

You should see this as a gradual process by which you present your argument. Listen thoughtfully to your physician's response. If you haven't established a relationship that allows for such a dialogue, but can only talk in generalities, you may only hear the same in return and miss learning how she may actually respond. As one doctor told me, "I've helped, but I certainly don't bring up the topic first." The dilemma, of course, is that you will never be helped unless you ask.

At this point, if your physician refuses to help, listen to her response. It may well make good sense. A refusal may only be for the present moment, given your current condition. If your suffering is not yet intolerable, you might do well to wait and bring up the topic again at a later time. You might also probe further by asking under what conditions your physician might reconsider. Or you might suggest that you could bring your partner or a close family member with you for your next visit or propose to your physician that she confer with your therapist about this next step, providing your therapist agrees.

If your physician is adamant in her refusal, you would do well to continue both with your treatment and with being open about any unresolved physical conditions. If your intention to end your life stays firm, however, you need to decide whether you can still remain open about this topic. Several interviewees, for example, expressed to me their fear in calling the doctor to report the death of a partner or family member—after the partner or family member had asked for assistance from the physician only recently and was refused. Their concern was over not knowing if the doctor would sign a death certificate claiming "natural causes" or if she'd share her suspicions about possible cause of death with authorities, thereby implicating significant others in a criminal act. This fear could have been eliminated if their partner or family member had opened a dialogue with his physician far earlier to test the waters.

Your physician may tentatively agree to help at some time in the future. Under such a condition it might be best for you to clarify what form this help will take and when it might be provided. The purpose is not to put your physician on the spot but to enable you to rest at ease and focus on the business of living until such a point is reached. This may well help you live longer. Moreover, knowledge of what drugs will be available to you later can do much to alleviate concern that others who'll be present at your death will not become unintentionally involved. This can reduce your level of stress and allow all of you to focus on achieving a sense of emotional closure.

FAMILY AND FRIENDS

In addition to doctors, the most important source of the means to die for many are those same family members or friends with whom they first discussed this option. The benefits of relying on friends are obvious. It allows all steps in the process to be scrutinized by those who have the most to lose by your death. The problem, however, is that this can insulate both you and others close to you, by creating a reality or world view that reinforces itself. This is why counseling or a professional opinion from outside the household or immediate family is so important.

An additional problem you need to resolve is that any involvement by others in providing you the means to die may be legally construed as "assisting" in a suicide. This, of course, is against the law. Under no condition should your partner or family member feel obligated to help you in any way to end your life. Although such a person may consider their help in this manner to be an honor or privilege, you need to discuss this and point out the legal considerations. Others often feel impotent when one they care for faces a life-threatening illness. They may see no other way to help you and may be vulnerable when they make such an offer. It may help them feel as if they're doing something, but later they may regret this action, especially if the drugs they provide you fail to work as planned.

Therefore, if you're considering using your partner, family, or close friends as a primary source—or as fellow searchers—for the means to die, consider:

- Taking this step and considering the help of another only after you've obtained the agreement of the person closest to you that this is an appropriate action

- Debating in detail the offer of another to help in this manner, explaining the seriousness of such an action and possible consequences

- Obtaining a guarantee from others that you will never be pressured by them into acting or accelerating the time for making the final decision

- Deciding together with the other and the one closest to you, if necessary, how this other is to participate in this search, and what drugs are acceptable as a means of dying

- Protecting yourself and others from suspicion of involvement in a planned assisted death by requiring full confidentiality and the need to approve in advance efforts to secure the means to die from any outside sources

- Contracting with this person that once the means to die are secured, she will have the opportunity to present any opposing arguments before you make any final decision to die

- Assuring those close to you that they will be informed of all aspects of your condition and any changes in it that might prompt you to make such a decision

- Informing anyone involved in this search to avoid making any street contacts or seeking the help of anyone outside your immediate circle without your approval.

With these provisions, and any others that seem relevant, you should be able to reduce the possibility of hasty, inappropriate involvement by others and protect all of you both emotionally and legally. Bringing this search process into your own intimate grouping requires a maturity on everyone's part. There's no room for manipulation. This is no contest about who loves you more, and there's nothing to prove. Instead, there is a shared realization of the gravity of what is being considered.

Nevertheless, these ideals are seldom achieved. People often wait until their decision is made by pain and suffering and then, when filled with fear and a perceived need for haste, they reach out to almost anyone to secure the right drugs. They begin with their partners and immediate families and then gradually branch out to nearly anyone within their circle.

Even the family "pariah" or "black sheep" can occasionally be selected for this special task. This was the case with Francess, who was approached by her former mother-in-law to get her the drugs to help her die. She said she was picked because of her known "liberal attitudes" and historical "involvement with recreational drugs." She explained:

> I was always the hippie and still am. So it was natural for them to turn to me. Mom and I stayed in contact even though Jeff and I divorced in the '60s and haven't really talked for a long time. The kids kept us together; she was their grandmother.... They've known all along about my lifestyle.
>
> When she asked, I found I didn't have the contacts I needed. I could get hallucinogens easy enough, but not this kind of

stuff. Then I got to talking with a friend with AIDS who said he had Dilaudid. I took it with me when I visited Mom in Boston. My ex-husband found out and took it away. He only gave it back when he could finally see she was dying. About a month later we got together again and she used the drugs. It took several hours but eventually it worked.

In far too many cases, however, family and friends without knowledge of—and access to—the right drugs, often set themselves up to participate in a death in a manner far different than they ever anticipated. They may be able to provide a few extra Haldane or Valium, but a resilient body, a strong heart, and perhaps an underlying will to live against all odds, can often defeat any but the most powerful lethal drug. As a physician friend once told me about Valium, "The only way to die from an overdose is to be run over by the truck delivering it." In this regard, another doctor, familiar with assisted death, once remarked, "I'm convinced the only way to overdose is to be a teenager and take the stuff accidentally."

What this again tells you is never to make the mistake of settling for second best or settling for someone else's hasty resolution to your problem. If you're going to make the decision to die, be certain that you enter into it fully armed with both the right knowledge *and* the right drugs. This means recognizing the importance of physicians in this entire process. Unfortunately, however, many with life-threatening conditions still avoid talking with their doctors about their concerns and desires. This prevents them from receiving the many benefits of this shared dialogue, and often means that they spend too much time dealing with issues of securing the right drugs.

This can be seen in the case of Jennifer. After five years of remission following a double mastectomy, Jennifer's cancer returned, and she began a regimen of chemotherapy that lasted for a year and a half. Nothing worked, and though she continued her treatments, ten months before she died she voiced her thoughts about "looking into it" with her husband, Bill. The two of them read *Final Exit* and discussed how they might obtain the "magic pills," Seconals.

After six more months of increased discomfort, additional discussion, and the failure of yet further experimental treatments, Bill finally decided to ask his uncle—a physician—about getting the drugs, "just in case, just for insurance." Bill didn't want to ask him, but couldn't think of any other source. Not surprisingly, his uncle responded and said that "if bad becomes worse and Jennifer's suffering becomes intolerable," he'd help.

Although Bill didn't want to use his uncle in this way, he knew that the means "were always but a phone call away." This took the pressure off. "It took away the fear, and she could always handle one more day, knowing that if tomorrow got worse" he could always call his uncle. This never became necessary as Jennifer eventually died a peaceful, natural death at home, her pain aided only by a little extra oral morphine.

There's a twist. A month after Jennifer's death I found myself in a conversation with her doctor, a well-known and respected oncologist. He told me that he'd only learned *after* Jennifer's death of her thoughts about assisted dying. As he shook his head, he added, "All she had to do was talk to me, but she didn't; I would've given her anything she needed." The moral of the story should be obvious.

INHERITING THE MEANS TO DIE

Another source of drugs you might be considering is the very real "underground" that exists among many with cancer or AIDS. This underground consists of networks of friends who share leftover lethal substances. This is most prevalent in urban areas with large populations of AIDS cases or women with breast cancer. In some cases, a person who is dying—who will no longer be in need of these drugs—may provide them to another friend he or she has met with a life-threatening illness. Or these drugs may make their way into a network where they're provided to someone designated "next in line."

For example, one man I talked with, a "member" of such an informal network in San Francisco, told me:

> Too often the hospice nurse asks for the leftover meds, especially morphine. They say it's for purposes of safety, and they

don't want to leave them around. Well, we have better uses for it than they do.

In the AIDS community, more expensive medications for treating certain conditions can also make their way into the hands of those who cannot afford to pay the high cost. For example, before my friend Barry died, he and his partner were paying more than $900 every six weeks for medications his insurance would not cover. One of his last acts was to instruct his partner to give a satchel full of these drugs to a friend of theirs who had the same condition, but who could ill afford them on his own.

This "inheritance" of drugs occurs even in cases of natural death. Two weeks after her mother died, for instance, Sarah called me and thanked me for my emotional support. Then she asked me what to do with her mother's leftover morphine and Dilaudid. She felt that I should have them, because I'd probably know some needy terminally ill patient who could use them or have them "for insurance" like her mother. Although momentarily tempted, I explained to Sarah that this offer, though thoughtful, was something I couldn't accept. I didn't want to be placed in the position of being a "drug supplier" or having to decide which one of the many terminally ill with whom I work would be deemed lucky enough to receive this gift.

STREET DRUGS AND STREET SMARTS

Another source you may be considering are non-prescribed street drugs. According to Derek Humphry, "Roughly half of the barbiturates made in the United States—the drug of choice in self-deliverance—find their way onto the black market." In addition, heroin, a strong injected form of morphine, which is potentially lethal in large amounts, is readily available to those with the right connections. These street sources are used rarely by the dying, but occasionally partners or family members may attempt to use them as a last resort.

Off the streets and away from any underground connections,

you or your partner or family may believe that what you need is only one drug user away. This is seldom true. Nevertheless, you may have the impression—compounded by film and television—that "heroin kills," and that even experienced users can die from having "just a bit too much." Or you may feel that other drugs can also be easily obtained. With this image in mind, you may feel like "hitting the streets" yourself in search of lethal means.

If you're considering this approach, I can only advise you in the strongest words possible *not* to take this step. The risks are far too high. You'd need to trust your source, and this means trusting individuals—who already are operating outside of the law—with both your safety *and* your death. First, unless you're a former drug user, you'd probably be seen as an outsider and would not be trusted. Second, you might be seen as a potential "rip off" victim, either to be robbed outright or sold substances other than what you desire. And third, even if you were sold the "right" drugs, in all likelihood these would not be in the right pharmaceutical dosages. One of my interviewees, for example, told me how he was supposedly sold four times the lethal amount of heroin, which his partner then injected. Several hours later, after repeated efforts to help his partner die, he finally resorted to using a plastic bag. He told me that he'd trusted his source. Obviously he was wrong. This was reinforced by another interviewee, a former IV drug user who told me:

> You can't get good shit on the street corner. The guy who deals in the "tenderloin" will rip you off one way or another. You won't get the real thing, or what you get will be cut so heavily you won't even get high let alone die!

In regard to Seconals, which supposedly are also available on the streets, Gary, a man dying from AIDS similarly commented, "I'm just a middle class white kid from the suburbs, where am I gonna get the shit I need? I know they're called 'reds,' but I wouldn't know what streetcorner to go to or who to ask, and I don't know anyone else who buys drugs this way." This sums up the problem. Derek Humphry writes:

> The average Hemlock member is not the sort of person who wants to hunt dark inner-city streets in order to purchase "reds" . . . illicitly. There is always the risk that drugs bought in the street are below strength or contaminated.

Unwilling to walk naively into unknown territory, Gary contacted an old friend in Spain, who was planning to visit the Bay Area, and told him what he needed. His friend brought sixty prescription phenobarbital tablets, some of which Gary used together with a potentially lethal dose of Dilaudid.

The only "safe" users of street drugs appear to be the former IV drug users. For example, my interviews in San Francisco included four former IV drug users who'd used heroin in assisted deaths, and who were planning to do the same for themselves when their own health further deteriorated. In talking about street drugs, one of these men told me that, like himself, "former IV drug users always go with their previous drug of choice even years after being clean." In most instances this was heroin, but he said that he knew one former "speed freak" who took all the drugs he could find and then "shot up a half gram of meth." He then added:

> They're not going to waste their time with prescription crap or trying to find some good Samaritan doc to help them. Former heroin users always use heroin. They still know where to get it. They know good shit when they see it. They know doses, and they've all nearly OD'd [overdosed] before. They go with what they're used to. They like the rush, the high; they go for the big dose.

THE HELP OF STRANGERS

There are no strangers who'll help you die humanely! Moreover, there are no foreign countries where you can secure aid-in-dying. Although physician-assisted dying exists in the Netherlands, it's available only to Dutch patients and is rigidly controlled. Similarly, although you might find the drugs you need in a few countries, you'd still have to contact a physician who speaks your language or track down a pharmacist who would help. Given the percentages of physicians who do assist their patients in countries like the United States, Canada, Australia, and Great Britain, it makes little sense to waste your effort going far from home. It might be easier for you to find another physician or take the time to make your case to your own doctor—the one person who can also best respond to your pain control and palliative needs.

Final Considerations

During the latter period of an illness, I've often seen a shift in awareness, where a person considering the decision to die moves beyond the detachment of philosophical discussion toward securing the means to die. At this juncture, I've heard in their voices terms such as *my* suffering, *my* pain, and *my* decision. There's a moment when one's "dying" is redefined, when one's illness no longer exists as the enemy to be conquered, and where death itself becomes personalized and even anticipated.

Novelist Sandra Paretti wrote of this redefinition in her own obituary, in which she said her cancer, "I embraced it and, behold, it was my last lover." Similarly, one woman told me how her husband moved from fear of dying to a sense of potential victory that she found disturbing. He talked about it longingly, equating it with a "sweet release." Finally came a balance, an acceptance of its gravity, what it meant, and what he still needed to accomplish before the end. But early on, she said, "death became his friend, almost a lover."

I'd come home from work and hear the excitement in his voice about some new discovery, some new possible source for a drug, a possible contact. In many ways I felt he became infatuated with his own death as if it were some not-so-secret mistress.

In a strange sort of way I began to feel jealous that he spent more time with her—with death—than with me. He spent more time talking about her—about death—than us. For a while I felt her winning, that she was going to take him away from me, because she could provide him something I couldn't. She could truly ease his suffering. I could only love him.

This seemingly strange fixation, however, soon ended. She explained that "this was his way in life, how he did everything."

This compulsion of his, like shopping for power tools or television sets, in a strange way kept him alive and gave him a purpose for his remaining days. He did everything just right, now he was going to do his death just right too. It kept him happy for a while.

Her husband's obsession soon ended after he found the means to die. He then began to "clean up his life," and when this was complete, he finally began to work on his relationship with his family. "Finally," she told me, "he heard another voice that, with a sense of calmness, he decided to follow."

Similarly, before my friend Ryland Jones died, he explained his thoughts on the subject in a *People* magazine article. The writer stated, "Now, [Ryland] has an odd sense of anticipation about death. While he no longer believes in heaven, he expects to enter 'a dimension that is bliss, completeness.' In the meantime, he hears a kind of siren call. 'The closer I get to death, the more compelling it is,' he says. 'The dying process has a ring to it, like a bell almost. When it was a new ring, it was unsettling to me.' Now, he says, 'it's becoming more and more pleasant.'"

Ultimately, there may come a time when you too hear this call, when you finally determine that "enough is enough," and move forward to end your life. Choosing this path when you're losing the battle against a life-threatening condition, and when you're no longer able to find any remaining quality of life or endure further suffering, is the most critical decision you can ever make. At such a time, there is no room for undue influence by others, for mistakes, or uncertainties. If you take this last step, it's crucial that you not act in haste or for the wrong reasons but instead take time to reflect, to be certain that your decision is unwavering over time, and then plan all details to reduce any potential negative impact on others.

Planning to die means preparing to sever many of the ties you've established during your life. This can be a harsh severance or one that is gentle. You can act in ways that are emotionally harmful to others and leave them with conflicts to resolve and work to complete, or you can reduce the impact, achieve a sense of closure, and provide others with a legacy of love and respect. Obviously, the latter is preferable.

To attain this requires more than information and lethal drugs. It also requires that you select, if you can, a time to die that reflects a balance between meeting your own needs to end your suffering and meeting the needs of others to be able to accept your death. It means trying as best and as early as you can, to complete the personal and financial business of your life. It then means giving serious thought to the entire decision and to the details of your death: time, place, ritual, methods, questions about the involvement of others, and the "discovery" and official cause of your death.

THE RIGHT TIME TO DIE

The place to begin is with a final assessment of your motives, one last look at your reasons for dying. You should know that it's not uncommon to experience a change of heart even at what you believe is the final moment. Although you may feel that there's a "flash point," "calling card," or "line in the sand," as others have termed it, this point can change and only you can make the final determination.

Study your journal entries and make certain that they are absolutely consistent over several days. If you have any doubts, *wait.* You won't have a second chance. Weigh your choice carefully. Take the time to ask yourself:

> *Am I absolutely certain that now is the time to die? How long have I felt this certainty? Did I select this date and time well in advance? If so, why? Have others in any way influenced my selection of a date and time? Has this decision been a hurried one? If so, why? Do I*

have any underlying doubts as to the rightness of this time? Could I wait another week? Another few days? Another day? Is my quality of life or physical condition absolutely intolerable?

Timing should be based on *your* schedule. You should never attempt to meet the schedules of others. To do so takes the full decision out of your hands, changes the potentially sacred nature of this event, and can leave others with a legacy of self-doubt and, in some cases, even guilt. You can only die once; do it in a way that feels right for you when you've reached a point of unwavering certainty. Bring up this topic in your discussions with others, seek advice from your therapist, and attempt to arrive at a resolution.

For this reason, predetermining a time to die in advance of the physical need to do so is unwise. I know of various cases where a date was selected for symbolic purposes, a birthday or anniversary, but this leans more toward suicide and seems driven less by necessity than self-determination. And while it's in everyone's best interest to plan the details early (thereby preventing mistakes and unnecessary involvement of others later on), it is similarly imprudent to make the final decision in a hurried manner unless your quality of life deteriorates and your physical condition becomes increasingly and irreversibly intolerable. Even then, advance time for discussion and closure should do much to set the proper tone and prepare others for this final act. In this regard, you would do well to reach out one last time to those you love and be absolutely certain that they too are ready for this step. This is especially crucial if you expect them to be present or to assist you in any way. The purpose of this act is to *end* suffering, *not* to create additional suffering for others you'll leave behind. Moreover, this is not a time for anyone present at this final time to be ill at ease or have less than a completely open heart.

WHOSE IDEA IS THIS, ANYWAY?

As you arrive at this decision, take special care to ensure that it remains firmly in your hands and that others are not promoting it. Your inner voice is your best counselor. The risk here is not so much that others will decide for you as it is that communication with supportive friends and family might be less than clear and open, or that you may interpret their emotional support as a recommendation for this course of action. Don't misinterpret exhaustion on the part of caregivers or their inability to communicate their feelings.

Be certain, moreover, that you are not following through to avoid disappointing others who are lending their advice, who've provided you the means to die, who might be present, or who you've asked to participate in some fashion. And don't let your own former expressions of opinion about your "right" to die in this manner oblige you to follow this path. This is what a "right" to die is all about. You may see your beliefs differently when the personal experience of a terminal illness intervenes. Remember, this is all about choice, in the same way that you might support a woman's right to choose abortion, yet welcome the birth of a child. There is no contradiction here. Ask yourself:

> *Do I know where the final decision is coming from? Am I certain that it is solely my own? Am I in any way dependent on others for making this decision or being influenced to act because of their recommendations? Do I feel any pressure to act by those I love or whose opinions I respect? Am I pressuring myself to act to "keep face" with prior statements I've made, or because others have "put themselves out" to obtain the means?*

How Effective Are the Means?

In the best-case scenario, you opened a long and thoughtful dialogue with your physician, determined together that further treatment would be ineffective or intolerable, obtained a second opinion from a specialist, received counseling, engaged in open discussions with your significant others, and at the right time obtained a fail-safe prescription to end your own life without requiring the direct involvement of anyone else.

The legally controlled and, therefore, "traceable" nature of potentially lethal prescription drugs, however, leads some physicians to underprescribe or provide other, less-than-effective substances for this purpose. Some of these less-than-effective drugs may pose a danger in the form of serious physiological effects in the event of failure. Talk to your physician about such effects before you finally select your drug of choice. Many physicians are willing to help, but few are willing to risk the suspicion of authorities, loss of medical license, or criminal prosecution. As a result, even if you receive a purported lethal prescription from your physician, you need to be certain of its efficacy. Such certainty is especially required if you secured these means from some other source. As a result, you need to:

- Feel absolutely certain that the means you've selected will be effective

- Know fully the potential physiological effects if they should fail to work

- Read carefully all "how to" materials and have someone you trust also read these materials and check the drugs and dosages for accuracy

- Trust completely the source of these drugs and their quality

Protecting Others

In planning to end your life, you have the responsibility to minimize potential harm to others—especially if they may be present at your death, involved in any way, or affected by it. After you arrive at this decision, you need to assess the emotional abilities and expectations of all who may be present.

You may need help in preparing or administering the drugs or more direct assistance if for some reason the means you've acquired fail to work. This is not idle fear; it happens in more cases than not. While advance planning and careful attention to detail can do much to minimize the involvement of others, you need to determine in advance what to do in such an event. Think deeply before you ask another person to step in to ensure your death should it become necessary. Many loving family and friends will agree or even offer to help, assuming that such an event will never occur. Unfortunately it does and too often. The willingness of others to help, however, does not mean that they are both practically and emotionally prepared to act or that they have the ability to cope with the results. You are asking another person to bear an emotional, legal, and moral burden for the rest of their lives.

There are only two choices: allow the possibility of failure regardless of the medical consequences or arrange to have others intervene. For those who may be present, the former may be as difficult to accept as the latter. Both have their drawbacks. Letting the drugs take their course may save others from any feelings of guilt for their involvement, but should these drugs prove ineffective other regrets can occur. There may be feelings that they failed you in your time of need, adding even more to the level of your suffering. And direct involvement carries its own regrets in the form of ethical, legal, and personal boundaries crossed, and the feeling that this was something no partner, child, parent, sibling, or friend should be forced to do.

To let the drugs take their course might result in anything from unconsciousness with gradual full recovery to serious, perhaps even permanent, physical damage that requires hospitalization. In such an event, your effort would most likely be looked upon as a suicide attempt, and the effect might well mean an investigation and no further assistance from your physician. This is a key reason why it is critical, if you finally decide to take this path, that you be cautious in exploring all the ways and securing the right means.

Having others intervene also carries the risk, however small, that someone will find out that your death was assisted. It is for this reason that I strongly recommend that you establish an open dialogue and relationship with your physician, and obtain not only a prescription for suitable drugs, but also a guarantee that he or she will sign your death certificate. I encourage group meetings be held in advance and that counseling be obtained, as this increases opportunities for closure for those who'll be affected by your death. Closure and acceptance reduces the risk that someone will feel the need to hold others personally accountable for your death later on. If others do not fully accept your final decision, you need to determine whether they should be present at your death, and, if not, whether they should be informed of any of the details. You might seek a promise from all present that anything they witness remains confidential.

Ask yourself:

Have I discussed with others the possibility of additional help? If someone has offered to step in to assure my death, am I certain that this person is emotionally prepared for this? Do I trust that this person will follow through as agreed? Does this person know exactly what this method of intervention should entail? Have we agreed to this method? Does this person know when to intervene, either in terms of an amount of time to wait or in regard to changes in my physical condition?

Do all others who'll be present know of this possibility? Are they completely comfortable with this potential for additional action? Are they completely aware of what to expect in such a case? How will this person who intervenes be protected by others present in terms of confidentiality?

If I've decided that no one should intervene, is this acceptable to all involved? In such a case does everyone know what to expect and do? Do they know when they are to call for emergency medical intervention? Are they comfortable with this?

To avoid potential difficulties, you would do well to determine both whom you *want* and whom you *need* to be present at your death. There may be persons close to you whose support you would like at this time, but who may be unable, emotionally, to witness this event. This is to be expected. You should discuss this with these individuals in advance and work together to find ways to resolve this possible conflict.

One method might be to divide the day into a time for personal good-byes and a group ritual, followed by a smaller gathering of those who'll be staying with you during the entire process. A second way might be to have everyone present in your home, with a private place set aside for those who need emotional support but who do not wish to participate in the final hours. Another approach might be to set aside two residences, one for your death, a second for those in waiting where they can obtain the emotional support they need.

For example, on the day my friend Barry died after a long fight against AIDS, he began by saying his farewells in a group setting and then adjourned to the privacy of his bedroom to take a lethal overdose. For the next eight hours his partner remained close by, while his parents retired to the privacy of an upstairs bedroom and his brother attempted to watch television in the office. I divided my time between Barry's partner downstairs and his brother upstairs. Several times the three of us checked on Barry's status. After his death, Barry's parents were notified and came downstairs to say their final good-byes to their son. We then all gathered, as we had before, to share our feelings. Only after this time of reflection was Barry's doctor called. This spatial division protected his parents from seeing their son unconscious and slowly dying, while the proximity ensured that they received both mutual support and the immediate relay of information.

Since it unlikely that your death will come quickly (unless your physician provides you a lethal injection), this time will not be easy for anyone. It is unlikely that those who care about you will be able to go about their business in any way that's normal, for they'll have difficulty concentrating, eating, or sleeping until the final outcome. Even then, however, they should have the opportunity to be with others. If your husband, wife, partner, or family members live with you, and elect to be absent at the time of your death, their return home later will be difficult. This return may be hard whether or not your body has been taken away. If your body is still present, they might have to face all the final details: the calls to the doctor or hospice, and mortuary or memorial. Even if your body has been removed, the house will still be filled with the remnants of your illness, such as medicines and medical equipment. You might discuss this in advance and provide your loved ones the option of having someone else take care of the details of cleaning the house. You might do well to:

- Ensure that others have the emotional support they need both during and after your death

- Arrange for a meeting to be held after your death for those present to be able to talk about the event, what occurred, and what reactions they may feel

- Discuss with your therapist the possibility of grief counseling for your partner or family after your death

SELECTING A LOCATION

For obvious reasons, most assisted deaths occur at home, though some do take place in hospitals, skilled-nursing facilities, hotels, motels, and even in residential hospices. Wherever it takes place, a fully conscious assisted death is one that minimizes the impact on others.

In this regard, in selecting a location you would do well to give some thought to possible premature discovery. People in residential hospices, hospitals, or certain residential retirement centers are checked on regularly. Become fully aware of the routines that have been established in these facilities as well as any possible emergency measures that might be employed. Study them. Only in this way can you prevent an accidental discovery.

The most critical concern, however, is protection of others who might be with you; a last visitor to see you in the hospital, for example, might instantly be suspected of involvement. So too would be a resident in whose home you took your life, unless, of course, your physician guarantees by his signature that your death was from natural causes.

This act is about much more than just accomplishing your death. It represents an opportunity for closure and for final farewells. More than in the case of a slow gradual death, an assisted death has the potential for being a rite of passage, not just for you, but for all who may be present. You might consider a location that provides for this possibility. This requires both comfort and a safe refuge from fear for all present, and this cannot be accomplished just anywhere. Ask yourself:

Where am I planning to die? Have I made this selection with full knowledge of the potential for intrusion? If this is at a location I share, have I warned other residents of my intention? Have I secured their approval? Might my death alter their feelings about continuing to live at this location?

Have I protected others from making an accidental and premature discovery? Have I checked my calendar and canceled appointments to ensure that no one will visit during the period of my death?

Do I have any neighbors or friends who might be worried if they don't hear from me for a period of several hours? Will someone be with me to divert any concern otherwise raised by an unanswered phone or door bell?

Do I have only a limited time in which to die? Am I certain the drugs I've selected will work within this time frame?

BEING FOUND

Whether you die alone or in the company of others, you need to be officially found by someone. If you plan to die alone, you would do well to arrange your discovery by some knowledgeable acquaintance. This person needs to be trusted to show up at the time you've designated and to be emotionally prepared for what he or she is likely to find. This person also needs to know what to do, whom to call, and when. This means informing this person of the means you've selected to end your life. This person also needs to have names, phone numbers, and back-up numbers handy, including that of your physician and the funeral home or memorial society with which you've made all arrangements. And if someone will be present at your death, this person needs to be strong enough to stand up to any official questioning in the event that you have not secured a guarantee of your physician's signature.

THE OFFICIAL CAUSE OF DEATH

In this regard, most assisted deaths by those with terminal illnesses are officially listed as "natural deaths" caused by their underlying condition. This is because they either have talked with their physician in advance, or they've worked out the details with others present to prevent their deaths from being suspected as suicides. Many plan to cover up the true cause of their death by ensuring that all evidence is removed.

In a small number of cases, however, evidence of direct assistance is removed, but the deaths are still officially determined to be suicides. Although questions may be asked of partners or others present, this protects them from what is obviously a worse stigma—that of being a criminal. They may still be asked difficult questions like, "Did you know this was going to happen?" and "Why didn't you do anything to stop it?" and "Are you sure you did nothing in any way to help this person?"

Whether or not you're planning to cover up your assisted death, it is important to consider writing a note in which you outline your intentions and state that no one else has been involved in your death. In the end, this may be the only thing that protects others who might be present. If you've secured the means of death from your physician, however, you should also think seriously about how such a note and official ruling of suicide may place this person in jeopardy both legally and professionally.

OTHER PRACTICAL CONCERNS

All of us need to take care of some basic practical matters whether we are preparing for a natural death or an assisted end. To the best of your ability try not to leave your spouse, partner, or family members with any unfinished financial business, expenses, or hardship because of your actions. To protect those persons, you should talk to a financial adviser, complete a last will or create a revocable trust, give written copies of your will to your executor, and leave adequate cash on hand or assured access to funds to cover unanticipated expenses. If you feel that completing such business is unimportant before your death, you would do well to explore again any unresolved issues or feelings (i.e., anger resentment, etc.) you may have toward those you leave behind.

Advance planning also extends to funeral, cremation, or memorial planning. Prior arrangements can do much to reduce the stress and emotional burden to others that might follow your death. Don't leave the actual details and payment for such services in the hands of family members or friends. They'll have too many other matters with which to contend. If at all possible, take care of these concerns while you're still physically able to.

This is not just another decision or task to accomplish. This is the last decision, and perhaps the most important decision you'll ever make. And the way it is made can set into motion a chain of other events and emotions that can continue long after you're gone. Your decision to act, and the way you plan and manage it, can leave a legacy of pain, guilt, and regret or a memorable gift of love. The decision is yours.

Chapter 5

WHEN THINGS
GO WRONG

There comes a time when the call to die becomes stronger than the desire to live, when one must follow his own call and listen to his own inner voice. This has not been an easy decision. As you know it has been several months in the making, and it has been as hard for me to get to this point as it has been for you to let me go.

In my suffering these past few months you have been the sole source of my will to live, but the inspiration for living must come from within.

Some of you have offered to care for me through my transition. Others of you have offered to help me die when you believe it's the right time. I am now at that point of transition, but since my body won't let me go, I have to nudge it along. . . . I'm quickly losing control and to wait any longer would leave me no choice but to involve you or linger in suffering until the end.

To those of you who have offered to help, I thank you, but I can't involve you. Ultimately, death is a lonely journey that we all must take one at a time. You can't keep me alive or help me die. These are both up to me.

Just remember that I love each of you. I will be with you during moments of celebration. I will be the gentle touch on your shoulder, the comforting voice during difficult times, the warm breeze that dries your tears. I will be the soft blanket that wraps you in love and lets you dream the blissful dreams.

Andy
Your loving son, brother, and friend

Andy's death points to the dilemma faced by many with life-threatening conditions who feel forced to choose between staying alive
for the sake of others or illegally involving those others in their
deaths. Wanting neither of these choices, there are those who act
by themselves before they'd be dependent on others for assistance
or be placed in a facility where an assisted death would be
impossible.

After securing a lethal prescription from his physician, Andy
came to a point beyond which he was unwilling to live. Suffering
from several AIDS-related conditions, he was quickly losing all
mobility, feeling in his hands, his sense of sight, and his ability to
swallow. Andy was bedridden, but had no way of knowing how
much longer he had to live. His doctor supported his decision to
die and, by providing Andy with the lethal drugs, gave him the opportunity to determine the time of his death. But he warned Andy
to "not wait too long." His partner told me:

> Andy's doctor trusted that he'd make the right decision. He
> gave him the meds and signed the death certificate. When I
> saw him after Andy's death, he said he was surprised Andy
> held out as long as he did. I told Andy I'd find a way to help.
> I'd do anything to have another day with him. I didn't know
> what, but somehow I'd help. He knew this was a constant
> burden for me, so he decided for both of us. His family faced
> the same difficulty in saying good-bye, so he said good-bye
> for them.

In the absence of legal opportunities for assisted death, we have
but three options: a "natural" death at home, or in a medical or
convalescent facility; a death like Andy's, self-enacted after receiving lethal drugs; or dying in the presence of your partner, family, or
friends with or without their direct assistance.

The first option—a "natural" death—is usually available and,
unless you've attained the support of your physician and have received access to the proper means, this may well be your only alternative. Moreover, unless you've also received the support of those
closest to you, it may be the best solution. At-home hospice care,

for example, with pain relief, palliative care and sedation, if such is necessary, can indeed provide for a peaceful end in most cases, while enabling those close to you to accept the inevitability of your death slowly. Less appealing, perhaps, is death in a hospital, convalescent-care facility, or some other medical setting. In fact, nearly 80 percent of deaths in America occur in such locales as there are certain medical conditions that are difficult to care for at home.

What this option does not provide, however, is guaranteed release from your suffering. Although a mixture of pain control and sedation may be available, the result—in terms of quality of life— may be little different from death. In addition, this option obviously does not ensure that you'll remain in control near the end or that you and others can fully and mutually participate in rituals honoring your transition. (I'll be addressing this possibility in detail in the next chapter.)

The second option—a "self-enacted" death—has other benefits and drawbacks. Most important, it protects significant others from further planned or unplanned involvement by excluding them. On the negative side, however, it eliminates the potential for their last-minute expression of opposition and for final closure. Moreover, it may leave them saddened that you died alone and always wondering if your last minutes were emotionally painful and if this were truly an illness-driven act or if you were motivated by something else. It also poses a significant risk for failure, if the proper means for your death have not been obtained. In the event of failure, the act of excluding others—who might otherwise intervene to ensure your death or call emergency response crews—can create a scenario worse than a death by drugs or natural causes. As I'll soon show, if the wrong means are used, severe physiological damage may result.

The third option, an assisted death in the presence of your partner, family, or friends provides the benefit of not dying alone. This can be important for you, given the fear that can accompany the final decision to end your life. This can also be important for your partner or family, who might otherwise regret not being with you at this critical time. The presence of others may also enable you to achieve final closure or hear words that may change your mind.

Although few assisted deaths are planned in careless, unfeeling ways, failings and errors can and do occur even with the best-made plans. These need to be addressed in detail.

When Events Go Wrong

Most of my interviewees who expressed regrets about their involvement in an assisted death did not attach these feelings to the other's decision to die, but to the event itself. Often their expectations of "helping" in only benign supportive ways were seriously altered due to the failure of the drugs to work or to work in any reasonable period of time.

Frequently, out of perceived necessity, their roles gradually escalated from "merely being present" to "doing anything necessary" to ensure the death of the other. As a result, the character of the event shifted from a positive and peaceful death in the presence of loving family and friends to one fraught with fear, uncertainty, disorder, and an unwanted concentration on the need to accomplish the task—to fulfill the other's last wish to die. In this way, their earlier expectations were often shattered.

When Drugs Fail

Many with whom I've talked blamed their problems on the failure of the means. In the end, the drugs didn't work, and as a "successful" death became less likely, others who were present saw no other choice but to intervene. Others told me that the problem was one of means and time; most simply, the drugs failed to work within a comfortable time period, and participants ran out of time or patience. At that moment intervention seemed "far easier than waiting any longer."

Other factors also came into play. These included: lack of preparation, elevated expectations, and inability by all parties to communicate about realistic possibilities. In nearly every one of these situations, the end result was further involvement by participants than they expected or desired. This occurred both where

drugs were obtained from nonmedical sources and in a few instances where physicians deliberately provided medications they
believed would be adequate to cause death. Each type of situation
needs to be looked at.

The most common mistake made is selection of the wrong
drug. This often is based on the assumption that if one pill can
help you sleep, then a hundred will ensure your death, or that if
Secobarbitals work then so will Pentobarbital, or if Phenobarbital
is used by veterinarians to put pets to sleep, then tablets of the same
substance will obviously help a patient die.

This mistake occurs most frequently when physicians have not
been brought into the equation, and when the person who is dying
and his or her partner or family members use themselves as the primary source for drugs, and add together an arsenal of substances
that "have to work" because of their sheer volume and variety.

This occurred most vividly in Bill's death. As his health deteriorated to where his doctor said he was but "weeks from death," Bill
came to a place of peace. After spending the day with his family,
they said their last good-byes and he went to his bedroom. He
began by taking antinausea medication. Then, selecting from a
storehouse of medication, he filled six syringes with Demerol,
which were to be injected later by his brother. He then applied to
his body several duragesic patches containing a synthetic form of
morphine. These were designed to provide continual pain relief,
and he normally wore four and switched one every day. Bill applied
twenty and concentrated them on his chest, near his neck, and
under his arms. Finally, he swallowed more than two hundred
tablets of Soma, Valium, Halcyon, and various other pain relievers,
including morphine. Within minutes he was unconscious, and
the family gathered in the next room and waited.

Three hours later, his brother injected the Demerol into the
muscle of his leg. Seven hours later, some ten hours after the process began, a cry came from Bill's room. The family rushed in only
to find him sitting up, conscious, and vomiting. For some reason,
the drugs Bill had taken had not been assimilated. A physician later
told the family that he believed the morphine "must've paralyzed

his gut." Whatever the cause, Bill fell back into a light sleep, while his family debated what to do next.

His brother argued that it was too late, that nothing would work, that Bill would "fight against the bag." His father disagreed, and said, "I know my son, he won't fight; he wants this more than anything." In resignation, his brother agreed to try. Bill had prepared for this possibility by taping together two white kitchen bags and setting aside an assortment of rubber bands. On the outside bag, with a marking pen, he had written the words "farewell," "peace," and "good journey." Although Bill was not unconscious when his brother placed the bag over his head and told him to "just relax," he managed one last word, "Okay." He died minutes later, without a struggle.

Though the family looked upon his as a "good death" and were emotionally prepared for the final act of involvement, the uncertainty about his near-conscious state and the possibility of his "fighting the bag" created an atmosphere of stress and indecision. Bill's brother told me later that this was "the longest night" of his life.

In a similar episode, Sheila described what happened when she and her sister helped their brother die in front of their parents. This case exemplifies what could've happened in Bill's case and what Bill's brother feared most. Sheila and her family knew in advance that the bag would be necessary and were prepared for it emotionally, because they knew from the start that "the drugs would never do it." What they weren't prepared for was what came next. Sheila told me how her brother "began to fight it," and how she and her sister "had to hold his hands down." She then said:

> I just smiled and pretended I was just holding his hand, but this was all for my parents' benefit, because I was using all the strength I had. Behind my smile, inside I was screaming. I looked over to my sister and saw that she was doing the same thing. She was using all her strength to hold his arm down, all the while looking into my eyes. Neither of us said anything. We just listened to his breathing and waited several minutes, hours it seemed, until it was over.

Only later did my sister ask, "What was that all about?" And I said, "Oh it was just a natural response." But inside I wondered, "Did I just kill somebody? Did he still want to die or was he changing his mind?" I had to tell myself, "He was unconscious, this was just his body trying to get air." My brother and I had talked about this forever and he never once wavered. If he had, I would've thought, "My God, this is all a mistake." So I came to accept that—although it was unpleasant—it was necessary and okay.

Too Little Time

In other situations, the results have been far less acceptable emotionally. In Peter's case, for example, a massive dose of Valium with bourbon was followed eight hours later with a similar decision to use a plastic bag. This was not motivated by obvious failure, but by a concern for time. At nearly 11:00 P.M., the participants—Peter's minister and two members of his prayer group—knew that Peter's wife, who wanted to know nothing about the death until after his body was gone, was due home at 1:00 A.M.

Although Peter had set aside a plastic bag and rubber bands for this purpose, "his eyes opened instantly" when they placed the bag over his head. "He wasn't conscious, and he didn't say anything, but he raised his hands to his face to remove it." A split second of confusion was followed by the joint silent decision of his minister and one of the others to hold down Peter's arms until his death. Doing so, they met their deadline; Peter's body was gone when his wife got home. Nevertheless, his minister told me later that it wasn't what he expected. "If he wasn't dying, and if he didn't want this so badly, I'd call it murder." He then said, "Still, it hasn't been very comfortable living with the images."

This situation developed in Peter's case because he had "no one left." A week before he died, he asked if I'd help him. I refused and told him he needed somebody closer.

He said, "I've buried all my friends." In response, I asked him if he'd discussed his plans with anyone. He replied, "Only Jesus, my minister, and my prayer group."

I said, half-seriously, "Well, you can't ask Jesus, but maybe you should talk about this whole decision again with your prayer group." With no one to help, I felt he needed more emotional support. He paused briefly and then said that he would.

In many instances, although the bag was visibly present, participants never wanted to believe in advance that intervention might ever be necessary. This can be seen by the fact that discussion of this possibility was often kept to a minimum. For example, when Bill brought up the topic his father commented, "The drugs will work, son; you've got enough to kill an army." Nevertheless, Bill talked with his brother and prepared the bag, giving it special thought and leaving it on the table next to his bed. Similarly, Peter's minister said they talked of it "but briefly." He explained, "I didn't want to listen to this, because I just knew the combination of Valium and bourbon would work, especially since Peter hadn't had a drink in more than ten years." He added, "If I'd known this would happen, I wouldn't have agreed to be there; I only wanted to give him support." And Sheila said, "The bag was our primary method, but I never thought he'd put up a fight."

In another instance where time took precedence, a man told me:

We realized the drugs weren't going to work, and as the hours mounted we began to comment, "Maybe we should do something." But no one wanted to take responsibility for the decision.

Finally, time made the decision for them.

It was getting toward dawn and we all wanted it over with. I wanted to leave before the sun came up. I didn't want any neighbors to recognize me later. So we talked about it, and finally I said, "Let's see what he's got." And we all went through his drawers until we found what we needed. The others clearly helped, but no one took the lead until I opened my mouth. Then we acted like a well-oiled machine.

The factor of time has another dimension to it. It seems to become more of a problem if friends are involved instead of family, if there are feelings of exhaustion, locational discomfort or wanting to be elsewhere, or if there is fear of being identified by neighbors. This component can be seen in both the above case and Peter's. One friend of a dying man said:

> I don't want to sound callous, because I really cared for him, but I had my own family, and my own plans, and I was scared, and I didn't want to be there any more, I was tired, and I wanted it over with and to go home.

SOMETIMES NOTHING SEEMS TO WORK

In some cases, fearing such possibilities, individuals plan for seemingly trouble-free death. But using sources of dubious quality, they still make mistakes. This was the case with Allen, who first called Hemlock for information about how to obtain lethal drugs to help end the life of his partner, Daryl.

Obviously upset, he told my associate that he was planning to give his partner a lethal dose of drugs by injecting them directly into Daryl's "central line." Like many AIDS patients, Daryl had a catheter surgically implanted into his chest during a month-long hospitalization. This was to ease the infusion of drugs as part of his treatment for CMV retinitis. This plastic tube—an "in-dwelling subclavian central line"—extended from his chest wall where it was implanted into a main artery leading into his heart. Because of the ease of access, Allen believed a lethal injection to be a "technically simple" matter, if only he could secure the drugs. He was told Hemlock couldn't help him, but to come in later if he "needed to talk." We arrived at the office within minutes of each other. He was nervous and visibly agitated.

Allen began by explaining that Daryl had just returned from the hospital a few days earlier following another month-long stay. Upon coming home, he'd stopped taking his medications and made it clear to his doctor that he wanted to die as soon as possible. Under no condition would he ever return to the hospital. Allen said that Daryl was "suffering intolerably," but refused to ask his physician for help because they'd recently fought about his decision to end further treatment. He added that Daryl's doctor knew of his plans, but only agreed to "not stop him."

Allen then talked in detail about how he was planning to help Daryl die. He finished by asking me if I knew anything about central lines or where to obtain heroin for this purpose.

I explained that my role was not to provide information, of which I knew little, but that I'd help him think about his decision. I asked him four questions: *Where is Daryl? Why didn't he come in? Why can't he wait for a natural death?* and *Why are you taking on this responsibility?*

He answered by explaining that Daryl had just been released from the hospital, was bedridden, would do anything not to go back, and was terrified of the possibility of AIDS dementia as well as suffocation from his next bout of pneumocystis pneumonia. He said, "We can't wait for nature to take its course; he's dying from AIDS, and I only want his suffering to end." It was "out of love for Daryl" that he agreed to help him die, and he'd "do anything to fulfill this promise." He said that he had to be involved as Daryl was bed-ridden and unable to search for drugs on his own. Without his doctor's help, Daryl had decided to take matters into his own hands. An injection of heroin into Daryl's catheter seemed "the easiest way for him to die."

The plan was devised because of Daryl's inability to keep food down. Allen explained that his friend would "throw up anything heavy enough to kill him." Allen had to help because Daryl wouldn't "be able to do it himself with one shot" of heroin before he went unconscious, and further injections would be necessary.

When I told him this might not be an easy thing for him to do or to live with later on, he replied that "it would be harder to live knowing that I let him suffer, knowing that I didn't help him." As to the possible legal consequences, he said, "I don't care, I have to take the risk." He then thoughtfully added, "You know, there are different types of prisons, and I'd be in one for the rest of my life anyway if I didn't do everything I could for him."

I expected that, like most callers and visitors, I'd never hear from Allen again. Five days later, however, I received his tearful call. He told me that Daryl had died on Sunday, only three days after we'd met. He explained that after he left our meeting, he saw an acquaintance who "dabbled" in street drugs. He informed him about their situation and asked him for "enough medication to kill someone." The next day, this man secured "a balloon with enough heroin to kill four people." Allen then told me his story.

On Sunday afternoon at 2:00 P.M., Daryl took four antinausea capsules. He waited thirty minutes and took four sleeping pills, waited ten more minutes and then shot himself up with one dose of heroin. He then said, "I'm starting to rush, you better help me into bed."

He went unconscious soon after the first injection. I immediately gave him a second injection, using an insulin syringe. I followed up with four shots of liquid oral morphine. I didn't really think about it at the time, but he'd been in the hospital for thirty-one days and must've had a tolerance to morphine. At about four, I gave him another twenty shots of oral morphine. At five-thirty, I gave him another heroin injection and twenty more shots of morphine along with ten shots of vodka. I thought the vodka would help. I was tearing up both my points [needles] and the line, with all the shots I was giving him.

At eight, after a final dose of heroin, I heard a shudder go through his body. Now I really felt this meant his soul had left his body, but he was still breathing. At nine-thirty, I finally gave him twenty more shots of morphine.

At ten he was still alive so I slipped a plastic trash bag over his head and held it around his neck with my hands. It only seemed to take about four minutes before he finally stopped breathing. As soon as he was dead, I called the answering service to locate his doctor.

It was here that their plan unraveled even further. He went on to explain that, although Daryl obtained agreement from both of his physicians that they'd "sign off on his death certificate," neither could be located. Allen went on to explain:

I was finally connected to a second backup who told me he wouldn't sign anything, and that I should call 911. Not knowing what else to do, I did. I told them I thought that Daryl was dead, but they arrived in full force only ten minutes later. I hopped in the back [of the ambulance], and they began working on him. One turned to the other and said, "I think I got a pulse." That did it. I began to cry, and I said, "Please, just let him die." They looked at me, and then stopped working on him, and slowed down all the way to the hospital. Later, after he was declared dead, one of the coroner's people asked me a few simple questions and then said that it looked like he "took his own life." I didn't say anything more, and though they sealed his house, they let me go in on Monday to take some of my belongings.

Allen finished his story by commenting—like Bill's brother, earlier—that this was "the longest day" in his life. "I'd been there for more than ten hours without a break; I had no one to talk to, and no one to relieve me." He added that giving the injections was the most difficult thing he'd ever done.

This was a lot rougher than I anticipated. I wouldn't recommend it to anyone. I'll never forget dulling all those needle points and tearing up his line with all those injections. His last words were, "Don't let me wake up." So I didn't. I also remember that when I put the bag over his head, I somehow expected him to struggle, but he didn't move.

Allen's situation was intensified by the excessive nature of the act—by giving, not one, but more than seventy injections—followed by the further unpleasantness of having to use the plastic bag, something he'd been trying to avoid all along. What also made this a "bad" death was his extreme isolation, his feelings of failure throughout, and his fear of being discovered as a result of the severe damage done to the catheter. His final statement summed up his experience. "I'd use a .38 before ever going through this again; It would have been quicker and a lot easier."

DOCTORS WITH BAD DRUGS

In a significant number of cases, physicians who decide to help are reticent to prescribe truly lethal means such as Seconals. This hesitation is out of fear that such a drug is tracked by government agencies and, therefore, the death of one of their patients might be investigated. As a result, some doctors provide what turn out to be the "wrong" drugs. The consequences of this can often be far worse than when partners, families, and friends take matters into their own hands and pool their own pharmaceutical resources. This is because, without physicians involved, most recognize that things may go wrong and they may have to intervene. If physicians are involved, however, the expectations of failure and potential family involvement are relaxed; a patient and others may place too high of a level of trust in both the physician's knowledge and in their prescription.

This occurred in the case of Jessica, whose daughter, Sally, called me one morning to talk about her mother's failed suicide attempt, and to discuss her own plans to help her mother do it right. Sally had but one question; if she helped, could the "true cause" of her mother's death be discovered? She explained that her mother's physician had assured her that the large dosage of Percocets he prescribed would be effective for this purpose. However, when her mother made the attempt she failed to inform the family of her plans and was found unconscious by Sally's sister. Assuming that her mother had a stroke, she called 911. Jessica was rushed to the hospital and, though her stomach was pumped, she was left in extreme pain with near fatal liver damage. Upon her release from the hospital, she was given only weeks to live because of her illness and liver damage. Nevertheless, because of her now-known suicide attempt, her doctor feared to prescribe any further drugs to help end her life.

In the case of Mark and his mother, Linda, however, the physician's help did not come in the form of a prescription, but from the doctor's own personal supply. Like Jessica's doctor, he felt that this was safer than leaving behind a lethal paper trail.

When Linda was diagnosed with stomach cancer, Mark's parents had been active in the Hemlock Society for years, and there was little moral debate that this would be the right choice for them both at the proper time. Nevertheless, the diagnosis came as a shock. She'd been feeling well and had gone in for a normal periodic checkup when her stomach cancer was diagnosed. "In just a matter of weeks, she went from feeling fine to surgery to never eating again to quickly wasting away." This made her decision easier about "when to die." Mark explained, "She probably would've died in another week if she hadn't taken her own life at that point."

During this time his mother began asking physician friends if they could assist her or help her obtain what she'd need to die comfortably and safely. As a health professional, she'd worked closely with a number of doctors, and it took little effort before one man, a personal friend, agreed to help.

Despite the fact that she was in pain, Linda had been staying at a cancer clinic in Mexico until the moment she decided to die. She'd been there for a week with Mark and his father, and that morning, still assuming that everything was fine, Mark drove back to their El Paso home to take care of personal business. He was planning to return to Mexico in a day to give his father a similar respite. This was not to be the case.

Only an hour after he got home, his parents arrived. They said that, shortly after he'd left, they'd had a serious discussion. His mother had said, "I can't take this anymore, and obviously the treatment isn't going to make any difference and the pain is too great and it's time." She called her friend who immediately came with a quantity of liquid morphine.

Their plan was to help Linda fulfill her last wish "to have something to drink." The cancer had crept up her throat and she couldn't swallow due to the pain.

> The physician suggested that a sufficient quantity of morphine, injected into her heart catheter, would first deaden almost all sensation, and there might be a little period where she could have a couple of last sips and nibbles like she wanted to do.

The physician told them that he could not take an active role but could "provide the medication" and would be "willing to stay in the house in case of an emergency." He said that Mark and his father should actively assist, but that it would be necessary for them to come to this decision together and "to know that no one forced it on anyone else." Mark and his father agreed. More than any-thing, they wanted her to be able to take a few sips of ginger ale. Mark continued:

> The bottom line is that nothing worked that day. We injected the morphine into her heart catheter and were very surprised that she was instantly made unconscious. We thought that there'd be a period of grogginess during which time we could say our good-byes. Then she would pass into unconscious-ness. Well, we injected it and she was gone.

Mark was extremely frustrated. They kept trying to offer her ginger ale, but it was too late and "there was no more communica-tion." But they rationalized that "maybe that's okay," because "she got to slip away easily and didn't have to face these last difficult moments of saying good-bye." He added, "After all, we'd been say-ing good-bye for weeks anyway, so it wasn't like we didn't say good-bye."

This was the least of their problems. After an hour, there was no change. Her heart rate continued strong. They consulted with the physician, who said, "Well I was worried about this; that mor-phine was something I'd been keeping around for myself for several years and maybe it wasn't potent anymore."

At that point they all realized they had to "do something more active." The doctor suggested that he could obtain a quantity of in-sulin for them, and that "a large dose of insulin injected in the heart catheter should induce death." The doctor left, and returned an hour later with several syringes which Mark's father took charge of, injecting them one after another.

> We waited and nothing happened. He [The doctor] had already said that as a last resort a very large syringe—which he'd also brought with him—could be used to inject air to induce heart failure. We ended up having to repeatedly inject air. It really was nightmarish, horrific, how this process seemed to keep on and on. But it finally worked and she passed on. It

took at least five hours from when we started. I stayed with her all of that time. This felt very important to be right there holding her hand and to be present with her to the very end.

When Circumstances Conspire

Sometimes even if drugs eventually work without further involvement of others, the circumstances surrounding the death can lead to dissatisfaction and regret, and family members or partners can be left feeling that they "didn't do enough" or that they "could've done better." This was the situation that followed Julie's participation in her brother Jerry's death.

Jerry had been suffering for years from progressive multiple sclerosis. In fact, besides her father, Julie was the only member of her family who'd not been touched by a chronic debilitating illness. She was driven to help Jerry partly because of this, out of survivor's guilt. A nurse, Julie was "the only one in the family who could talk to him about his dying." He'd first asked for her help five years before, but other than talk, nothing more was done. They discussed it again over the next four years and she finally agreed to "get what he needed." With her mother's knowledge and support, Julie secured what she believed would be a lethal dose of Demerols.

Jerry kept the drugs for several months, until Julie's next visit for a long-planned family celebration for their grandfather. During this time, Julie became increasingly "worried that he was taking so long in making the final decision." This was rooted in her knowledge that Jerry's condition was worsening. Soon he'd lose the capacity to swallow or even to "open the bottle of pills." This was critical to Julie, because the final act itself had to be Jerry's. She wasn't going to assist him actively, but she was afraid that if he waited too long he'd plead for her to help him directly.

On the day Julie arrived, Jerry decided it was time. Although nothing was said in advance, her presence helped him make the decision. "Being there," she said, "gave him the sense of security he needed." In the early hours of that day, Jerry took the forty Demerol tablets. When his mother found him in the morning, she removed the pill bottle from his bed. With his nurse soon to arrive, Jerry's mother wanted no evidence of a suicide in progress. However, about noon Jerry awoke and called for Julie and his mother. When they discovered that his attempt had failed, they called Jerry's doctor for advice. His doctor told them that, most likely, the pills had lodged in a pocket in his throat and hadn't dissolved. Though Jerry was upset and confused, his physician told them all to do nothing until the next day. During this time the drama was known only to Julie and her mother. Neither the nurse nor any other family member had been informed of the attempt. As a result, later in the afternoon, Julie had to leave to join her father for dinner "as if nothing was happening." Julie's mom remained with her son, fed him more food, and this "washed down the pills." He ended up dying only two hours later. When Julie returned after dinner, she found an ambulance and three police cars in front of the house, and "a total of nine people in uniforms."

> They asked questions about his pill bottles, and we heard them say to the coroner that "It looks like we might have a suicide here." They let it go when they confirmed with his doctor and nurse that he'd been sick a long time. It went down as a natural death.

Later, Julie wrote me to share more of her feelings. She said that what bothered her most was that Jerry "had to go through that horror of awakening" after he'd finally gathered the courage to make the attempt. For Julie, "the horror of those hours and the look in his eyes" was something she couldn't forget.

> For me, the guilt that I experienced about his suffering during that time is something that has been an integral part of my grieving and something about which I have worked to forgive myself.

Another regret was that her brother "had to do this alone, that no one was at his bedside when he took the pills." But the largest factor of her guilt is rooted in the secrecy of the situation itself, which prevented his death from ever being the special event it might otherwise have been. This was due to the "illegality of assisting," and the need to "keep it hidden from significant family members" and "proceed as though nothing was happening." A month after Jerry's death, Julie realized the "insanity of the situation." She said, "I've really struggled with how could I have left him and how awful for him to be left." She realized that she would like to have been with him when he died to have completed what they started five years before.

SEEING NO OTHER OPTION

Situational factors leading up to an assisted death can also be sources of regret. This occurred in the case of Frank, who made the final decision to die, and his wife, Marie, who agreed to help him only because "convalescent care" was breathing down their necks and Frank "saw no other solution." In their case, the failure to see other possibilities became the defining factor of "what went wrong." After building a life together for more than fifty years, they were forced to leave the home they'd built for themselves in the country because of Frank's progressive difficulty with Parkinson's disease. Moving to an urban retirement community that gave little allowance for the disabled, they stayed for the next seven years until Frank's condition worsened.

With Frank's increasing number of falls and trips to the emergency room, Marie was being pressed by the administrators to "do something about Frank," to move him to a long-term care facility. As a long-time member of Hemlock, Frank didn't see this as an option. To him, being taken from his wife of more than fifty years was "akin to divorce and would've broken the marriage." She explained, "I was part of him, and he was part of me; to end that would've been too hard."

> We would lie down beside each other on our bed with his arm across me, and he'd say, "This is living." You can't do that in a convalescent hospital. You can't have a family. It's

broken up. It's not only being warehoused, it breaks up the relationship.

With availability of alternative housing for both of them, with innovative care that could've allowed them to be together, with other economic resources, this man might not have found it immediately necessary to take his sleeping medication, and this eighty-year-old woman might not have needed to carry through with her end of the bargain, to use a plastic bag after his pills took effect.

Other kinds of situational factors can also go wrong. When Steven Shiflett died, one minute before midnight on Good Friday 1992, it was not as he'd planned. Late that afternoon his "small" farewell party soon filled his living room to overflowing as his friends gave him a "final toast." All of this was documented in text and photos in a *San Francisco Chronicle* article six months later.

After most of the celebrants left, his plan was to take enough medication to sleep and then to have his "surrogate"—the term Steven gave to the man he'd asked to help him—inject him with a lethal dose of drugs. This man, however, had now been drinking for several hours. Before the party, "he seemed the perfect candidate," as he too was infected with AIDS and had admitted to helping four others die, "smothering one by holding his hand over his mouth and pinching his nose."

"I am not a pillow for hire," he told a *Chronicle* reporter. "I wouldn't do this for everyone, for a stranger." But Steven had selected the wrong man, whose resolve "had been weakened by alcohol" and who was nervous that too many people at the party knew he'd been appointed to help Steven die. To make matters worse, Steven was unable to digest the sleeping pills he'd taken. The climax occurred when someone walked into Steven's room while this man was giving the first injection. Unknown words were exchanged and Steven's surrogate rushed from the home, abandoning his effort to help Steven die.

The others present panicked, and one called a physician who knew of Steven's plans. The doctor told the others over the phone "how to finish" what had been started. "It crossed the line for me;

I was involved way more than I wanted to be," the physician later told the reporter. "It should have remained just between Steve and me."

When Motives Fail

Although drugs might not always work and circumstances might be less than positive, these can be overshadowed by a larger issue, that of motives. This applies both to the person who is dying and to the one who has agreed to help.

COERCION UNTO DEATH

Opponents often argue that if physician-assisted dying is legalized, the most vulnerable persons will be coerced by unscrupulous family members into ending their lives. In talking with hundreds of terminally ill over the past few years, I've yet to hear this complaint voiced. Nevertheless, what I have heard on more than a few occasions, both from the dying and from surviving participants of an assisted death, pertains to two other forms of "coercion." The first, and most common, is an often not-so-subtle coercion by the dying themselves to ensure the participation of others in their deaths.

When Peter, a long-time member of my support group asked me to help him die, I refused. I told him that I couldn't cross that boundary, that he wasn't "close enough." It might be different in the case of a wife or family member, but even then it would be a difficult decision to face. To help him, I explained, would be too much of an emotional burden. I also worried that it might make it too easy for me to help others. I said, "Where would I draw the line? Whom would I help? Whom would I turn down?" He immediately replied, "But I have no one else I can ask?" In that moment, I realized up-close the emotional conflict a physician can face when a patient makes a similar request.

Later, instead of having a discussion with his minister and prayer group about his decision, as I'd earlier suggested, he just asked for and received their assistance. I was surprised by this turn of events, and in talking with one of these participants after Peter's death, the first thing I asked her was "Why did you decide to help?" In response, she explained, "Peter was very persuasive about having no one left to turn to." She added:

> I felt a bit coerced, I was definitely torn two ways about this. I didn't want to see him suffer, but I didn't necessarily want to be the one to put him out of his misery. I think we were all torn, but decided to share the burden.

This idea of "sharing the burden" is not uncommon. One man told me, "My partner said that since he was paying the ultimate price with his life, the least I could do was to pay my dues by helping him die." Similarly, another man said that his wife was "angered" over his hesitation to help, and told him, "You're part of this relationship, and this is what I need. I can't do it without you. Next month you'll still have a life. I won't!" He explained that "she used guilt, love, and tears," but ultimately he decided to "equalize the burden."

The second form of "coercion" is when the dying feel the need to consider the schedule of others in timing their own deaths. This happened in the case of Barry when he decided to time his death to occur before his physician left for vacation. His partner told me, "Barry was always watching out for me; he didn't want to take the risk of having some other doctor refuse to sign his death certificate."

This form of coercion is much more apparent when a trade-off is necessary for the assistance or attendance of others. This can be seen in the case of Carol, who, at eighty-six years of age, decided to die because of severe emphysema and her fear of ending up in a nursing home. Increasingly frail, Carol had taken several falls and had recently been released from a convalescent facility, to which she never wanted to return. She'd shared her desires with her nephew's daughter, Anna, who was her primary caregiver. Carol had received a large prescription of morphine and percocets from her physician for the purpose of ending her life, and Anna offered to be there with her in whatever way she might be needed, including "using a plastic bag" after Carol was unconscious.

Carol was nervous about using the drugs alone, and Anna's father, though supportive of his aunt's decision, didn't want his own daughter to be alone when she helped Carol die. He'd offered to be there to give his daughter any support she might need, but his work and travel schedule meant that he could only be there on Friday, or Carol would have to wait an additional three weeks to die. I heard all this on a Thursday afternoon, the day before her planned death. Carol called to ask if I thought the medication she was planning to use might upset her stomach because of her ulcer.

In asking her about her ulcer, I discovered that it had only become a problem the week before when she found out that she either had to die on Friday, or wait. Talking further, she admitted to feeling "rushed," and that she wasn't yet ready, but afraid to wait any longer. I told her that this was the most important decision of her life and, obviously, it should be given more thought. She also might do well to share her feelings with both Anna and her nephew, I suggested. Carol called me back a week later to say that her stomach was "feeling much better."

QUESTIONABLE REASONS TO HELP

In some instances, those who are dying seem only concerned about their desire to die and appear to have little regard for the needs of others. At the same time, others often only see the need to help, regardless of the consequences. This co-dependency can be accentuated by the private relationship that caregiving often entails, and can especially be intensified by the privacy and secrecy that often develops when two individuals begin talking of the option of assisted death. This can be seen vividly in the case of Michael and his father.

Michael told me that he became his father's caregiver and finally helped him die as a way to "show his love" and to "redeem" himself for his "failures in life" and for disappointing his family years before. Michael's involvement began after his father was diagnosed with colon cancer and had a mass removed from his liver.

For the next year Michael worked to "secure the right drugs," but his task took on special urgency when the oncologist informed him that his father would gradually "waste away from liver cancer."

As his father's cancer worsened, and he required more care, Michael took a leave of absence from his business and moved back home. He felt he was the only one his father could rely on, as his doctors rebuffed him. "This became our secret pact," Michael said, and his father didn't even want his own girlfriend to know of their plan. The two of them also kept their plans secret from Michael's brother, who's never been told how his father died. Michael told me that he felt a mixture of "pride" and "a heightened sense of awareness and duty," but still resented the fact that "this wasn't the loving act" he wanted.

During the last month Michael reached burnout. He'd taken on the sole responsibility of caring for his father, because there was a lack of continuity of care with "day attendants changing every few days." As his father's death drew nearer, his workload increased and, to fulfill his duty, he began excluding others. As he saw it, he "couldn't take the risk of others getting in the way."

Eventually, his father's liver began to press on his diaphragm, causing uncontrollable hiccups. The oncologist "didn't know what to do." The options got fewer, and Michael's inability to take time off increased his isolation. His father would awaken at night and fall while making his way to the bathroom. Michael "was traumatized," and would shut the door so as not to hear him fall and cry out for help. "I knew I was over my head," Michael said, "but what could I do?" The pressure built and one night, feeling chest pains, he even checked himself into a hospital emergency room.

Weeks earlier, he'd obtained the drugs and gave them to his father to use whenever he wanted. Without warning, his father took them, and Michael found him later in bed. "It was a cosmic joke," he said, "because it didn't work." When he awakened, his father "was pissed that it'd failed and he again was in pain."

Matters worsened. One night his father fell behind the bathroom door and was badly cut. Michael forced his way in. "Dad was naked, but I got him bandaged and into bed." The next afternoon his father announced, "Today's the day." Just before, Michael had called an estate planner and tried to get his father to wait until after their appointment. Michael was crying, but his father was "clear headed and said, "No!" Michael finally agreed, got the pills, ground them up, and mixed them into his pudding. "He got it down, even though it hurt."

Michael explained that he was in a "profound and heightened state of consciousness." He said that at that moment, after his father had taken the drugs, he began to ask him all the questions for which he wanted answers.

> I asked him questions like, "How did you make it through life?" and "Do you have any advice for me?" But he was getting tired, and gave me no secret that changed my life.

Michael's life was soon changed anyway. Death didn't come. Michael repeatedly entered his father's room in disbelief that the "drugs weren't working." His fear and isolation built. During those hours an old girlfriend called. She had known that Michael was back home and caring for his father. He immediately told her what was happening in the next room. At 1:30 A.M., he called his business partner and asked his advice. Finally, two hours later, he made his decision.

> I got two dry-cleaning bags and placed them inside one another. I didn't think I could do it. It took me a couple of minutes before I could go ahead. But I forced myself. I felt I had no choice. I said some kind of prayer that it would be okay. This was clearly a loving act, but it seemed like forever.
>
> I then took off the bags, put them in the garbage behind the supermarket. I'd been careful not to tie them too tightly around his throat. I didn't want to leave any kind of mark. Then I called the mortuary, who called the coroner, who called the mortuary back. A sheriff's detective came and took pictures. He called the doctor, who told him it was a natural death.

Michael went into "a state of shock" until the funeral was over. His sleep disorder continued. He began to second guess his decision. During this period, he wasn't helped by the secret he carried or by the fact that his father's girlfriend blamed him. "I got no support for all that I'd done," he said.

A month after his father's death, Michael entered a treatment facility for his insomnia and depression. He was put on medication, but the effects continued. Michael knew it was from the "mix of emotion," the "profound nature of the experience," and "replaying the event over and over again."

> I would think about the plastic bag, of asking him questions, of waiting for his breathing to stop, of watching him die, of pushing people away in the last days, and of being the gate-keeper.

Though he "couldn't stand it" and wanted his father to die, he also explained that he "wanted to recapture and somehow share the clarity of what happened at the end," which had been the "peak experience" of his life. "In retrospect," he told me, "I wish there was a pill that could alleviate uncertainty and anxiety and help people make the right decisions."

For Michael, the opportunity to care for his father, and the bond created by the pact, enabled him to "redeem" himself for his failures. In a subtle way, by agreeing to help his father die—and by following through—Michael was able to obtain validation from his father, which, he felt, had eluded him for twenty years. It was this secret pact that held the promise of a father's love, forgiveness, and admiration. For this self-professed prodigal son, this temptation was too difficult to ignore. It was both "bittersweet and refreshing," and a source of both guilt and pride, a peak experience and one filled with regret.

Michael's case exemplifies several, though not all, of the features of what can go wrong in an assisted death. These included, the failure to obtain support from one's physician, the inadequacy of the drugs obtained, the need to take additional measures to ensure the death, and serious lasting effects for those involved—the most obvious of which were exemplified in his depression and sleeping disorders. In addition, several other factors came into play.

These included: secrecy and isolation, exhaustion from caregiving, absence of support from others for the decision, fear of discovery, and differences between Michael and his father about the final timing for his death.

In addition, his need to prove his love to his father, to redeem himself in his eyes, to be the competent son, obviously affected both his decision and his ability to work with others to ensure the best quality of care for his father while he was alive. Nevertheless, Michael was not alone in this; his father participated in this mutual conspiracy of silence and used his son's need to prove himself as a way to coerce the help he so long desired.

Like Michael and his father, some relationships are filled with the shared belief that what one wants, the other must provide. To me, this co-dependency unto death, defines what can go wrong far more than any amount of wrong drugs or plastic bags. This is a greater tragedy.

Perhaps those who are dying need the agreement of others to help as a way to gain a sense of power in the face of their impotency toward death. This demand for help can be partly false bravado—a way to confront death head-on—and partly a means to extract a promise that the other will do anything for them out of love. If nothing else, the agreement to help, unless too eagerly provided, can serve as a sign of that love, and as an insurance policy that there's a way out if it should become absolutely necessary.

Help from Those a Step Removed

There are less obvious cases that still trouble me even though family members and participants themselves may have defined these experiences as "good deaths." What troubles me the most is when I find myself second-guessing the motives of another, when something doesn't fit, although one person may want to die and another willingly offers to help.

This was my feeling in hearing the case of Jessie, a friend of the family, one-step removed, who assisted in the death of her close friend's mother, Kathryn. In talking with her daughter Carla about her desire to die, Kathryn suggested that they ask Jessie, a Hemlock "life member," for her help. Carla had already secured enough drugs for her mother to ensure unconsciousness, but they felt it was too risky for Carla to be further involved. Instead, they asked Jessie, who readily agreed to help.

Jessie arrived at Kathryn's high-rise wearing a wig and dark glasses to prevent being identified by the building doorman. She also brought along a pair of white cotton gloves that she obtained from a gardening catalog. Jessie put on these gloves as soon as Kathryn opened the door. She wanted to leave no fingerprints. Once Kathryn was ready, she began by trying on various plastic bags and made her selection. The plan was for Jessie to use the bag on Kathryn once she was unconscious. Kathryn then called Carla to leave her usual night message on her machine, and then placed "her Hemlock books and suicide note" on the dining room table. All of this was to take away any suspicion of involvement by others.

When Kathryn was finally ready, Jessie handed her the pills, and both worked rapidly so that Kathryn could swallow the last pill before the first took effect. As soon as Kathryn fell asleep, Jessie laid her back on her bed, put the bag over her head, tied it with string, and arranged her hands as if Kathryn had done all this by herself. A half an hour later, Jessie left. On her way out to the elevator she removed the gloves, but continued to wear the wig and dark glasses.

The next day Carla arrived with another friend, who supposedly helped his own mother to die. Instead of calling the authorities to report her mother's suicide, however, Carla untied the bag, put her hands into a "natural pose," took away the evidence, and then called Kathryn's doctor, who ruled it a natural death.

When Carla shared this change of plans, Jessie was disappointed, as she'd "done so well" in covering up this assisted death. Eventually, she realized that "this way was better for the family" as Kathryn was Catholic. In discussing her feelings about helping Kathryn die, she explained:

> I've been wonderful ever since. I wish I could do it again, and wish I knew somebody else to help. I would like my mission to help others out of life. I'm proud of myself about this. It's

given me the most self-esteem I've had in my life. It was heal-ing to help someone who needed me.

She also talked of her preferences, saying, "If it were legal I could just do it; I wouldn't have had to get nervous or wear a wig." Nevertheless, in describing her feelings, she seemed to express an almost proprietary attitude, suggesting the importance that this was *her* plan, *her* death, and no one else's. She said:

> I wouldn't have done it with others present. There'd have been too many people saying, "No, do it this way." It's wrong to involve too many people. I wouldn't have felt right. I loved doing it by myself.

Jessie never told her boyfriend of several years what she did, but she did have a session with a therapist since she "had to tell" somebody. "I told her that I felt funny, not sorry, but funny, just not right; nevertheless, I'm proud of it!" Her therapist told her she "did the right thing."

Missionaries and Hit Squads

Jessie's desire to "do it again" is not all that uncommon. Some who take on this task of helping are seduced by the experience. I've seen this occur only rarely among family members, except where fami-lies are struck with multiple lingering deaths. But I've heard of it on several occasions among those a step removed, who lack true inti-macy with the one they've helped. There is an exception within the AIDS community, as I'll soon discuss, but the very nature of that disease, of course, has created exceptional circumstances in both caring for the sick and bringing them release through death.

Those who have taken on this "calling" are driven both out of love and something else. This "something else" is frequently the desire to recapture some earlier excitement or inspiration. Several have told me that this act of helping another to die, of being so close to something as powerful and awe inspiring as death, was a "peak experience." It became so important in their lives that the need for repetition transcended the risk of exposure, arrest, and imprisonment. This evolves partly out of the belief that their participation has given them a special knowledge or ability that shouldn't be wasted. I believe this becomes especially important if other aspects of their daily lives have failed to provide them with this same sense of personal worth and accomplishment. Maybe this partly explains the actions of Dr. Kevorkian.

Without legal opportunities and strict rules for who should and should not receive or *provide* aid-in-dying, those without any knowledge turn at times to those with a little, and these individuals may not always be the best. There are a number of such men and women who have stepped across this boundary into a secret world of assisting others outside of partners, immediate family, and close friends. Unlike Kevorkian, however, these individuals, with but a few exceptions, have had no interest in going public about their special talents. It has been their close association with the dying that has brought them some kind of special identity.

Barring nurses and physicians from this equation, such individuals can be found in both metropolitan regions and smaller cities, wherever a population with terminal illnesses reside. They include women helping women with breast cancer and others who reside quietly among cancer support groups. They especially can be found in areas where there are large numbers of AIDS cases, like San Francisco, where more than 14,000 documented AIDS deaths through mid-1995 occurred. This volume of death has come to affect nearly everyone in the Bay Area, as workplaces and neighborhoods have been decimated and extended families and friendship groups have been shattered. The nature of the disease, seen by most patients as always terminal, allows for easy cover-up, because many physicians participate and others don't fully investigate or even want to know the true cause of death.

AIDS, more than any other disease, has lent itself to this practice because patients are highly sophisticated about the course of the illness, which too often consists of multiple severe, painful, and disabling conditions. In addition, the proximity of patients to one another and to numerous AIDS support organizations allows all but the most isolated patient to discuss alternatives among themselves, to constantly exchange stories, and measure themselves against each other. Unlike typical cancer patients, many with AIDS claim that they see their future daily in the faces of friends, those on the street, and in multi-page obituaries in an active gay press where articles on assisted suicide also frequently appear. One man told me:

> A lot of us don't want to hang around till the end; we don't see a cure on the horizon or hope for recovery. We fear we'll become incontinent, rot away, vegetate, or get dementia. In the early '80s no one knew what it was or whether it was curable. People held on longer, and suicides were rare. Now they know what's in store for them, and they don't like it.

Although most assisted deaths occur with the help of partners, family, and only close friends, there are others who lack such close ties and who may only have their peers to fall back on. For example, one man, who admitted helping four of his friends to die, told me about his very early "awakening" in 1983, when he turned down his friend's request and never forgave himself. As a result, when asked by another friend in 1985, he hesitated for just forty-eight hours—only long enough to be certain of his friend's true intentions.

> When he asked me again, I got a big three-quarter gram bag of heroin. He'd never shot up before. I was paranoid about the syringe, and made sure I wore gloves to get in and out of his apartment. I shot him up and put his hands on the syringe and made it look like an overdose. It took about two minutes to really hit, because heroin builds to a big bang.

In talking about his own impending death, he said he'd made "a mutual assistance pact" with four of his friends, one a physician, all of whom have AIDS. He said he told one of these friends—one closest to dying—to let him know if their physician friend couldn't do it, because he would. The reason he gave was "love" and because "it's the compassionate thing to do." He added, "People know when they want to go, and they should be able to do it; If they can't, they should be able to ask those they love for help." He underlined this, however, by saying:

> I couldn't do it to just anybody. It'd have to be someone I love, and I'd have to be sure they weren't depressed. If they asked me to help I'd have to talk to them again in a few days. After all, friends help friends, because doctors often won't, and birth families are seldom there.

This man used the knowledge he'd gained from being a former IV drug user, and watching people overdose, to refine his skills. Others, without this type of experience, have developed other knowledge. One gay couple, both active in the AIDS community, who assisted in the deaths of more than a dozen of their friends, made the discovery that plastic bags are vital. "Drugs require a long time without interruption," one of them said, "sometimes up to two days." They didn't often have this time and couldn't take the risk of failure. They told me about their favorite bag, by size and brand, and how they use a painter's mask first to prevent the plastic bag from being sucked into the mouth.

They also described some of their exploits. One involved a near escape when a former lover of the dying man called 911 without informing anyone. They escaped just before the emergency crews arrived. Still, the bag ensured the death. In another case they encouraged a friend with no place else to go to make a reservation at a San Francisco landmark hotel. When he checked in "he paid for his room in cash and placed his drugs in the hotel safe." Only then did he call the couple for their help. When they arrived, they found him in a weakened state, helped him shower and dress, and led him down to the front desk "to retrieve his stash." One of them then went to the gift shop where he bought a small souvenir frying pan. Back in the room they used the pan, together with the bottom of a beer bottle, to crush the pills. After waiting several hours, they still had to use the plastic bag, which they took with them when they left, all the while worrying about being seen by the hotel maid.

The Wrong Emphasis

In listening to such stories, I'm especially torn by the human tragedy that creates the perceived need to die and the desire to help. Obviously, there is a need for another way, for a middle path between what's legally available at present and any underground technology of death that can only offer release, quickly and secretly, without aesthetics and grace. I'm torn when I see that achieving death becomes more important than attaining peace and closure, and when the nature of the experience becomes less than sacred.

I'm aware that the problem resides in my own notion of the "good death," and reflects my personal difficulty with current legal choices and the availability of alternatives. Some of my concern has to do with the treatment of death itself within our contemporary culture, the fallout of which obviously can affect the experience of assisted death. As I'll show in the next chapter, however, there are those who—even at the end of their lives, and even selecting an assisted death—are still able to achieve a personal transcendence from the mundane and expected to the extraordinary.

Part of what "goes wrong" in assisted deaths is that the very nature of its illegality often raises barriers to positive experience in the form of fear, inadequate knowledge, and lack of appropriately trained practitioners. How does one "do" an assisted death unless one has done it before? And where does one learn—not just methods but manner and appropriateness—without prior experience? And what would such manner and appropriateness look like? In this way, the lack of models, known experience, and opportunities for training partners and family members makes this an action that must be constantly reinvented. Every death is new, every experience is fraught with its own fears, hesitancy, and ignorance, and nearly every one who participates is an actor with an unrehearsed script.

This, more than anything else perhaps, creates the potential for error and dissatisfaction on the one side, and on the other an attitude rooted in fear, a focus more on methods of death and a concern for secrecy than on a sense of awe, sacredness, and respect for what is actually occurring.

In some instances, therefore, I'm reminded of an introductory statement in François Truffaut's film, *Confidentially Yours,* in which the viewer is informed that:

> Death is a strange thing. When people die of illness it's cruel and unfair, but it's really death. When it's a crime or a killing death becomes abstract, as if the solution to the mystery had priority. It's like reading a thriller.

I think for many, the act of assisting in a death can take on this quality, albeit in a reverse manner. A crime is being committed, but the "solution" is to hide the fact of its occurrence. It's a mystery that needs to be solved in advance by those participating in it. In so doing, however, the importance of the life that is ending can be temporarily forgotten. The question is not "How do I help you die in a manner that's right for both of us and reflects both our love and the importance of this final farewell?" Instead, it becomes "How do we construct this death quickly and safely for all involved?" or "How do we make an assisted death look natural?" The solution becomes the emphasis, perhaps in the way that some doctors separate illnesses from patients, and see the mystery of symptoms instead of the human suffering they create.

For example, when I asked Randy what he remembered the most about Ralph's death, he didn't say, "The loss of my closest friend." He said, "Shooting the rubber bands out the window and wondering if they could be fingerprinted." Similarly, Danny told me that his only thoughts at the time were about his "fear of discovery, and wondering when to leave, and where to dispose of the trash bag." And then there was Greg, who said that he could only think of "not being around when the hospice nurse arrived." Others have told me of their apprehension of "someone coming over unannounced before it was all over," or of being "stopped on the way home by the police while carrying" a plastic bag, syringes, or extra drugs.

One man I talked with, who'd participated in two "plastic bag" deaths seemed more interested in the "problems" of plastic bags than the people on whom they were used. In several interviews with him, I could never break through to emotion. And whether this was a result of false bravado or machismo, he was more concerned in sharing his worries about covering up the asphyxiations of his friends. He asked me, "Do you think the coroner could test tears for plastic residue? Toxin tests are so good they can pick up parts-per-billion in water; what if they test for plastic?"

I gave him no answer. In response, he described how he'd resolved this worry by washing the faces of these two individuals after their deaths, "just in case." He then talked casually of possible innovations, and joked that "perhaps Hemlock could market a plastic bag with a cotton liner."

Perhaps such thoughts are normal, given the illegality of the act and the secrecy represented. And perhaps it's the only way some individuals can distance themselves from the gravity of the death and the seriousness of their actions. To me, this distancing—this transforming of the end of life into abstract mystery—more than anything else, fills me with a mixture of repulsion, sadness, and regret. For how can a death be good, if the one who is dying is the only person to have dealt with his or her fear and feelings of regret, and if even loving family members can now—in the final moments—only focus on "cleaning up the evidence" or "getting their stories straight."

This, to me, depicts better what can go wrong than any wrong dosage or plastic bag.

Chapter 6

RESOLUTION, RITUAL, AND THE GOOD DEATH

Dennis died late on a Sunday night. The morning before, he'd received the news from Janet, his general practitioner and close friend for years, that his final chemotherapy treatment wasn't working. She told him that his kidneys were failing, and it was "but a matter of days" before he died. Both Dennis and his wife, Grace, had been expecting this for some time, but he'd refused to give up his battle, pinning his hopes on this last effort. After all, only four months before he'd been told that he'd "beaten" the prostate cancer he'd endured for years. But now he was bedridden and in pain, even though he had a pump that fed a steady dosage of morphine into his hip, and could also give himself an additional dosage every hour by using a hand-held button.

I first met Dennis and Grace several weeks before. I came over to discuss his desires to die. Janet, his doctor, was also present along with his minister, who was another long-time friend. At that time, Janet assured Dennis that she'd help him die when he felt the time was right. She explained that she'd come over to increase the base dosage of morphine and give him full control over the button.

At that first meeting, Dennis thought he was "almost ready to take the fast train." Nevertheless, he still talked about "licking" his new cancer, if only his "blood levels" would get to where he could endure more chemotherapy. Grace wasn't ready for any type of death; she hadn't accepted the possibility of losing him. She'd been depressed, was playing with the dosage of her antidepressants, and was now taking sedatives to "get back in control." Janet was supportive emotionally but was professionally noncommittal about the chemo.

Dennis turned to me and asked, "Do you think I've got six weeks?"

Pausing, I said, "Not if you take the fast train." I then added, "What do I know? Ask your doctor; she's sitting right here."

Janet took over and told him, "Probably. There's nothing now to indicate you don't."

Then I told him he'd been doing some great work, which he should continue, but added that he needed to talk more with Grace, to complete whatever was still necessary, and to "do the chemo" if that's what he needed for peace of mind. "You've got the support of your physician here, and it's good to talk about this, but it's premature to make any plans; when the time comes you'll know it."

Janet agreed, telling him, "I'm but a call away when you need me."

Weeks later, on a Saturday afternoon, he made his decision. Grace had finally come to a place of peace over the previous few days. Dennis made several calls. He asked many of his friends to visit, telling them they wouldn't have much time. He also made a long call to his brother to tell him good-bye. It was but a few months before that these two formerly estranged brothers reconciled after several decades apart. Dennis's brother had come out from the east coast for a "short visit" that ended up lasting weeks, and they spent more time together than they had since they were children. "We didn't appreciate each other then," Dennis told me. "Now we do."

Late Sunday afternoon, their minister arrived, and Janet came for a "last house call." Grace and six of Dennis's friends were also there. When he was ready—after final words, tears, laughter, and farewells—Janet increased the dosage on the morphine pump and gave Dennis full control over the hand-held button. He kept pressing it until he relaxed and drifted into a drug-induced sleep that was seemingly filled with "peaceful visions." After Janet left, the button was turned over to the seven others who were present.

Later, Grace told me that Dennis didn't want her to press the button. Hers was to be a special role, and she held his hand until close to the end. "We lost three of our people at eleven," she said, "and after that Dennis was left with what he called his 'little harem.'" These were his "inner circle" of four favorite women: a blond, a redhead, a brunette, and one with gray hair. With the departure of the three, Grace's role changed. "In the last couple of hours I was the pilot," she explained. "The four of us were like a team of 'birthers' and now we're bonded for life."

During the last hour, Dennis's heart rate increased and "his breathing was like that of a woman in childbirth." They knew he was getting close. Grace decided to turn him on his right side "as in *The Tibetan Book of the Dead.*" The moment they did, he finally died.

After Dennis's death, Grace sobbed at a level she "never experienced before." Then the women bathed and dressed him in freshly ironed pajamas, and Grace removed his wedding ring and placed it on her own finger. "The room was strangely filled with a warm glow, a radiance," Grace explained, and they all "knew that he was still near." Comforted by this, they went to bed. Early the next afternoon, they sensed that his spirit left. "At 1:00 P.M., it went cold, the room emptied." An hour later, they called the funeral home.

"Like a birth, a death is not an easy thing," Grace told me two days later. "I felt no guilt or regret; this was a sacred time only affected by the uncertainty of how long it would take." Without Janet's presence, the uncertainty continued, but they knew she was but a phone call away. And the sharing of the responsibility by these women, who took turns pressing the button, allowed each to participate in a joint act that enabled them to rationalize that no one hand carried the burden. This act also provided the necessary ritual to move it from the realm of helping to die to that of spiritual birthing. Together, they took on the common role of midwife and molded this experience into something personally transformative. No lonely rooms, or fear of discovery interfered with the sacredness of this moment. And the gift that came later, in what they felt as the warm glow of his presence, reassured each of them that they'd done the right thing.

Defining the "Good" Death

Can there be such a thing as a "good" assisted death? To Grace, the answer is obvious. To others, any death is wrong if it results in a life being shortened "unnaturally" by a single breath. Doctors are taught to "do no harm," and act only out of beneficence. But many people believe that a patient's autonomy should extend to the determination of what constitutes "unnecessary" suffering, and that it's up to the person to make this final decision. In this way, we each carry within ourselves an ideal as to how we'd like to die. We also carry feelings and beliefs about how others should lead their lives. These ideals are deeply personal and touch at the core of where we live. They reflect our spiritual beliefs, our feelings of control and independence, our fears about death, and our issues around abandonment, holding on, or letting go.

The concept of assisted death is both supported and vilified. It goes to the heart of the question: *To whom does a death really belong?* Does it belong to the person who is dying or to others? None of us want anyone we love to make such a decision without us. We want to know that our desires and our feelings matter.

How Do We Decide?

To evaluate a death as "good" requires that we look at it from various sides and listen clearly to how others who've shared in such an event express their feelings about *what was missing, what was right, what went wrong,* and *what made it special.* Only by analyzing their words, thoughts, and actions, is it possible to develop some criteria for evaluating the experience. This goes for both "natural" and assisted deaths. At a minimum, it requires that everyone involved be practically and emotionally prepared for whatever happens, and that they follow a course of action that's true for them. Beyond this, it's important that they be able to accept the death, however it's managed, and that those left behind feel a sense of completeness in their relationship. This isn't always easy.

For example, when my friend Tom died a natural death from metastasized lung cancer, his partner told me that she saw his as "a good death" as she'd been able to accept it and use *The Tibetan Book of the Dead*, and because Tom achieved a reconciliation with his two teenage sons. Nevertheless, Tom suffered severe pain and discomfort for several weeks and achieved this closure with his children nearly a month before he died, about the same time he secured the lethal drugs from his doctor to use in case he decided to end his life. Three weeks before he died, he repeatedly begged me to convince his partner to "let him" take the pills that sat on the table next to his bed. I told Tom that this was his task, not mine. While we often meditated together until he slipped into a coma, I was painfully aware of the severity of his suffering. But I also understood his partner's need for him to die in a more natural way and remember her telling him that she'd "have to move" from her home if he "took his life" there, because she couldn't stay in a place with "such negative energy."

In Tom's case, I felt the conflict. What was "good" for his partner was not necessarily the same for Tom, who wanted a different end, but also respected this woman's needs. This became the dominant emotional theme in that room. For him to do anything else would've left his partner with an immense "spiritual" pain and suffering that might've been worse in its own way for her than Tom's own physical suffering.

As we've seen in the previous chapter, a "good" or positive assisted death can be jeopardized by several factors. These can include lack of planning, use of the wrong drugs, a rush to action, inadequate time, improper setting, coercion, inadequate emotional and practical preparation by all parties, and questionable motives of participants. Even when deaths are "less than aesthetic," however, many participants with whom I've talked still expressed to me the feeling that "the experience was positive." This occurred in Bill's case, described in the previous chapter, where seemingly no amount of oral drugs, duragesic skin patches, or Demerol injections would end his life. In desperation, his family finally decided to use the plastic bag that Bill himself had decorated with slogans and set aside next to his bed. Similarly, several other individuals have told me of feeling no regrets or personal ill effects after making their own deeply personal decision to intervene to help the person they loved move from unconsciousness to death.

After reflecting on these stories and events, from that of Bill to Tom, I'm convinced that the manner of death itself—whether assisted or not, and though at times unpleasant—is less important in defining a "good" death than for all involved to be able to accept fully the necessity of the decision and to feel a sense of completeness in their relationships.

These two factors are closely linked. The achievement of *closure* or *resolution* first requires that there be "a good reason to die." This implies an acceptance of the death by all concerned as both rational and reasonable. But more than this, it's critical that all involved be provided practical opportunities—well in advance—to reach this point of acceptance, resolution, and a sense of completeness.

Overcoming Barriers to Closure

Several factors related to the very nature of assisted death can combine in ways to create obstacles to closure. For example, the rush to action and the neglect of more emotional concerns by the one who is dying can hinder resolution. In addition, unless other occasions for closure are provided earlier, the illegal nature of assisted death and the perceived need for privacy and secrecy often result in limiting knowledge of the intended action only to those who can be trusted. Those who aren't expecting such a death may be left with no one to whom they can express their love, regrets, and good-byes.

Nevertheless, even in such instances of secrecy, it seems that a "good" death is still possible. When Maggie died, for example, only three of her four children knew the timing in advance and were present on that final day to help her die. The fourth, Jackie, a fundamentalist Christian, was strongly opposed to Maggie's "tentative proposal." As a result, Maggie backed away from the truth, and explained to Jackie that she'd "just been thinking about it." Instead, as the final act drew near Maggie told Jackie she was "getting worse," and the two spent time together and shared their love. The next evening, before she finally died, Maggie expressed the thought to her three other children that perhaps she'd "made a mistake" in not bringing it into the open. "She didn't like secrets in the household," a daughter explained. "After discussing it, we all felt it would cause Jackie too much pain to know." They were also worried that Jackie might intervene and force Maggie to stay alive. "We love her," said one of her sisters, "but this might've been just too much." As it was, "Jackie was able to say a peaceful good-bye, without worrying" about the fate of her mother's soul. Moreover, her siblings told me that they all saw their mother's death as a "good" experience. One added, "Although Jackie doesn't know how mom really died, she's at peace with the knowledge that the two of them had come to a loving acceptance of each other."

SHARING ALL WORDS

In addition to accepting the inevitability of a death, I believe the most crucial factor necessary for achieving closure is for partners, families, and friends to have opportunities to share their thoughts and feelings openly. As we saw in the previous chapter, this place of relaxed dialogue is not always reached. In times of perceived urgency, those in supporting roles often get caught up in the drama and feel the immediate need to give themselves fully to the one who is dying, regardless of their own needs for emotional completion. Moreover, one who is dying can also get captured by a quickly evolving situation, and feel too awkward to shift from what may be a comfortable lifelong pattern of noncommunication. Several partners and family members, for example, have told me that they didn't wish to say anything to "upset" their dying partners, parents, or siblings. And as one woman told me, "I wasn't about to work out my issues while my husband was suffering in pain; it would've been wrong."

Unfortunately for this woman and many others, unless they begin early, there is often no other chance. This was certainly the case for Jim and Susan, who had months to talk about their relationship and lives together, but didn't. Although Jim's treatment for lung cancer and final planning for an assisted death gave them this opportunity, Susan failed to follow her "intuition" and now feels that she made a grave mistake. "Now that he's gone," she said, "the opportunity to talk about it is also gone."

While such comments are frequently made by survivors of any intimate loss, these statements take on special significance in cases of assisted death. This is because the decision to die requires talk and the death requires planning. As another woman told me, "Damn it! He could talk day and night about how he was going to do this, but he wouldn't spend a minute saying good-bye." Similarly, Susan said, "It feels like a door's been slammed shut, and Jim's on the other side, and I'm over here with all the words I wanted to say and with all the questions I wanted answered."

In the case of Susan and Jim, it was not so much a lack of time, but their lack of ability to express feelings of sadness and loss. This is a common occurrence and has various sources. It can be a trait people bring into a relationship, can develop as a pattern over time, or become especially visible when faced with death and loss. Whatever its source, in some unspoken way participants often agree to honor the silence. Susan described her experience to me:

> I didn't want to talk about his death, because it would make it real. Oh, we could talk about his drugs and techniques of dying, but we couldn't talk about the life we lived together, or what his death would mean to me and the children. I remember thinking at the time that it would be too final to say good-bye, so we didn't. Now I don't know how to.

Avoidance of final conversations means avoiding resolution. Some wounds need attention to heal, and often the healing balm of resolution best comes from the other half of a relationship. Death takes away this opportunity, and means that any completion—out of necessity—becomes one-sided and can only occur during a subsequent grieving process, when final words and responses can no longer be heard.

These final conversations and opening of hearts can, and do, take place. When Bruce finally died it was only after months of counseling with his partner, where each obtained an understanding and acceptance of the other, and after Bruce had reached a similar place of peace with his father, who'd physically abused him as a child. Similarly, when Jason died it was only after his family had taken advantage of several opportunities for sharing their feelings. Not only were they all present at his death, but they'd joined him at his home days earlier. Each family member had time to be alone with him and, in the two days before he died, they all met on several occasions to talk about his life and his decision. Since much of the emotional work had been done earlier, these meetings took on a more relaxed nature, and there was much more joy and laughter than tears.

Finally, when Bill Meyer helped his father die, and told me later that he felt "no grief or guilt," he explained that it was because his father had always been his "best friend and adviser," and they had just spent the previous two days reminiscing about the decades they had together. As Bill helped his father slip a plastic bag over his head and then held his hand, he heard his last words—"I'll see you someday." Now, years later, Bill still has no regrets.

KEEPING PROMISES

To some partners and family members a sense of resolution can only be obtained by fulfilling a last wish or promise. This can take on symbolic import. Remorse over failing to fulfill a loved one's last wish, or regret over missing words *and actions,* is common among survivors of any type of death. As I described in the previous chapter, Mark's greatest regret was his inability to say good-bye to his mother one last time and ensure that she had achieved her final desire to have a few sips of ginger ale before the morphine brought unconsciousness. Others have expressed similar regrets. For John, it was not being able to make love to his wife, Leslie, one last time before she died; and for Gary's dad, it was not being able to take his son to Hawaii.

In some cases, however, we have to question the meaning of these "unfulfilled promises." They may well be symbols for other regrets or unfulfilled aspects of a relationship. In talking further with John, for example, he admitted feeling that he hadn't done enough during his marriage with Leslie to show her that he was "really there." He added that "making love" was always their way of proving that the marriage was on firm ground. "Leslie wanted this to know that she died with a good marriage; and I wanted to show her it was true." Similarly, Gary's father told me that he "never had the time" to take Gary on "a proper vacation" when his son was growing up, and that "Hawaii would've been this trip."

Regardless of their true source, these unfulfilled promises are often what survivors cling to, thinking that they somehow did not do enough. This belief can last for years regardless of whether the desired act really would have meant that much to the deceased. This can be seen in the case of Helen and Lawrence.

When Helen told me over several meetings about helping her husband Lawrence to die, she never expressed regret over placing a plastic bag over his head. Instead, her greatest difficulty was realizing that she'd failed to tell her husband of more than fifty years how much she "loved him" and that she was "going to miss him." His final statement to her before he went unconscious was, "You've been a good wife." To this she replied, "We've been a good team." In reflecting on this later, Helen felt that this "didn't say it." She needed more. Two other regrets added to this. First, before Lawrence took the sedatives, he pulled her into his lap as he sat in his favorite chair facing a large picture window. In response, Helen "quickly got up," embarrassed that some neighbor might see this expression of their affection. Later, she blamed herself for worrying more about what some stranger might think than returning Lawrence's affection. "He needed me to show my love, and I didn't." She also felt remorse for not helping Lawrence fulfill his wish of having one last walk in the garden. "During his final days he always said how good the garden looked and how he'd like to go outside, but I was so exhausted from caring for him that we never seemed to have the time." She explained:

> When we did go on short walks, I worried about him falling. Once he tripped over a small curb in the park and fell. He

shattered his wrist. I never really thought that we wouldn't take that last walk, but toward the end I was emotionally numb, experiencing burnout, and operating on automatic. But now he's gone, and my not taking him out to the garden is something I constantly think about and feel guilty about.

These cases suggest that much can be overcome by the combination of full and open dialogue, early acceptance of the inevitability of death, respite for the caregiver, and delaying final action for as long as it's physically possible. Respite care, for example, might've enabled Helen to step back from round-the-clock caregiving, overcome her emotional numbness and burnout, and reflect on what her husband's death would mean to her. Although respite care alone provides no such guarantees, it still provides the potential.

Taking the Time

Closure requires conscious effort. When my friend Robert died, for example, he'd already spent months suffering from an intolerable AIDS-related condition and had lost more than forty pounds. He held on for as long as he could, however, until his mother both understood and supported his decision. She told me, "I don't want to let him go, but I don't want him to suffer anymore." During these final months, the two of them went away together twice even though this was physically painful to Robert. He did this, he told me, "so the memories won't be all bad." He then made certain that she'd be taken care of financially after he was gone. Only then did he make the final decision to die.

In looking at these examples, it would seem that closure, in its ideal form, comprises several additional elements that facilitate the sharing of final words, the opening of hearts, and the expression of last wishes. Whether you are deciding to die or anticipating the death of one with whom you are close, make sure you do the following:

- Take the time for reflection about any unresolved emotional issues between you and your loved ones

- Take the time to locate specific sources of such emotions as sadness, anger, guilt, or regret

- Set aside multiple opportunities to communicate with each other about these issues

- Establish the goal of accepting the other fully in the here and now, regardless of whether either of you can or should apologize for your own actions and can or should forgive the other for theirs

- Take special time to get to know each other fully as individuals—outside of your specific role relationship (e.g., father and son)

- Share with each other the lessons each of you has learned in life and what each of you has been given by the other

- Take special time to get away from home together, if this is physically possible, to be fully with one another and to create memories that are unrelated to any medical treatment or to the dying process

- Grieve the loss individually and together, with each of you reflecting on what this death means

- Reach for a point where each of you feels that you've done your best to obtain a sense of closure

- Ensure that the final decision to die, if physically possible, comes only after adequate opportunities have been provided for both reflection and discussion of unresolved issues, and after the inevitability of the death has been fully accepted

PRIVACY, DISTRUST, AND SELECTIVE DISCLOSURE

Lack of final resolution can occur, not only in deaths that are driven by a perceived sense of urgency, but where there is secrecy, limitation of knowledge, and restricted involvement of significant others in the death. As in the case of Maggie and Jackie, information is not always shared with all who might be affected by the death. It's not unusual for a particular child, sibling, parent, or close friend to be uninformed or kept out of the inner circle to protect them from difficult knowledge or to prevent problems.

Mary, for example, who at sixty-five helped her eighty-seven-year-old mother die, said she kept the true cause of her mother's death a secret. "This was between mom and me." She explained that she told her son only "two or three years later." His immediate response was to cry and then say, "Don't tell the girls," referring to his sisters, Mary's two daughters, who were "fundamentalists with very strong beliefs" about assisted dying. Mary explained that she and her mom were far more open and liberal. "Mom believed that God was good and love and I always felt the same way."

In some instances, the real fear is that the secret of what is about to—or just did—occur might be disclosed inadvertently to outsiders. Until laws change, the potential continues to exist for criminal indictment and prosecution. For many, this has been a risk too great to take. The negative effects of sharing secrets can be seen in the case of Bill Meyer, who helped his father die with a combination of drugs and a plastic bag. Two years after telling me his story, he shared his experience "off the record" with a journalist, with the result being that Bill was convicted by a Connecticut court for assisted suicide after the journalist violated his promise and published the full details.

In a few situations this selective disclosure also means *selective closure*. This can be seen in the example of Julie and her brother Jerry, whom I discussed in the previous chapter. Most members of the family were kept from the knowledge of Jerry's intentions. It was this secrecy that prevented his death from otherwise being a "special event."

Such secrecy of intent appears to occur more commonly among those who have had difficult or strained relationships with their biological families. For example, many AIDS sufferers, who moved away from their families years earlier to support lifestyle choices, often become both geographically and socially distant. I've also seen this occur among some single women with cancer. In support groups over the years, I've often been told that this distancing resulted from family conflict, unresolved issues of abuse, or a lifestyle or sexual preference at odds with the values or religious heritage within their own families or communities. As a result, many turn to others within their own friendship groups—their *families of choice*—for support and final assistance.

This independence of lifestyle and identification with self-selected "family" has the potential to reduce opportunities for biological relatives to obtain closure. This can especially occur when the one who is dying was once considered a "prodigal" member, or when overtures for reconciliation—from either side—are rejected. Although many families take the step to reach out to their dying children and, as I've shown, even take over roles in providing care and final help, there are other families who refuse to alter their views. For example, Charles told me that when his sister informed the family about his AIDS, his father replied, "That can't be; our son died years ago."

Some families do make the effort to achieve closure years after a rupture of relations. In such instances, proposals for reconciliation can be met with mixed feelings, depending on whether the one dying is welcomed back with full acceptance or more conditionally. Some come to enjoy the love and support that alluded them for many years, while others see these as attempts to "control" them. One man explained that his parents had never accepted him, but said, "Now that I'm dying and no longer sexual, all is well; once again I can be a good Catholic and return to the fold—as long as I never talk about killing myself."

This is one of the major reasons why "hit squads" and "mutual assistance pacts" have come into being in some segments of the AIDS and breast cancer "communities." As a woman told me, "There often is no one else who'll provide caregiving, unconditional support for the decision, and also help carry it out." If the original split with the family was particularly harsh, families are not always welcomed to share in the knowledge of the planned death. Instead, the "secret" is kept hidden beneath a cloak of silence. This especially occurs if there are religious differences between the family and the one who is dying. Carolyn, who was dying from cancer, told me:

They had years to get it together, but they didn't. My father abused me, my mother let it happen, everyone denied it and, self-righteously, they still go to church. I don't owe them a thing. They don't want to say they're sorry, and they don't want my forgiveness, because they're still in denial. They're emotional vultures who only want to come here now to inter-vene for my soul and ruin my death like they fucked up my life for so long.

Full disclosure of one's plans for assisted death, therefore, is not always included as a part of final resolution, especially if issues of family control over past or present life choices still exist. John summed it up the following way: "They wouldn't let me live, now they won't let me die; they don't care about my suffering, only their own." He rhetorically asked, "If my family really cared, wouldn't they let me talk and be myself?" Like others who depend on their friends for emotional support and final assistance, John said he had no desire to speak with his family about his thoughts regarding an assisted death.

And for some, resolution of past wrongs and full disclosure of an intended assisted death are not always seen as good. Instead, out of necessity, closure has to be more one-sided, and is achieved when the one who is dying accepts the circumstances of her life and that others may never change. In this way, closure comes from within and cannot always be resolved by the actions of others. Car-olyn stated:

I have no desire to ever see my father again. I couldn't possi-bly confront him about the abuse, the incest, and his alco-holism, because it's still there. It might let me vent my anger, but I'd have to spend valuable time and energy dredging up things better left alone. I'm not going to spend the last days of my life trying to create a silk purse out of a sow's ear. And I couldn't pretend that it never happened. Either way would just open up too many wounds for me. I've reached a place where I've accepted the situation and myself, and that's enough. I don't have much time, and what time I have left I want to spend in peace. I'd rather go within and find peace and a deeper connection with God.

Until the laws change, secrecy will remain one of the most dominant features of assisted death. Opponents argue that one of the major drawbacks of legislation is that no proposals for legalization have yet to require that families be informed of an intended death. Nevertheless, the cases of Charles and Carolyn provide strong counterarguments. To them and many others, the concept of family is an emotional—not a biological—bond, one that implies mutual love and respect.

I remain hopeful that if the decision to die can be arrived at thoughtfully, then opportunities for resolution can also be arranged in a more conscious manner. With this in mind, it would seem that if you are deciding to die you should:

- Reflect on how others, even those with whom you are estranged, may be affected by your death

- Determine the emotional and physical energy required to make the effort to open the lines of communication with these others

- Reflect on what you hope to achieve, and what each of you stands to gain, but be realistic in your expectations

- Weigh various "safe" steps to open lines of communication to those with whom you're estranged, such as making preliminary contact through letters or using others as intermediaries

- Think about providing these individuals with more direct opportunities for reconciliation and emotional closure by arranging a tentative meeting

- Explore alternatives to achieve resolution within yourself about the circumstances of your life, if your overtures for reconciliation with others fail to achieve positive results

- Separate the final decision to die from any unresolved emotional issues or feelings of loss that you may have

- Question your own decision to die, and talk to your therapist, if you view your death as a way to punish or prove something to others

- Ponder the emotional impact of—and *all* your motives for—sharing your thoughts about assisted death with others who might be opposed for moral, religious, or personal reasons

- Consider the possibility that, once informed, others opposed to assisted death may intervene to prevent it, thereby increasing the legal risk to those who have agreed to help you die

- Decide whether you need to keep your intentions secret and, if so, don't let this keep you from exploring alternative ways to provide others with opportunities for reconciliation or closure

- Assess *all* your motives in requesting or accepting another's help in dying, if this person was one with whom you either were formerly estranged and may still have emotional work to complete

- Avoid using such assistance as a way to "punish" others for past wrongs, to have them "prove" their love, or for either of you to reconcile past differences

- Prevent needless emotional problems for others by taking responsibility for a successful assisted death thus minimizing involvement by others and ensuring that they will have the emotional support they need after your death.

In this regard, I'd like to add three caveats: keep your own counsel; avoid alienating those close to you if you attempt to reconcile with others; and know that closure may have to be one-sided.

In terms of the first point, it's important to balance what feels right to you with the advice you may receive from others. Although it's often easy for those close to you to give advice about relationships you may have with others, especially with others who have disappointed or hurt you in the past, you need to do what feels right in your heart. Your partner, family members, or friends may wish to protect you from further disappointments, but they also may harbor fears that they'll be replaced emotionally by those with whom you were once close. In this way, new partners may feel threatened by ex-partners, close friends may fear displacement by old friends, and a devoted wife—never accepted by her husband's family—may feel personally rejected by her husband's efforts to reestablish family ties.

Second, if you decide to reach out to others, it's important not to alienate those with whom you're close. You can achieve this by: affirming your love to them; explaining your need for resolution; acknowledging their concerns; and promising to stand by them and to keep their needs in mind always.

Third, it's important for you to be open-hearted and realistic, and understand that, even with the best of intentions, you may not achieve the sense of resolution you desire. What matters most is to give it serious thought and make the effort if it feels right, understanding that closure also means accepting what you can't change outside of yourself.

The Timing and Conditions for Resolution

At a workshop a few years back, I asked participants to describe their perfect death. About half talked of their desire to die without warning—in their sleep—and to feel no pain in the final moments. The others envisioned gradually drifting away. They saw their deaths to be absent of suffering, but occurring in a favored location, while surrounded by those they loved. Both groups shared a common desire to die at a *point of completion* where nothing would be unresolved. Unfortunately, this didn't mean that they wanted to do this work early. In fact, some liked the idea of knowing when they were going to die so they could start the process as late as possible.

This exercise reinforced my belief that while we all may want *completion*, most of us do little to achieve it. We talk the talk, but avoid the tasks required. To die this way requires us to live this way, in a state of *resolve, deliberation,* and *completeness* in the here and now. Ideally, it means living a life rooted in an ongoing appraisal of who we are and how our actions affect ourselves and others. It suggests an appreciation of the full texture and significance of each moment and an understanding of where we are on our chosen paths. To live in other ways makes it too easy to reinforce *incompleteness,* to remain focused on the past or the future, in unnecessary regret or in fear or unrealistic anticipation.

Part of the problem is that we define closure in different ways. To some of us it represents an end, a door that slams closed, locking out our hopes and unfulfilled desires; we reach out only when we resign ourselves to death. In this way closure is seen as something that's to be dealt with as late as possible—if ever—so we can maintain the myths of our lives and relationships as long as possible. To others of us, perhaps a minority, closure means living in a way that shuts out myths instead of hopes, and lets us constantly close the door to resentments, regrets, and unspoken words. It suggests living in an emotional present, knowing that—while death can take us at any time—this, perhaps, is far less important than constant reflection and acceptance.

Those considering an assisted death, and those who help, are often like everyone else. Although concerned with the manner of their deaths, not all pay attention to the need for completion in their relationships. Some reach peace and want to move on, while others are seemingly concerned only with a quick and painless end to their suffering, with "beating" the dying process.

Knowing that a life may end at a certain time threatens the complacency both of the one dying and of others. It suspends our taken-for-granted assumptions about the world, and puts an end to the belief that there will always be a tomorrow when we can reach those we care about with a simple phone call. There may be no phone calls if we wait too long. And there may be no death-bed reversals, because there may be no final death-bed; it may never get that far. As a result, this attention to the inevitable also carries the knowledge that there may be no better time than the present to resolve the unresolved, to reach out, to accept, to find closure.

Through all of this, I've come to believe that, although resolution is ultimately rooted in the acceptance that comes to each of us from within, it also represents a general attitude that we carry in life toward "endings." Some of us have harder times letting go of the emotional energy we've invested in others because it also means letting go of a major part of ourselves and of our own life situations and unfulfilled dreams. This goes farther than love. It includes letting go, not only of shared experiences, but experiences we never had time to share; and it also means facing our own sense of mortality, seeing time instead of timelessness, and realizing that some opportunities will never return.

It's because of this that some are so repulsed by the concept of assisted death. It forces them to pay attention quickly to the inevitability of death and presents the possibility that someone they care about may choose to die before they choose to accept this person's death, to reach out to them, and to say their good-byes. In such an event, resolution, acceptance, and closure may come slowly, long after you're gone. For this reason, the end of your life is not a time for stubbornness, a battle of wills, or continuing long-lived negative communication patterns. Instead, resolution is best facilitated in each other's presence by a mutual desire for understanding.

Resolution for others can also be tied to the circumstances of your death. The nature of the event, the level of their involvement, and the effort you place in practical and emotional preparations can help others define both your death and their own role in it as "good." The reverse is also possible.

How people arrive at such a conclusion varies. It first requires accepting the death, either in its inevitability or in its actuality. In this way, for those who help, it can come at various times, simultaneous with the death, or attained much later. Further, it requires that one also accepts the correctness of both the decision to die and their own actions in helping. These and other variations of experience can be seen in the following examples.

How Resolution Can Parallel
the Dying Process

Resolution comes easier to those who begin early and work on issues throughout the dying process, using this time as a special opportunity to come closer together. Under such circumstances, the
life-threatening illness of one is experienced fully by the other, and
the eventual decisions to die or to help can evolve naturally from
this shared experience. In this way, the decision is not interpreted
as selfish abandonment or escape, but often as "the right thing to
do." The decision to help can arise out of the relationship, not out
of duty or expectation, but as a natural extension of the love and
care of one for the other. I saw this in the case of Edgar and his
wife, Rachel.

Edgar was diagnosed with prostate cancer only two days after
his own brother lost a seven-year struggle against the same illness.
That night Edgar told Rachel that he didn't want to go like his
brother. Rachel, a nurse and a hospice volunteer, said, "We both
knew that death by cancer is neither quick nor clean." Seeing this,
they at once opted for surgery and treatment. This kept the cancer
in check for four years, but it then spread and later it became "obvious he was dying." Edgar held on for another six months and,
though he was radiated for the pain, "this caused such massive
vomiting that on three occasions we had to rush him to Emergency,
but they couldn't help him."

Edgar had waited to tell their children about the cancer until
it spread. When he shared the news, they immediately asked
him about his plans. He told them he had some pills that he would
take when things got bad. "When the kids were informed of
this," Rachel said, "they never complained that it was the wrong
decision."

Now nearly a year later Edgar began to slur his words and they
suspected that the cancer "was in his brain." This was confirmed
with another scan. That day, when they got home from Radiology,
Edgar made his decision, and he and Rachel talked for two hours.
At 7:30 P.M., she "got out the photos" and they went through them
and had a drink. Edgar then asked her to "bring the pills"—some

forty Seconals. He took them and went to bed. Just before 9:00 P.M., he died. Rachel said, "It was that quick; he was ready to lay his burden down and die, and he did."

After calling his doctor and the Funeral Society, Rachel called the children. They asked what happened. "I gave him the pills and he went to sleep," she said. They responded, "How wonderful." Rachel then stripped the bed and "slept better" than she had in years.

Rachel told me that she'd been working toward closure since his diagnosis, and didn't really shed any tears after his death. "After all," she said, "we talked and cried for years." After forty years of marriage and being a nurse and hospice volunteer, she knew "he wasn't going to live, and there comes a time when death is no longer the enemy."

How Resolution Can Be Achieved Through the Death

In some instances, participation itself in an assisted death seems to provide this opportunity. This happened in the case of Joseph's death, which enabled his family and ex-wife to achieve resolution as a result of their involvement.

Joseph and Anne had been divorced for more than two decades when he wrote to tell her about his diagnosis and hospitalization for liver cancer. In his letter, she explained, "He said he was in severe pain, had lost a great amount of weight, had difficulty holding any food down, and was terrified of dying in the hospital alone." Though divorced these many years, Joseph and Anne had remained "close and loving friends" because of their three children. Anne now lived in Florida, but made a point of seeing Joseph on her trips to Louisville to see their son. During these visits she and Joseph "always spent a day or two together," and the two of them always took time to be with their son "as a family."

Anne told me that, a few days after receiving his letter, Joseph called to ask her if she could do two things for him. First, he wanted her to come to Kentucky to help him get discharged from the Veterans Hospital "so he could die at home." Second, he wanted her to "put him to sleep" when his pain became unbearable and he could no longer function. She immediately agreed to both requests. A month later, when his suffering increased, Anne made a quick trip to Louisville to help secure his release and to arrange for him to be cared for at his home.

Joseph's condition continued to decline, and a month later Anne returned to care for him and then help him die. After she arrived, she called their three children to explain what their father wanted her to do. "At first they were shocked and angry," Anne said, "but after discussing it they agreed" that if he wanted this and she could do it, "then it would be okay." Their one son, who lived locally, visited often. Their other children, who lived in other states, would come later when called. Nothing more was said for two weeks. Finally, Joseph told Anne that he'd like one of her "special" meals.

> He asked me to fix him chicken and dumplings, turnip greens, black eyed peas and cornbread. He ate every bite and washed it down with iced tea. We talked and laughed all day, and Joseph had a wonderful time. But that night when he went to his bedroom we both knew the end was near.

The next morning Joseph's pain had increased to where "he couldn't be touched or moved," and he asked Anne to call the children. They arrived by evening. That night and throughout the next day "Joseph talked with them and they all took turns sitting with him." By that evening Joseph's condition worsened, and he told Anne that the time had come. Early the next morning, she woke the children and told them that they "needed to let their Father know it was okay for him to go." They all took turns "talking to him, hugging and kissing him, and holding his hand." Then, at 6:30 A.M., Joseph asked Anne to bring him the pills.

> Much to my surprise the children came in and together said, "We'll help you, Mom." We all gave him the morphine and stood holding each other and talking to him until he slipped

into a coma. But just before he did, he opened his eyes and said, "Thank you." He died at 12:15 P.M. that day, quietly and peacefully.

What pleased Anne most was that this joint effort brought the family even closer together. "It's like we now share a bond even deeper than before," she explained; none of this would've happened if they had waited for him to die a natural death. "In all likelihood, the kids would've come on different days," and any later "Joseph would've been too drugged or would've slipped into a coma." She then said:

> Of course we all grieved but the grieving was made easier because we saw his suffering and agony and knew we helped to let him die at home, surrounded by his family and without any fear at all. Now, since their father's death, they've told me that if and when I need them they'll be there to help me, and be with me, so I won't have to be alone.

Although the gathering of families, and mutual opportunities for joint closure, can and does occur in cases of more natural deaths, families who are geographically distant often come together at different times according to their own schedules. In some cases members gamble on time and lose. Or they might be told: "Don't come now, wait till she gets better," or "He's conscious; plan your visit according to your own needs." In Joseph's case, this was avoided. His decision to die at a designated time brought clearly into focus the knowledge that there could be no gambling. All realized there would be no later time for good-byes.

SOMETIMES RESOLUTION COMES LATER

For some survivors of an assisted death, resolution may come only after a death, after they've had time to reflect on the experience. In this regard, the supportive attitudes and actions of others can do much to define an event as positive or negative, and this can play a major role in easing grief and helping partners and family members achieve a sense of peace.

I found this especially to be the case with Allen who, together with his friend Jim, helped his partner Mike to die. For Allen, "peace of mind" came only later during the grieving process, and as a result of the support he received from his father. He said that in growing up he'd "always had a love-hate relationship" with his "macho type" father. Nevertheless, they became particularly close after Allen "came out" as a homosexual, and of all the family he handled it best. "Dad's main thing," Allen said, "was how much courage it takes to be openly gay; he takes pride in it, and now mentions it freely when introducing me to his friends." As a result, Allen's father looked at him as "his brave son," and this attitude carried over after Mike's death.

His father told Allen that he was "proud" of him for helping Mike die, that he "knew it was difficult, but was the loving, right thing to do." Allen said that "these words helped a lot" to accept Mike's death and to "come to peace" with his own role. To Allen, the little things helped most of all, like hearing his father tell him that he'd "been lucky" to have Mike in his life, or just to hear his father say, "I thought about Mike the other day; I felt his presence."

In fact, this perception of Mike's "presence" ended up playing a key role in helping Allen reach resolution. This occurred most vividly when he had what he "thought was a dream." A month after Mike died, Allen went away for the weekend to a friend's cottage and fell asleep. He said:

> I had a dream. I saw Mike standing in front of a brilliant bright background. He looked at me, and he smiled and said, "I don't want you to worry anymore, everything's fine. See? I'm going into the light." And Mike walked into the light. I sat bolt upright in bed shocked and disoriented. Then I had this incredible feeling of warmth and peace and I knew that everything was right with the world.

A few months later, Allen was having dinner with his friend Jim when he heard Jim tell him "a nearly identical story." Allen said that he hadn't told Jim about his own experience, but "here it was, almost word for word, and I blanched." Jim described to him how he'd seen Mike and a bright light, and Mike said to him, "I want you and Allen to please stop worrying and tell Allen everything's okay." Allen went on to say:

> I don't know if my friend had the same initial conflicts and worries about Mike's death as I did, but this made me feel that I'd done the right thing. He said, "It was all so spacy; I didn't think it would be comforting to have such a visit, but it was." Again to me it showed that this was a loving act. I now know I did the right thing.

Whether these were dreams or something else, Allen and Jim grasped onto them as ways to validate that Mike's was a "good" death, and that their own actions were right. Combined with the words from his father, these "dreams" did much to bring Allen to a point of resolution.

Opportunities for Ritual

To some the option of an assisted death provides the benefit of consciously dying in the presence of others at a time designated as special. Instead of envisioning a lingering death, or one that's filled at the end with severe pain or unconsciousness, the one who is dying perceives that he or she can become an active participant.

Moreover, many who assist in a death often feel that, had they not helped, they would've become merely impotent observers to suffering. Although much can be gained by such a role—by just being present, by witnessing the natural transition from life to death, and by individually arriving at a place of acceptance—others have been able to gain from the opportunity that the experience granted them.

SPECIAL EVENTS

For many, the time before an assisted death provides mutual opportunities for closure in the form of special features, shared moments, or in gatherings that honor one's life and transition. In this way, the nature of a death can be transformed into an experience that can ease the loss. Combined with earlier opportunities for reconciliation, the time for a more ritualized good-bye can do much to help externalize grief by converting thoughts and feelings into expressed words and acts.

To achieve this, of course, requires a willingness on the part of all participants to share emotions, both physically and verbally, and without thoughts of embarrassment or self conscious consideration of what others present might think. This can be a tall order. Nevertheless, many reach for and achieve this goal.

Among those whose friends often become self-selected families, elaborate events may be planned to coincide with a death. These serve as wakes or memorials at which the honored guest is still alive—at least for a time. Such a ritualized passing is often viewed by the one dying and their friends as a necessary way to mark a person's life, to show that it had meaning. One woman who'd been present at several such events told me,

> This is crucial when so many are young and without children
> or personal accomplishments. Often we've made a ritual out
> of the death with flowers and incense, and with people getting
> their favorite music together, or having the food they'd like
> their friends or family to eat both before and after their
> deaths. They might all talk, look at photos, and share stories
> until the person feels it's time to die.

This happened in the case of Steven, described earlier, who planned his own "small party" for late in the afternoon on the day he decided to die. The living room filled to overflowing as guests responded to his handwritten invitations. Steven told a *San Francisco Chronicle* reporter: "I could have had the usual wake and you could all come look at the body, but I didn't want to miss a good party."

For some, like Steven, this is their last party. For others, having one or two close friends with them is enough. In most instances, the social nature of the event takes on a more private and, at times, sacred character, as people share their love for one another and honor the life that is about to end. One man told me:

> We think of birth as a miracle and we all want to be there, but we've looked at death as ugly and undignified. Death is honorable and holy, and to be there, to support them emotionally in calming or reassuring them, in helping them physically through a hug or a back rub, or actively assisting them in dying by helping administer the drugs—all this is a gift. In this way death is as holy as birth.

For others, like David Lewis, there are multiple events. He began his final week on a Sunday by holding a barbecue at which his family and friends came to say good-bye. One participant said, "We laughed and joked and David told ribald stories." The following Friday evening, however, was "more subdued," with tears and private good-byes by his closest friends, and with a reading from Stephen Levine's *Who Dies*, and the playing of Louis Armstrong's "It's a Wonderful World."

SYMBOLIC ACTS

At the simplest level, a ritual can involve merely a special act between two or more people, the one who is dying and the ones left behind. Such an act can symbolically express the importance of one's life and the love that is shared between them. For example, in one case it came in the form of a gift from a physician to a couple, a bottle of wine presented along with a prescription for morphine and Seconal. When the time finally came for one partner to take the pills and die, they followed the "doctor's orders" and toasted their love for one another with the wine.

Such simplicity and thoughtfulness can also be seen in the case of Barry, who made his final decision only after months of family counseling, repeated hospitalization and surgery, and after his physician held his hand and said he'd "used up all of his magic." Barry waited until his discomfort became uncontrollable and he was no longer able to eat. The final straw came with increasing night sweats and medication every three hours, which made it impossible to sleep. He then spent the next two weeks getting closure. "When he finally let go of his anger and found an inner peace," his partner said, "we all knew he was ready, and when I accepted this, I was able to let him go." During his final two days, his family gathered. Each had several opportunities to talk alone with him. Finally, in a circle, each made statements that were filled with both tears and laughter. In return, Barry presented each of them with audio tapes he'd made over the previous week with special words and advice.

Barry had kept a plate full of "angel cards" in his living room. This was a set of small cards, each with a drawing of an angel on one side and a one word message on the other. Every day he would take a card from the plate and turn it over; that message became his thought for the day. The morning after Barry died, the family gathered in the living room and found that one of Barry's last acts the day before had been to turn over a new card. It contained the single word "freedom." In Barry's case, these little rituals and special acts did much to help the family find a sense of peace in his death.

In some cases, the families continue to maintain a special vigil after the death. Such was the case with Robert's death. The evening began with "take out dinners" for his wife and children and was followed by a group farewell and his favorite music. After his death, Helen shut off his morphine pump and left him in his bed through the night. In the morning, the family entered his room to find that his expression had changed from an almost-constant look of pain to one of peace. "He was smiling," Helen said, "so I decided to let others see him one last time. She called hospice to cancel his bath, while his son and daughter picked flowers from his garden and arranged them in his room. Then they lit candles and called his closest friends. As soft music played throughout the day, visitors came and paid their respects. Only later in the afternoon did Helen finally call the authorities to describe his "suicide."

RITUAL AND RESOLUTION

Ritualized opportunities for closure, especially those that occur before or simultaneously with an assisted death, can only work if they're thoughtfully planned in a manner that coincides with their intention. For example, if the intended purpose of such an event is to ease your death for yourself and others, you need to ensure that the event doesn't betray this intention by becoming something else. This means paying close attention to both what it means, what it looks like, and who participates. And it means paying even closer attention to the needs of those you'll be leaving behind. If you make the decision to provide yourself and others with this ritualized opportunity for closure, you would do well to:

- Realize that a ritual by itself doesn't ensure a "good" death, that this comes from acceptance of your death by others and their support for your decision

- Give those closest to you the time for anticipatory grieving, letting them talk about what your death will mean to them

- Set a timetable for dying that's independent of any ideas you might have for a ritualized gathering

- Determine whether such an event is to occur independent of your death or linked to it in some fashion

- Consider how others may be emotionally affected by such an event, and the personal and legal risk to them if they're planning to assist in your death

- Decide who should and should not be present at such a moment, and whether the attendance of some may negatively affect those closest to you

- Think about how those closest to you may feel the need to be protected from the presence of others who are more emotionally removed

- Assess the emotional and physical energy required of those closest to you to participate in such an event

- Ask yourself whether a joint gathering before or at the time of your death can actually help both you and others obtain a sense of closure

184 · FINAL ACTS OF LOVE

- Make the decision as to whether this event is to provide others with a safe time for sharing and grieving or is designed for other purposes

- Assess whether you and those closest to you might be better able to achieve a sense of peace by the addition of special shared words or acts

- Establish whether this is to be a sacred time and reflect on how you might guarantee this meaning

- Ensure the meaning you desire by assessing the features of this event and the particular roles others might play

- Respect the spiritual needs of those closest to you in designing it

- Choose someone who can quietly serve as your "director" to take charge and shift responsibilities away from those who need to focus on sharing or grieving

- Ask those closest to you what they might like to accomplish from the event and what elements they'd like to include in it

THE ROLE OF CLERGY

It has become increasingly apparent to me that those who decide to end their lives with the help of physicians or family members could well use the spiritual and emotional support that clergy are trained to provide. Except in a minority of cases, most dying and their families are reticent to share their thoughts about assisted death with their ministers, priests, or rabbis, especially if their religious affiliation opposes assisted dying. They are even less likely to invite clergy to the final act. Instead, fearing the risk of discovery and perceiving the potential for a negative response, the dying and their families often stand outside of their religion, isolate themselves further, follow their own hearts, and act alone. In doing so, some make hasty choices. Others experience a gulf that they later perceive as a form of "spiritual abandonment."

Many facing such decisions could benefit in the final days and hours by having the opportunity to discuss the decision once again, and by feeling that they are still part of a larger spiritual community—regardless of the actions they finally choose. Until religious organizations recognize this need, however, this perception by some of their spiritual separation will still exist. And instead of providing the additional opportunity for a more ritualized transition, the dying and their families will see no choice but to create their own last rites.

This may seem an impossible demand for some clergy, who believe in the sanctity of life. But for others there may come a time when they see that the heart of their religious calling is to minister and support, not to judge. If clergy could find ways to do so, they could also counsel, provide social guidance, serve as a further control against wrong-minded actions, and then give ritual support for the dying and their families. Later, they could aid survivors in their grief processes.

THOUGHTS ON THE "GOOD" DEATH

The idea of the "good" death is not owned by any one approach or institution. In doesn't only occur within hospital settings or with availability of hospice care. The idea of "good" is affected by the nature of the experience wherever it occurs and whatever model of dying is finally selected. It evolves out of the experience itself by the opportunities that are taken by all participants. In this way, an attitude of awe and sacredness toward death doesn't necessarily depend on "how" or "where" one dies, as much as on "who one is" and "what one carries" into the experience. Though any death can be managed in better ways, if we desire that a sense of awe, respect, and sacredness be present, these must be brought to the experience by the participants themselves.

Although opponents of assisted dying often say that this deliberate act is unnecessary as nearly all "pain is controllable" and that models such as hospice "restore dignity" and can bring families together, this is not always the case. This model, like any other, is only as good as the experience, the quality of families, and how well it matches the self-determined needs of patients and their families. Although an assisted death can have serious drawbacks, these often evolve from its illegality. Other models are not necessarily always better.

The hospice model, for example, can also include extensive sedation, ineffective pain control, or pain-relief efforts that must be applied in such dosages as to cause either death through "double effect" or a dying experience that can involve severe drowsiness, and loss of cognitive skills, meaningful control over life, and even "personhood"—those elements that many of us equate with being human. These elements, however, are not always given the level of importance they deserve. A 1990 resolution of the National Hospice Organization opposing assisted death stated, "Family members can often use this final period of peaceful, pharmacologically-induced sleep to begin to separate from their loved one in preparation for the time of actual physical death." The assumption here is that an assisted death excludes such opportunities.

This resolution went on to say, "Achievement of comfort through intensive symptom control prior to death is less of a burden to the family and the caregivers than having to directly cause death as the only way to relieve the patient's suffering." For many families with whom I've talked this is true, but many others felt no such burden and thought any other option would've been wrong.

I'm convinced that the means we use to die remain far less important than the right-mindedness of our actions on this path. Assisted death cannot be excluded from—or be predetermined to lie outside—a "good" death. To make claims to the contrary reeks of spiritual elitism, for there is no guarantee that home, hospital, or hospice deaths are any more enlightened or centered on the "right" path than those midwifed by loving family and friends.

The problems that are obvious in assisted death come from barriers to positive experience in the form of fear and inadequate knowledge. Given the fact that assisted death is not a practice that's been institutionalized, it's remarkable that so many "good" experiences with it have occurred. This suggests that the main problem resides more in how we view death than how we do it. It further suggests that the problem is in how well we reach out to resolve our personal issues, and live as fully as we can until the moment we die.

A Final Exercise

Before you make the final decision to end your life, take as much time as you can to consider once again the reasons for this action, to seriously consider its effects on others, and to then take some time to reflect deeply on the course of your life and how this may in some ways be affecting your decision.

Another way for you to achieve this work is to step outside of yourself and take the role of another, hearing your arguments from the other and giving theirs in return. This can be done either alone or with another or, preferably, in a therapeutic setting. By attempting to take the feelings of others as your own, you may gain insights about your decision and possible objections that you hadn't previously considered.

A second way is to imagine yourself in the future, looking back at your current life, your decision to die, and your final act of assisted death. By placing yourself on the other side of this act, take time to reflect on when and how it took place, what roles were played by others, and how your death affected them. Then, ask yourself the following set of questions, and take your answers into consideration when both making your final decision and in living the rest of your life.

- Was there any other way I might've achieved release from my pain and suffering, or was it absolutely necessary to take this action?

- What were my primary motives at the time and do these now seem all that important to me?

- Did I have to take this action at the time that I did, or could I have waited another month, week, or day?

- What else might I have accomplished had I waited longer?

- To whom didn't I say good-bye, and with whom didn't I obtain a sense of closure?

- Who now would I have contacted, seen, called, or written?

- What previously unspoken words do I now wish I had said?

- Whom would I have forgiven, how difficult might this have been, and how might this act have changed their lives?

- Did I come to a sense of peace and forgive myself for the regrets in my life?

- If I'd had more time, what final business would I have completed that I left for another?

- Did I share with others the most important lessons of my life?

- Had I shared these lessons, how might this knowledge have affected them?

- What music, films, or books do I now wish I could've experienced?

- Looking back on how others thought about me, is there anything I could've done to make them think differently about me, had I more time?

- What parts of my life that I kept secret, what feelings and thoughts, do I now wish that I had shared with others?

- Could this secret knowledge about me, my joys, passions, and beliefs, have provided others with something of value to help them in their own lives?

- What could I have done better to achieve a sense of closure with the many people I touched in my life?

- What could I have done better to achieve a sense of peace within myself?

- If another person helped me to die, do I now feel absolutely comfortable with my request, with their motives for helping, and with their action?

- How did my death and the actions of others affect those closest to me?

- What aspects of my death do I now wish I could've changed?

A "good" assisted death requires more than opportunities for discussion and resolution, more than an open dialogue, feedback from others, and thoughtful reflection on your reasons to die. This is only half of the equation. The other half is that since your death is bigger than you, the effects will outlive you. As we'll see in the next chapter, those who help you, those who participate in your death, will be faced with surviving, with overcoming your loss, and reestablishing some kind of lives for themselves. As such, your death, the way you die, and how others come to make their decisions to help is not something you want them to look back upon with regret. Remember, their decision to help should never result from an act of seduction on your part, but should always be an act of love.

Chapter 7

DECIDING TO HELP
ANOTHER DIE

Whether or not to assist in the death of one who is close to you is among the most difficult decisions you can ever face. It can inspire a full range of your emotions, which often reflect the entire history of your relationship with this person. All the love, regrets, disappointments, and anger you've experienced with—and because of—this person are brought to the foreground. This is even more so than in any other death because you're not just a caregiver or an observer, but taking on this added and, maybe even unwanted, responsibility of helping another person to end his life. Not only are you losing one who is close to you, but you're also considering participating directly in the loss. As a result, this decision doesn't come easy.

Most who assist in the death of a terminally ill partner, family member, or friend usually do so only after long and serious deliberation. As I've shown in previous chapters, there are those who don't always hold to this ideal. Some may act out of a perceived sense of urgency without paying close attention to the full range of emotions that motivate their decisions. Moreover, swept up in these emotions, there are those who don't always fully consider the seriousness of this action, to the likelihood of mistakes, or to the possible emotional or legal consequences.

Understanding the Impact

Before you embark on an irreversible course of action, look again at the guidelines in Chapters Two and Three as well as the positive and negative stories in Chapters Five and Six. By knowing what others have come to define as either a "good" or a "bad" death, you can do much to influence your own actions. And it's also important to see what factors others have defined as critical in their personal experiences.

LEVELS OF PARTICIPATION

In the end, the way in which you participate in a death, and the amount of time you spend preparing for closure, will directly relate to the intensity of your response. If the decision to die comes slowly and is thoroughly discussed and accepted beforehand, there is an increased likelihood that you can avoid a negative experience. Being prepared for further involvement is also important. In this regard, the factors of time, closure, preparation, and expectation all combine in either positive or negative ways.

With all else equal, however, the level at which one participates is also a vital factor. Overall, any direct assistance is far more difficult emotionally than either "just being present" at a death or merely helping one to secure medication or even to prepare medications for self-administration. Those who have the greatest difficulty accepting their involvement are partners or immediate family members who are emotionally unprepared for it but still actively assist by either providing a lethal injection or by using a plastic bag. The most profound negative effects are in those cases where overdoses are ineffective and are followed by several hours of lonely, anxious waiting and uncertainty before these other means—sworn never to be used—are finally employed "out of necessity." The negative quality of such an experience is only intensified when participants act alone and lack the practical and emotional support of someone they can trust.

Negative effects are less often experienced when the person who assists expects this course of action and has a firm understanding of the time period when other methods are to be used. The only exception occurs when drugs initially used are inadequate to bring on full unconsciousness. In such an instance, the person who agrees to assist is faced with an additional moral and emotional dilemma. To do nothing ensures failure, while any efforts to intervene further to ensure death might be fought by one who is now drugged and no longer rational and competent. Participants who have faced this dilemma have told me that their use of a plastic bag under such circumstances often felt—and looked—too much like killing.

Those who have used the plastic bag method have described it by a range of terms that are seldom positive. It's been called "ghoulish," "grotesque," "necessary," or simply "disturbing." Also, because of the sheer volume of plastic bags in our culture, this method of death provides the person assisting with frequent reminders of the act. One man reported "difficulty later walking down that aisle in the supermarket without thinking about it." And a woman told me that "It makes every trip to the market difficult, and the simple question 'paper or plastic?' becomes a constant reminder." Yet another told me that he saw "every bag" as an "implement of death," and fantasized being arrested for even having his own trash bags at home. In explanation, one woman told me, "The simple household bag has been changed forever in my eyes."

SECRETS AND FEARS

We've seen how secrecy is often thought to be required before an assisted death to "protect" oneself from intervention or others from the knowledge of what is planned. Beyond this, the effects of secrecy continue. Those who participate often continue to carry the fear of arrest for years to come. This begins during the death with the fear of interruption and even with the distrust of some who may be present and might decide to "tell" others what they've witnessed. Moreover, if the cause of the death has been covered up, the fear of investigation and possible arrest often continues until a death certificate is signed or a funeral or cremation occurs.

One of the ways that people normally deal with their grief is by talking about the death. This option is closed to them in an assisted death, unless one has participated with other family members or close friends. Those who assist may come to feel that they've no one they can talk to, no one with whom they can share what may well be one of the most powerful experiences of their lives. They may be too frightened or ashamed to tell others in their own family or their closest friends, who might not be supportive of such an act. One woman, who finally shared her story with a few friends, told me that one responded, "Now I understand. We couldn't see why his death hit you so badly."

Those who assist also can begin to feel the regrets that they "could've had family and friends around," or they "could've planned an open farewell event," or that "grieving can't be done in full, because only a few know the truth." Outsiders may attempt to console, but consolation is hard to accept from others who "don't know the truth," or don't know that the experience was "more than a natural death." In this way, secrecy means that participants become members of a special tribe, initiates into a private ceremony that can't be discussed. One person explained, "We carry the trauma of what the death was all about, and it can only be dealt with in a limited way, because we don't get support for it." Where it's especially secret, it can also interfere with some family relationships. One woman said, "It's a constant lie; and though I'm tempted to talk about it with my dad, we've had a difficult relationship, and this is another barrier that I'll eventually have to deal with."

Overall, the effects vary according to what others expect and what they bring into the experience. Those who bring fear, second thoughts, or feelings of resentment, carry away the same, while those who bring a sense of its sacredness, and a feeling that it's the right decision, are often rewarded in a similar manner. For some, it's an experience they'll long regret, others see it as a "bittersweet" experience, and still others define it as "special," and even as a "spiritually fulfilling" act of love.

Practical Considerations

You need to be absolutely certain that participation is right for you. You need to look closely at the other person's motives for wanting to die and requesting help, attempt to assess the validity of such desire and needs, and give thought to what you too might carry into such an event and how you might be affected by such participation.

Begin by paying close attention to the fact that assisting in a death, whether by securing and providing the means to die or by directly engaging in the act itself, is a crime in most jurisdictions around the world. And even in those few areas where legal provisions enable qualifying patients to request and receive aid-in-dying, such assistance is strongly controlled. For example, in the Netherlands, such acts are carried out with the assistance of physicians who follow strict guidelines and prepare reports for legal authorities who still have the option of bringing criminal charges against doctors who violate these guidelines. Moreover, while physician- and non-physician-assisted deaths have become increasingly common in English-speaking countries, few cases have come to trial. This is because of the often secret nature of the act and the special nature of the cases that have been brought before the court. Yet the act of assisted death remains a crime and is still typically covered under homicide statutes.

Without a legal option, nevertheless, you may still feel that you have no choice when the one you deeply care about is suffering intolerably, wants to die, and asks for your help. You may ask yourself, "How can a requested act of mercy be a crime?" Obviously, this is a question only you can answer. And while I can't condone or recommend this action, it is my hope that you strongly consider the full range of factors, described below, before you make your final decision. You should:

- Broaden your perspective as much as possible by opening a dialogue with others, avoiding isolation and seeking outside counseling

- Obtain all the facts about the person's physical condition and emotional state, and open the lines of communication with the person who is dying

- Understand fully the other person's motives for wanting to die

- Assess your own ethical beliefs about assisted death and define your own personal boundaries

- Examine your own motives for agreeing to assist

- Determine the necessity of your help, specify your role in providing assistance, and what this will actually mean

- Think about the possible emotional, legal, and other effects on you

- Become aware in advance of all details before and after the death, and assure yourself that the mutually agreed upon plan will succeed

- Reach out for emotional support both before you agree to help and after you participate in this event

Broaden Your Perspective

The imminent death of a person close to you is one of the most difficult and powerful experiences you can ever face. And it can only be made more so if an assisted death is being considered. The decision to help another die is often guided by the strongest emotions of the moment. While these can be love and an unwillingness to see another suffer needlessly, the decision can also be influenced by physical exhaustion and feelings of helplessness in the face of another's suffering. You may not necessarily want to help, but see no other choice. You may view any resistance to helping as somehow selfish or of small concern in light of the enormity of the other's experience.

Ordinary time and life has stopped. Nothing else matters at this moment. Job responsibilities and participation in social events seem irrelevant, and this action of helping another die can seem more important than any cold sterile laws in some book. Your relationship with this person becomes your law, your government, your court; after all, what has any other government, court, or law done to ease this person's pain or bring current quality of life to this person.

For all these reasons it's critical that you broaden your perspective, and realize that your viewpoint may be strongly influenced by a mixture of emotion that prevents you from looking at your best interests in the long run. Increased communication, however, and opportunities for counseling and further reflection, can do much to provide you the balance to make a well-reasoned decision.

Open the dialogue. Often the relationship between one who is dying and his or her partner, family, or close friends is so special—as in the case of a husband and wife, long-term life partners, a parent and a child, or close siblings—that they discuss the idea of an assisted-death on several occasions throughout the illness and dying process. Together, they may talk with one's physician, obtain a better understanding of the course of the illness, engage the assistance of a counselor, become clear about their relationship, and work to help ensure honest and open communication and equality of power before any final decision is ever made.

Many cases, however, fail to hold up to this ideal. Too often there are broad gaps in honesty and openness. Those who are dying may not feel comfortable sharing their fears, concerns, or preferences until they believe that it's absolutely necessary, while others may avoid responding to any initial talk about the issue as they may feel that it interferes with the treatment process or it's simply too painful to discuss. In their efforts to protect each other, or themselves, the feelings, motives, and needs of each party are left unquestioned, and the final decision is rushed. Only later, after the fact, is the decision second-guessed and, in some instances, regretted.

For whatever reason, not all decisions about an assisted-death are arrived at through open dialogue. Not all final aid-in-dying evolves from partnerships of mutual concern. As a result, this may well negatively affect the one who assists—the one who's left behind. And this occurs even in cases where all parties involved agree that an assisted death was the only alternative. Some have said, "I didn't know I was going to be *that* involved" or "I supported this and was willing to be there, but I never thought it would come to *this.*"

The best time to talk about participating in an assisted death is before the need arises. Open and early communication is crucial to avoid less-than-thoughtful requests, misunderstandings, and all-too-willing assistance. Last minute requests and decisions to help are too often rooted in feelings of duty and helplessness rather than in mutual awareness of the needs and feelings of each party. Don't let this happen to you.

Open dialogue increases the likelihood that all of your motives and desires can be better known. It's vital for you and everyone else involved to have opportunities to share your feelings, intentions, and needs. Fully opening up the dialogue, allowing others to raise the topic of an assisted death, however, should not be misunderstood as meaning that you or anyone else has given their final approval to this action.

Communication with all involved parties is also necessary for you to obtain a firm grasp of both the decision to die and its possible effects on others beyond you. Who is an involved party? Nearly everyone who'll directly be affected by the person's death. For example, if you have siblings and yet you've been the one asked by a parent to help them die, then your decision to help is a matter that goes beyond your own personal relationship with your parent. Only by knowing the feelings of your siblings can you determine if such an action is right both for you and for everyone else involved.

In this way, another's opposition shouldn't be easily ignored. Instead, you should make every attempt to understand it. Similarly, don't let your own beliefs about the needs of one who is dying interfere with his other relationships that don't include you. It's not up to you to judge those relationships, or tell yourself that only yours is special. Each has its own dynamics. Yours may let you help a parent or partner die. Another's may require that she oppose such an act. Ultimately, none of this may change a person's decision to die, or your final decision to help. But it may bring you the insight you need to know that, after all, these two interrelated decisions were the right ones.

Seek counseling. This is where group counseling and family meetings pay off, as they can help all of you better understand the root of either your support or opposition. Moreover, counseling also sets the stage for each of you to begin work on any unfinished business that can be influencing your actions.

For this reason, if at all possible, you should avoid making any final decision to help until you take into account the feelings and potential reactions of others, who'll similarly be affected by the loss. And if you safely can, clear your final decision with them. If you're absolutely certain of the validity of the request and the need for your involvement, then at the very least give others ample warning. Enable them to resolve any of their own unfinished business with the dying person who's asked for your help.

Avoid isolation. Isolation increases the potential for the wrong decision to be made. Without opportunities for discussion, this shrinking world can insulate both you and the one who's dying and prevent you from obtaining a better understanding of what other options may exist.

Fear of communicating with others can also lead you to listen only to your own counsel and to the very few you trust. If those you trust are similarly isolated in fear, and if their knowledge of options is limited, then what you hear may sound very much the same.

OBTAIN ALL THE FACTS

If you're asked to help another die, the enormity of this responsibility should allow you to make your own demands in return. If another is asking you to bear the weight of this action as an emotional burden, then you should similarly be able to demand such things as full medical information, an additional diagnosis, participation in any medical discussions about prognosis and, if you believe it's required, full participation in counseling.

Assess the other's condition. In this regard, you might do well to accompany this person to her next medical appointment, and ask her physician some questions of your own.

If you believe that assisted death is warranted under specific conditions, you need to be certain that this case meets your own personal criteria. Learn about any treatment options that may be available. You need to know this person's condition, diagnosis, and future prognosis with certainty, and whether further treatment options, with a minimum of invasive procedures, might be helpful in alleviating further suffering. It's vital to find out why another wants to die, and whether it's become easier for this person to die than to fight assertively for the best pain control and palliative care available. You should determine:

> *Am I relying solely on this person for medical information? Could others know something I don't? Has a terminal or irreversible prognosis been confirmed? Is this person refusing further treatment options? If so, why? Could treatments improve his or her quality of life? Does this person's physician agree? Have all possible pain or other symptom control measures been explored?*

Probe the other's emotional state. Some requests for help in dying stem from depression or other emotional sources. I've addressed some of the symptoms of depression in Chapter Two. Review these, as it is critical that you do not help anyone who is unable to make a well-reasoned decision.

As we've seen, some depression is normal in terminal illness. It is often transient and needs no intervention, but a certain amount can affect judgment if left untreated. If you have any doubts about the person's emotional state, talk to others who are close to the case—including the physician—and do not hesitate to demand counseling. Make your needs known to this person, set your personal boundaries, and don't cross them, as you don't need to ever second-guess the "rationality" of two decisions—this person's *and* your own.

Similarly, a person may decide to die because of emotional exhaustion. One who is dying may tire of fighting both an illness and the social service and medical systems. It is normal at times to feel like giving up. Provide whatever emotional support and practical help you can until you're absolutely certain that nothing more can be done.

It is important that you don't become the sole judge of another's competency and rationality. You may be emotionally too close, and your ability to assess the other's emotional state and to even make your own well-reasoned decision to assist in their death may well be colored by your own desire to see this person's suffering end. It is key that you talk to others and obtain their opinions.

Others who have assisted in such deaths often placed an enormous trust in the rational decision-making abilities of those who were dying, and who asked for and received their help. And in a few cases, it appears that they may have been wrong. For example, I've seen several instances where individuals with AIDS dementia were assisted in their deaths, and some of these individuals made the request to die *only after* the onslaught of their symptoms. While most were supposedly helped *because* of their previously expressed desires, in none of these cases, even where therapists themselves assisted in the deaths, was there any psychiatric or psychological assessment of mental competence made prior to these acts. In such instances these acts take on the flavor of "mercy killings." This is a far cry from a conscious act of assisted dying and legally is an even greater risk to take.

Close relationships become insular and isolated. The outside world can often become a place of disappointment and suspicion. If you become too close to the one who's dying, it may become easy to accept their view of the world and take it on as your own. Therefore, at a time when talking to others is most critical, it often is seen as "too risky" or as only confirming an "opposing" perspective. In this view, others often stand "outside the veil," "don't or couldn't understand," or "would only get in the way" and "put up barriers."

The only way you can know for sure if this position toward others has merit is to keep the lines of communication open and, if possible, include counseling and group meetings within your circle. You should ask yourself:

Can I make proper judgments about the rationality of this decision? Has this person obtained counseling or emotional support? Might emotional exhaustion play a role in this decision? Might my efforts be better spent providing emotional support? Might I better serve as this person's advocate?

Assess the Other Person's Motives

Before you agree to help another to die, it's absolutely vital that you become as fully cognizant as you can of what motives are driving this person's desire to end his life. Find out as much as possible about this person's stated reasons for wanting to die and his need in requiring your help. Also assess if anyone else may be influencing this decision. You should consider:

Whose idea is this? Might someone else be persuading this person to die early? Is there any possibility of economic or emotional coercion? Might this decision be based on a desire to please another or to relieve others of a perceived financial or emotional burden?

Although you may feel honored or privileged to be asked to help another, you need to look closely at the reasons that underlie your own selection and discover if someone else was previously asked. If so, think seriously about finding the reasons why this other person turned down such a request. Maybe this person knows or learned something about which you're not yet aware.

Why I am being asked me to help? Why won't closer friends or family members assist? What might others know that I don't? What aspects of the situation or personal effects of assisting have others considered that perhaps I haven't?

How enduring is the request? It's crucial that the final request for your help be explicit and persistent. I would advise that both you and someone else be witness to it on various occasions, and that you take the time to discuss it again fully in an appropriate counseling or group setting. Study the request, how often it is made, and whether there is any hesitancy. Then reflect:

How many times and over what period has he expressed the desire to die? Could this person really be asking for emotional support? Could he be testing me to see if I think it's time to die?

Assess Your Ethical Beliefs About Assisted Death

Begin by examining your own moral and ethical beliefs on the subject. Decide whether you think assisted death is ever appropriate and, if so, under what conditions. You may conclude, for example, that no one should be helped to die simply because they fear future pain and suffering but should be helped only if their condition is terminal with intolerable and irreversible physical suffering. For your own sake, establish your own personal guidelines as to who should ever qualify for assistance in dying and under what conditions.

Initially, you must decide whether helping another to end their life—with or without your direct assistance—could ever be an ethically correct act for you. These concerns reside at the very core of any such decision, and can be both a starting and an ending point. They may keep you from proceeding, or they may follow you throughout your decision-making process. You need to address these concerns at the beginning of the process, before your relationship with another person becomes too focused on assisted death as an inevitable outcome. Consider the following:

- Ask yourself whether anyone ever has the right to decide matters of life and death for themselves

- Decide whether it is ever right for a person to end his or her life and, if so, under what conditions

- Determine whether it is ever right for another person to help another end their life if they meet those conditions

- Consider whether assisted death under these circumstances is the same as an act of suicide or murder, and if you view all assisted deaths to be wrong

- Consider whether it could ever be right for you to help end the life of another, either directly or indirectly, upon their request, and under certain conditions

- Assess your ideas about assisted death and spirituality and whether you believe in an afterlife or reincarnation that may be affected by an assisted death

- Reflect on your attitudes about the sacredness of life and whether you might be able to help another die in a way that respects your beliefs

Examine Your Own Motives

If you are seriously considering helping another person, think about your reasons for wanting or agreeing to do so. If you believe you "should" help out of some sense of duty, or because of the nature of your relationship, then you need to ask yourself: (1) if this is a good enough reason; (2) whether you really want to help; and (3) if you would feel comfortable doing so. If you don't truly want to help, don't! Trust and follow your feelings. Otherwise you may be burdened by this decision for years.

> *Is it my "duty" to risk prosecution, fines, attorney fees, imprisonment, loss of income, and the effects of this on my career and my other relationships? Do I view this request to assist as an honor or a burden? Do I look at it favorably or with grave reservations?*

Similarly, if you feel that you do want to help, then you should also be suspicious, and look deeply at what you hope to accomplish *for yourself* by participating in this fashion. At this point it is vital that you spend time exploring the nature of your relationship with this person. Look at your history together and see if there are difficulties in your past or aspects that you somehow hope to complete. Although this may be difficult for you, it is best at the present time to assess how you actually feel about this person. You may realize, for example, that you were expected to do things in the past against your better judgment or desires and that your current decision to help may in some ways reflect this old pattern.

> *Do I love, merely like, or in some ways dislike this person? Have I done things for this person in the past that I came to resent or regret? Might I come to resent or regret my actions in the future? Will I look forward to this person's death, to the end of this personal burden, and to the end of his expectations of me?*

Think about the financial implications of your involvement. Perhaps you stand to gain financially, or the illness creates a financial hardship for you, which the death would end. Or you may have economic obligations to this person. At some deeper level, you need to be certain that saying "yes" is not just a way of repaying this obligation. If you are named as a beneficiary in the person's will, under criminal laws, there is a risk that you could lose any moneys you stand to inherit from this person if your role in his death is discovered and the will is challenged by others.

> *Is possible financial gain influencing my decision? Would I take money to help someone die? Is this person a financial burden to me? Would I rather help this person die than help him financially?*

If you are not a close friend or family member, look even more carefully at your motives for helping. It's vital that others who are closer have the opportunity to attain whatever level of closure is possible. If they have not been given the opportunity for counseling or involvement in any group discussions, then perhaps such opportunities should be provided. And under no condition should you agree to help another to die if any loose ends such as these still exist. Far too much is at stake—for others emotionally, and for you emotionally and legally.

You should never help another die because of subtle manipulation by the one who's dying, because "there's no one else," or because other family members may feel that you're "best qualified" to perform this role. Avoid coercion and manipulation by anyone. Ask yourself:

Why am I considering this action? Is this my responsibility? Am I motivated out of pride or a sense of being honored by the request? Might someone else be more appropriate? Can this person act alone and seek only my moral support?

Given the worse-case scenario of involvement, without the right motives on your part and without being fully present with an open heart, there is little that separates an assisted death from homicide. If no differentiation can be made now, then most certainly you won't make it later on, during the grieving process, when you reflect back on this action from new surroundings and from a broader perspective. Avoid later regrets for the wrong decision by paying close attention to your motives now. This act of helping another die can either be something you regret the rest of your life or, in its own way, treasure as the most powerfully positive moment and even spiritual act of love in your life. The difference depends on how you make this decision now.

ASSESS THE NEED FOR YOUR HELP

If you decide to help another to die, you should be certain that this person is unable to perform this act alone. Throughout life, individuals often ask others to do things they find uncomfortable doing themselves. In an equal relationship we might be more willing to refuse "rescuing" another from what is obviously their responsibility. If the other is facing a terminal condition, however, it's often tempting to step in and do more. The planning for an assisted death is no different; an individual may ask for help in securing the right drugs, in preparing or administering them, or in having someone take more "active" measures should self-enacted attempts fail. Except for the latter—if it should prove to be necessary—the dying person might well be able to perform most tasks alone.

If you know this up front, you can then establish a balance of power in the relationship and set your own boundaries. You can still be present at this person's death, but can "negotiate" your role in a way that meets your own needs without surprises later on.

Why is my involvement necessary? Is this person physically unable to perform these tasks on his own? Am I comfortable with all aspects of the request? Has this person contacted his own physician? Has this person attempted to complete these tasks alone?

What will it mean to assist? Most critical in any discussion of "assisting" is for everyone to know what to expect of each other. If you agree to "be there," it is vital for you to communicate clearly to the other person what this means to you. If you will only provide emotional support, specify this. Know your limits, explain them, and stick to them.

To reduce the potential for deeper involvement than you desire, discuss the plans for the event well in advance. To not do so, to ignore the possibility of failure, is one sure way to become more involved. Avoid this by doing your own homework, learning the methods this person intends to use to achieve her death, and determining on your own the potential for success or failure. Obtain input from those who possess more knowledge on this subject than you.

Have I been informed of the plan? Am I certain that the method chosen will be successful? What will be required of me if the plan fails? Have I explained my limits and will I stick to them? Am I certain that I will not become more involved?

If you decide to "actively assist," you should be certain that this person has made every effort to reduce any possibility that might make this necessary. Moreover, when you discuss "active" assistance, both of you need to know what this might mean. Talk about the possibility of failure: it often happens. Then discuss alternative methods and what they might entail. If you feel uneasy with your possible role, think again:

Why is my involvement necessary? If failure occurs, am I comfortable with further involvement or do I view such as a crime or as murder? How far am I willing to go? Have I discussed what other methods are unacceptable to me?

Moreover, if others will be present with you at the time, you also should discuss how far each is willing to go to assist should the person's efforts fail. Most important is for everyone to be in agreement, know what could go wrong, and not ignore this possibility merely because you don't want it to happen.

Have we discussed in detail what role we each will play? If I will be there only for emotional support, have I made this clear to everyone? Am I certain others will not pressure me to do more?

This is not a time to impress anyone either with your bravery or the depth of your love. This is not a contest about who cares the most for this person. At this point it's important to care for yourself also. This is a time to trust your own feelings about what is right for you. Follow your own heart not the demands or expectations of anyone else.

THE EMOTIONAL LEGACY

Before deciding, think hard about how this may affect you emotionally. Consider how you may feel next week or year, and if you might feel guilt for helping the person in this rather than in some other way. Also think how your involvement might affect your ability to mourn. In normal grief, for example, we often unburden ourselves by talking about the details of a death. Remember that you might not have this luxury.

How would others react if they knew of my involvement? Will I be able to share the details of this death—of my loss—with anyone? If necessary, can I keep a secret of this magnitude?

Visualize yourself with this secret looking back at the details of the event. Feel the emotions of both losing this person and helping in their death. Think what it might be like to be alone after this person has died.

Do I feel that I did enough while this person was alive? Did I violate my own moral standards? If I violated criminal laws, am I comfortable having done so? Am I worried about possible discovery of my involvement?

THE FINAL DETAILS

You also need to make contingency plans in case something does go wrong. If you just agree to "be there," unless you're a medical professional, you have little to fear, as there is no law prohibiting your presence at a death, even a suicide. Nevertheless, if no attempt is made to mask the cause of death, your presence may result in an investigation. If this death was obviously assisted, then you may face possible arrest, prosecution, and all the unwanted publicity that could surround such a situation. If you're not ready for any of this, then you should step back and reconsider.

If others are present and "things go wrong," there may be little to protect you if you overstepped your own boundaries, especially if the continued silence of others cannot be guaranteed. All of you need to feel that what each of you has done is morally the right thing, and the only way to ensure this is to talk about it in advance and in detail.

You need to agree to such matters as who's to "find" the body, who's to be called, and whether this is to be reported as a "natural" death or a "suicide."

Will this be an official suicide? Do I have an explanation for my presence in the home? How will I be protected from an accusation of assisted suicide? Will a "suicide" note be left? Will I help hide evidence of a suicide or assisted suicide? Am I comfortable with this? Will I have to answer questions for authorities? Do I trust others to remain silent about my actions? Do I know who to call and what to do after the death? Has the physician agreed to sign the death certificate?

AFTERWARD: REACH OUT FOR SUPPORT

Before you embark on an action of this magnitude, it is crucial to prepare emotionally for the seriousness of what you may be required to do. In a best case scenario, all who'll be involved in this action would do well to receive counseling in advance. You also would do well to find a trusted outside confidant with whom you can talk and share the details as they develop. Get feedback from this person and listen to any advice she might have.

In addition to this, however, be sure there is someone to turn to after the fact. Remember, everyone facing a loss can use emotional support, both before and after, and this especially applies in the case of an assisted death. This is because of the personal moral and ethical boundaries you may find yourself crossing, and because of the "secrecy" that can interfere with the normal grieving process.

Continue a counseling dialogue with a private therapist or reach out to grief support groups in your area. If you feel a special need to talk about assisted death, you might also reach out to other organizations where you can safely broach such a topic. A few of these are listed in the Resources section of this book.

Grief, Loss, and Assisted Death

Whether a death is assisted or not, most of us will experience some form of grief after a loss. This is defined as the combination of the thoughts, emotions, physical symptoms, and behaviors that result from the severing of the ties that bind us to someone or something outside of ourselves. Grief shows us that our connections with others are not easily altered, and that love does not die quickly. Grief can be seen as the way we honor the depth of our union with someone else.

THE SYMPTOMS OF GRIEF

Grief is a mixture of raw feelings that range from numbness to sorrow, anguish to disbelief, anger to relief, guilt to resentment, and despair to regret. It includes these and other responses, such as anxiety, loneliness, emptiness, longing, yearning, pining, fear, and deprivation.

Pangs of grief. Researchers have found that the sensations of grief occur in waves that last anywhere from twenty minutes to an hour at a time, and can include sobbing and crying, tightness in the throat and chest, shortness of breath, the need for sighing, an empty feeling in the abdomen, lack of muscular power, and intense tension or mental pain. This constellation of feelings has been referred to as the "pangs" of grief, and they may begin shortly after the loss—a few hours to a few days—and last upward of several weeks. Over time, these pangs occur less frequently and eventually are expressed only when there is an anniversary or other reminder of the loss. Sometimes these pangs don't begin immediately. People can frequently feel numb or in shock—without appropriate feelings—for the first few days or couple of weeks following the death.

Grief is experienced in all aspects of our being. We can feel it emotionally and physically within our bodies, and it also affects the way we think and how we behave.

Physical symptoms. When we feel grief physically in our bodies the symptoms often include: exhaustion, nausea, loss of appetite, tension, and sleeplessness. More specifically, the most common physical responses are: a dry mouth, a hollow feeling in the stomach, a tightness in the chest and throat, a feeling of breathlessness or shortness of breath, muscular weakness, lack of energy, even an oversensitive reaction to noise.

Emotional responses. The emotions that we experience can include shock, numbness, apathy, sadness, depression, despair, sorrow, denial, anger, relief, guilt, loneliness, and acceptance. In addition, in the case of assisted death, some individuals also experience fear, anxiety, and distrust of others. In experiences defined as "positive" assisted deaths, there can be an overwhelming sense of peace, serenity, and what some describe as "bliss," which can alternate with feelings of severe sadness and acceptance. By contrast, in "negative" experiences, where direct assistance has been required, it is not unusual for a person to feel a mixture of numbness, regret, sadness, and acceptance.

Mental responses. Grief can also affect the way we think, the content of our thoughts, or what are termed "cognitive" responses. These normally include disbelief, confusion, preoccupation with both thoughts of the loss and even the dying process, "psychic" encounters with the deceased person in ways that make him seem alive, and a tendency to go over the events that led up to the death again and again.

In the case of assisted death, however, there can be other responses. These include a need to share information with someone about the event and to "confess" one's role, while at the same time constantly feeling the need for secrecy and the instinct to discuss nothing, including one's own grief. There also can be a general feeling of distrust toward others and a need to maintain emotional distance due to the fear of opening up and describing something that might be held against one later. Moreover, if one failed to take an active caregiving or patient "advocate" role during the other's dying process, there can be thoughts of not having done enough, of questioning one's own actions, the decision to help, and the inability to find other options. Or, if one also directly helped another die, there can be a tendency to go over the events of the death itself again and again and question whether this action was helping or killing. Nevertheless, in a "positive" assisted death there also can be a secret pleasure in knowing that one helped end the other's suffering, fulfilled the other's last wish, accomplished a selfless task that others couldn't, stood up for one's own values, and disregarded legal authority for a higher good.

Behavioral responses. Finally, in addition to all these others, the grief process may include a great deal of sighing, crying, and irritability, inability to eat, restless overactivity, and sleep disturbances in the form of insomnia or sudden awakening. There also may be absent-minded behavior, aimlessness, social withdrawal, self-criticism, searching for the object of loss, either avoiding or visiting places that are reminders of the loss, and either hiding, giving away, carrying, displaying, or treasuring objects that serve to remind us of our loss.

During this period, moreover, there is an increased risk of substance abuse, in the form of drugs, alcohol, or tobacco. Those with other addictive tendencies can also experience intensified cravings. Interestingly, however, for many there comes a time when the loss itself and increased abuse of substances can combine to promote reevaluation of lifestyle and eventual positive behavioral changes to "improve" one's life, or to live in a way that would meet the other's approval.

THE PROCESS OF GRIEF

The characteristics and symptoms of grief change as you move through the process. Much has been written about the stages of grief, and researchers agree that there are either three or four distinct phases through which a person moves on their way to recovery. These include: (1) shock or denial; (2) protest, despair, anger, guilt, or pining; (3) depression, withdrawal, or disorganization; and finally, (4) recovery or acceptance. Although there is no set time for each of these stages, the first phase of shock or disbelief usually wears off during the first two weeks, but the entire grief process may take as long as two years.

The grief process should be seen as a wheel that turns back upon itself. It can move from one stage to the next and back again. You may feel that you're well on the road toward recovery only to succumb once again later to the same symptoms you've experienced before and the behaviors you engaged in weeks or months earlier. For example, you may find yourself "pining" for the deceased and being preoccupied with thoughts of this person even after a period of apathy, long after you've begun to take on new interests.

Grief is a wound that must heal, and this process takes time and attention. This emotional pain is not constant but can seem that way if you put energy into suppressing your feelings. It is vital that you admit—not deny—how you feel. To express normal grief, that is, grief that is not inhibited, delayed, or distorted, is to work toward a positive life. Although it can be debilitating for the time after the loss, it cannot be hidden, closeted, or ignored. Instead, its effects will be felt until it's resolved, until you process it, until you reach closure.

Process is a good term, for you must take the raw material of your loss and gradually transform it into something else. Although you never stop feeling, and you never stop caring for what you've lost, you can transform your loss into something manageable and acceptable. In this process you don't just recover, you are transformed. Much of this work, however, can be accomplished earlier, before the death, if you take the time to reach closure or a point of resolution while the other person is still alive. In such instances, grief can be lessened or transformed before the fact. This explains why "positive" assisted deaths, those occurring after acceptance and resolution, seem to lack the intensity of grief that's experienced even in many "natural" deaths.

In cases of both "natural" and assisted deaths, however, some types of losses can be more disruptive than others and more difficult to recover from. In *Necessary Losses,* Judith Viorst points out that, in the death of a life partner, for example, you may mourn a "compendium" of different losses, including your companion, lover, intimate friend, protector, provider, and fellow parent. Combined in this way, you may mourn the "shattering of a whole way of life." Add to this, the secrecy of an assisted death, especially one that's less positive, and you may similarly lose a sense of self as caregiver and loving partner, child, or parent.

In any instance where two individuals are intertwined, the death of one can result in the loss of identity of the other. This is because you may lose more than a person; you lose your best friend, sexual partner, problem-solver, advocate, handyman, financial adviser, spokesperson, and housemate. In the case of a "negative" assisted death you may feel that you've both lost *and* helped kill the only one: who understood you, made you laugh, shared your worldview, and with whom you planned to spend your future.

When you lose such a role partner you also lose much of yourself. In a very real way, you can't be a husband without a wife, sister without a brother, or parent without a child; that is, your roles are often interdependent.

The need to mourn. While *grief* is the term for how you feel, *mourning* describes the ways you may express your loss through behaviors, and in the funerals, memorials, wakes, or other events in which you may participate. How you mourn is influenced by your culture and your religious and family traditions. Many cultures, for example, require that you dress in particular ways and require a special mourning period that may last as long as a year. Some communities and cultures have stronger support systems than others, provide more emotional nurturance, and make it easier to grieve. In a "negative" assisted death, however, you may feel unworthy to accept such support or experience a sense of detachment from your former religious affiliation. This is especially the case where you sense the need for secrecy, feel guilt or regret over your involvement, and failed to achieve resolution. Moreover, if your religious affiliation is vocally opposed to assisted death, you may feel further alienated from it by your own need to maintain secrecy. As a result of your experience, you may now see your church's beliefs as naive or self-righteous. Furthermore, in countries like America, you may find that you're often expected to return quickly to a normal life and be productive at work as soon as possible. In the case of a "negative" assisted death, you may feel this to be impossible as this was not just a loss or a death, but a significant life-altering event, requiring adequate time for reflection and healing.

When necessary, mourning should be a period when you can set aside your everyday activities, reassess your life, and take the time for healing and regaining your capacity to live fully. This is a time when you examine every aspect of your relationship with the other person over and over, when you study the very nature of your attachment, and when you review your every emotion, thought, memory, and regret for the past, present, and future. In the case of a "negative" assisted death, it's also a time to review the event, your participation in it, and the events that led up to it.

The tasks of mourning. To recover from grief it is crucial that you complete four tasks. In *Grief Counseling*, William Worden suggests that you need to:

- Accept the loss as real and acknowledge the end of the relationship

- Realize that grief is emotionally painful, face the difficulties loss creates, and understand that avoiding your emotions only delays the healing process

- Adjust to a world that no longer includes the other, take on new tasks, and begin to do alone those things that were once done with the other

- Shift your emotional energy from the one you've lost to new activities and relationships

In addition, in the case of an assisted death, you need to accept both the other's decision to die, the inevitability of the death, the extensiveness of the suffering, the nature of the death, and your role in it.

Preparing for grief. It is easier to describe the process of grief than prescribe the means for recovery. Indeed, there is no way through grief, but by feeling, by way of the heart. Nevertheless, you can make the journey less strenuous by knowing: (1) the signs of grief and its process; (2) that most of your emotional, physical, cognitive, and behavioral reactions are normal, and; (3) the impact of a devastating loss can be decreased by using—instead of avoiding—the supports that exist in your environment, by separating your grief from the circumstances of the death, and by engaging in activities that can add meaning to your life even as you grieve.

One way to prepare for grief and lessen the magnitude of its effects is to assess the various ways in which you're actually connected to the person whom you either are losing or have recently lost. These include:

- Economic concerns and how dependent you've been on this person for income, financial advice and decisions, and daily fiscal management

- Practical concerns and how dependent you've been on this person for daily activities and household chores and decisions

- Social life and how dependent you've been on this person for connections to friends, social networks, and invitations and activities

- Future goals and how dependent you've been on this person for connections to a future life and goals, and plans on where and how to life

- World views and how dependent you've been on this person for your ideas, philosophy, and outlook on politics and social and personal life

- Perception of self and how dependent you've been on this person for your own sense of worth, beauty, and value in the world

Once you make this assessment, and actually understand the level of your dependency on this person, you can then begin preparing for or meeting this loss. If given adequate time, some of this preparation work can take place during the dying process.

If this period is extensive, you may already be taking over some of these economic and practical responsibilities or finding others to help you out during the process. You might also do well to reach out and begin exploring possibilities for a new life, a little at a time. This may include finding your own support network or reestablishing ties with your own friends or engaging in some activities alone.

Recovering from grief. It's seldom easy to recover from grief alone. It often takes reaching out to others. The first step might be to turn to those to whom you have immediate access. These might be a family member, neighbor, friend, counselor, minister, priest, rabbi, spiritual adviser, and even your family physician. Use these contacts both for immediate support and to help guide you to other resources, including organizations for grief counseling, private therapists, and even groups that provide a range of social activities where you can participate as much or as little as you wish.

It never hurts to have professionals with whom you can talk and discuss the depth of your loss. In various areas, for example, this service is provided by local organizations geared to grief counseling. These include suicide-prevention centers, local churches, and hospice programs, all of which often provide individual counseling and bereavement support groups. So too do some senior centers, community mental health programs, or local chapters of the Widowed Persons Service Program. You might also seek referrals from your local mental-health association or from health or social-service agencies. In addition, some local chapters of the Hemlock Society and right-to-die organizations in other countries offer support over the phone to callers needing to talk.

It's possible—and perhaps necessary—to separate talking about your loss from talking about an assisted death. Don't deny your need to talk about your loss, however, simply because of the nature of the death that you're grieving. Once you develop a close relationship with a good therapist, this topic can also be safely discussed.

The third place you might turn are to men's or women's groups; look for local ads, or talk to your own private counselor. Again, to talk more freely about an assisted death, you might also contact a local Hemlock Society chapter in America, or one of the right-to-die societies in other countries, to see if they offer a support group or contact person for counseling purposes in your region. In any case, avoid those persons who look at grief as a disease to be treated primarily with drugs. Although medication can be helpful in certain instances, by aware that grief is a natural part of healing from loss, and that medication often only blunts the feelings that eventually need to be acknowledged.

Once you feel ready, you might think about moving from *being* to *doing*. In this way, you might do well to take up new activities, engage in exercise, join others in group activities or cultural events.

218 · FINAL ACTS OF LOVE

Such endeavors can be helpful, especially physical activities that help get you out of your house and help you meet people not associated with your loss. You might also consider using any free time to join a community organization, and volunteer to help others. What all of these activities have in common is that they break patterns of behavior that also get linked to thoughts and feelings. Physically getting away from your home helps you get away from reminders of the loss and away from reminders of how to think, feel, and behave.

The value of solitude. It's also valuable to spend time alone, and especially engage in personal pursuits that help you reflect on your life and your relationship in other ways. After all, healing requires reflection, and whether you're receiving counseling or not, reflection is best done alone.

Various things can be helpful, including: meditating, reading thoughtful books, listening to music or self-help tapes, writing to yourself in a journal, writing letters to others, drawing or painting, walking, gardening, exercising, even cleaning.

Spending time alone is not always easy, especially if much of your recent life has been spent focused on the needs of another. But being alone can help you move from *reacting* to *acting*, to taking control over the rest of your life. It can also teach you to do things without help, to achieve, accomplish, and succeed. These are things that you may find extremely important at this time. And finally, solitude gives you the opportunity to be alone with your thoughts. In this sense what you do is secondary to the inner dialogue that accompanies what you do. Ultimately, it's through such inner talk that you may accomplish much of your healing.

Tips for Grief Recovery

- Allow yourself to move in and out of pain naturally. Know that confronting grief shortens its duration. To be open to the grieving process, recognize the full range and intensity of your feelings and talk or cry as much as you need.

- Find a trusted intimate with whom you can discuss *all* aspects of the death if you feel this need.

- Don't attempt to control or reshape your emotions out of fear that you might hurt other survivors, lose control, be misunderstood or seen by others as vulnerable.

- Self support is a form of self love, and both are necessary for healthy recovery and reestablishing your life. Give freely to yourself by trusting and following your inner voice and by respecting your feelings and your desire to express them.

- Know that grief will change you regardless of whether you want to or not. You can't prevent change. It's a part of surviving loss.

- Realize that grief will change you whether or not you express your emotions, and that your feelings will affect you in varying ways until you express them. The way to healing is to tolerate and accept your feelings, by moving with them for as long as it takes the wound from your loss to heal.

- Grief ends when you can finally let go of the intense connection you have with what you've lost. This is not the same as the end of love. Your love may never die, but the pain of loss can eventually diminish.

- To mourn completely, be aware of your needs, honor them, and take time to grieve. Caring for yourself is vital. You're not being self-indulgent if you rest, eat well, or pamper yourself.

- Major loss can seem unfamiliar and overwhelming. This is because we often deny the extent to which we feel grief in our everyday changes and losses. We can avoid some of the intensity following a major loss by allowing ourselves to feel *all* of our losses—major or minor—at the time they first occur.

- Find the right vocabulary to express your grief. Move beyond statements of fact such as "She's gone" or "He's dead." Replace these with those that express your actual feelings, such as "I feel, I need, I wish, I miss." Moreover, in the case of a "negative" assisted death, nothing is gained by using terms like "I killed" or "I failed."

- Your grief is special. Others are not always right in their advice, and they do not always know the best way to support you. You might do well to ignore them if they: tell you that talking about your feelings doesn't do you any good; counsel you not to be weak or not to express your pain or sadness; urge you to think of others who are worse off; see your expression of sadness or despair as "wallowing," a "waste of time"; tell you to "stop grieving" because the other's death was "for the best"; urge you to "focus on tomorrow" and "forget the past."

- In the event that the death was officially declared a suicide, or if another is aware of the assisted nature of the death, but opposed, you might do well to ignore his comments if he: tells you that the act was "irrational," a "sin," or a "sign of weakness"; accuses you of killing or murdering this person; blames you for causing the death; attempts to argue with you about the ethics of the action.

- Recovering from loss is often easier if you reach out to others, even though you may feel like withdrawing. Think about what family members, friends, or organizations might be sources of emotional support for you.

- You might need to mourn, to externalize your grief, in ways that feel right for you. Funerals or memorials are only one method and only one-time events. Your mourning doesn't have to end when a memorial is over. Find your own ways to express your grief, and use your own emotional timetable.

- Think about using your own creative skills to help you through the grieving process. You might consider expressing your emotions outwardly by painting or drawing, verbally through poems or letters, musically through songs, or physically through some form of movement or a pilgrimage to a special place.

- You might also consider creating your own personal rituals or group activities to help you through this time. Our ancestors combined art, music, words, and movement together with sacred objects in their own mourning rituals. You still have the opportunity to create your own constructive and personally meaningful ceremonies, celebrations, and ritual activities.

- Think how can you give your own everyday activities a more ritualized and sacred quality by being present in the here-and-now and by performing daily actions with a conscious deliberation. This can be anything from preparing dinner to taking a walk. There are special qualities in everything you do. Your ancestors engaged in these same endeavors over countless generations. This can reinforce your connection to the past and to others and reaffirm the sacredness of all your actions.

Helping Others Grieve

- The person who is grieving needs friendship and support. Start by acknowledging her loss and then by asking the other what she needs from you.

- Give your presence as long as it feels comfortable to the other. This is far more important than any knowledge or advice you may wish to give. You can begin by sitting near her. If it feels right to both of you, hold her hand, or give her a hug.

- If you can, be a willing—and completely trustworthy—listener who will in no way judge the other's actions.

- If you can cope with strong emotion, accept your friend's tears, and then share your own feelings, and shed your own tears of support.

- Without displacing the other's depth of feelings, share your own experiences and memories of the deceased person and, without pushing your beliefs, gently share your own spiritual ideas.

- Provide practical assistance and incidental acts of compassion, such as performing mundane chores and activities or, with her permission, even serving as her spokesperson or intermediary.

- If you can't cope with strong emotion, help in whatever way you can. You can do this by helping with outside chores and errands or even making necessary phone calls from your own home.

- When visiting, know when to leave, and respect the need for the other to be alone or to have periods of silence.

- Do not withdraw your support without warning; it can feel like another loss.

- Follow through on all your promises; this is not a time for further disappointments.

Chapter 8

HELPING A PATIENT DIE:
A Physician's Guide

If you are a physician who currently provides aid-in-dying for a terminally ill patient, you do so outside the boundaries of legally protected medical practice. Whether you're motivated by compassion or not, you face a wide range of legal and professional risks. Without legislation and clinical guidelines to draw upon, you may also feel hesitant to discuss this practice with other physicians and, therefore, feel either unable to help a patient even in the most appropriate of cases or less than certain as to what factors to consider if you ever decide to assist. As a result, you may feel alone. At the present time, there are few places to turn to for help, and most hospital ethics committees are reticent to discuss aid-in-dying in practical ways that are supportive if you're grappling with such a decision.

Nevertheless, physician assistance widely occurs, and most doctors who assist in the death of a terminally ill patient usually do so fully considering the seriousness of such an action. This decision is typically based on balancing the patient's medical condition, prognosis, degree of intolerable and irreversible suffering, and persistence of the request for aid-in-dying. The relationship between a physician and an incurably ill patient is so special and often of such long duration that assistance is usually provided only after a patient's condition becomes increasingly intolerable, her quality of life diminishes, and available treatment options are no longer effective in relieving suffering. At this point, a patient may decide that death is the only possible release.

Seeing this, some physicians—responding to their patient's request—discuss the issues involved, communicate openly with the patient and her significant other about the seriousness of this action, and finally agree to help. In doing so, some doctors see their help as a legitimate part of the practice of medicine at the end of a continuum of medical care. The decision by a physician to assist a patient in dying is most often based on this understanding and is made out of compassion and medical necessity regardless of the consequences that she could possibly face later on.

In many instances, however, a physician may respond too willingly to a patient's request for help, or too hesitantly, and thereby deny the request at a time when it's too late for the patient to do anything else but seek the help of significant others. Both scenarios leave much to be desired. In the former case, the request may come at a point too early in the dying process, while there's still a possibility for further treatment options and for the patient to enjoy a substantial quality of life. In addition, agreement to help may be made without full knowledge of all factors that might need to be taken into consideration. To maintain secrecy—to protect from scrutiny, legal action, or intervention—the physician and patient may be similarly hesitant to explore the range of psychological, familial, social, or economic issues that might influence the patient's desire to die. In the latter case, when physicians respond too hesitantly and deny the request late, the possibilities for failure are increased as is the potential for serious negative effects for those significant others who may feel the need to intervene.

PRACTICAL GUIDELINES

These risks can be reduced by use of procedural and practical guidelines that physicians can follow to ensure they'll not act in a precipitous fashion. Procedural guidelines can specify a patient's qualifications to receive aid-in-dying from a physician, the process to be followed, the need for consulting opinions, psychological-social assessments, waiting periods, and so forth. In addition, practical guidelines can provide physicians with ways to assess their own possible responses in particular cases.

Assisting in a death is not the same as performing any other medical procedure. In the current absence of legal and procedural guidelines, there's an absence of a more practical guide to help physicians address their ethical, emotional, and legal concerns. Such a practical guide can enable a physician to follow a self-guided set of questions to ensure that she has thoughtfully and thoroughly explored the diversity of issues involved.

The following guide has been designed for this purpose—to help you, as a physician, examine the range of concerns that are best addressed before you ever agree to help a patient to die.

A Decision-Making Guide

The following practical self-guide has also been designed to reduce your risk as a physician of any wrongful actions involved in assisting in the death of a patient. In this regard, it can be looked upon as an ethical map. In this way if, as a physician, you find yourself being asked to help a patient die, you will not feel compelled to provide assistance without adequate reflection on your own beliefs, motivations, and needs. You might also use this self-guide later on, after a change occurs in the legal status of physician-assisted dying, to help you throughout the decision-making process.

In preparing to help a patient die, it is important for you to:

- Examine your moral and ethical beliefs about assisted dying

- Become fully aware of all legal and professional considerations

- Open the lines of communication with your patient, and be absolutely certain that you understand each other completely, regardless of possible differences in cultural background, language, or ethnicity

- Obtain all the facts to understand your patient's physical condition, perform appropriate diagnostic assessments, and ask for a consulting (second) opinion in order to be absolutely certain of the intolerable and irreversible nature of your patient's condition

- Assess your patient's motives for wanting to die and, if you have any doubts about his request or psychological/emotional condition, make a referral to a psychiatrist or psychologist to see if depression is present to the degree that it impairs judgment and could warrant medication

- Determine the enduring nature of the patient's desire to die in light of his current medical and psychological status

- Evaluate your motives for agreeing to assist, and be certain they are appropriate and sound. Be sure you are not being unduly moved to assist, perhaps because of the nature of your relationship with your patient

- Specify your role in providing assistance, whether you will be providing a prescription for lethal medications, will be taking a more active role by being present to monitor the outcome when medications are being self-administered and, if necessary, intervene by administering further medications

- Determine the extent of involvement with which you are most comfortable, weighing your patient's needs and agreeing to take no action for which you are emotionally or practically unprepared

- Think about all possible emotional, legal, and professional effects on you

- Become aware of all the details in the planning for this death to ensure success of this effort, while minimizing the potential of harm to others

- Prepare emotionally for helping your patient by obtaining feedback and advice from a *trusted* third party (a counselor, the hospital ethics committee, or another physician), who poses no risk to you or your patient.

ASSESS YOUR BELIEFS ABOUT ASSISTED DYING

If a patient asks you to assist him in dying, you need to examine your moral and ethical beliefs concerning the treatment of terminal patients. First decide whether you think physician-assisted dying is ever appropriate and, if so, under what conditions. Explore your beliefs and establish your own guidelines as to who might qualify, in general, for any aid-in-dying and, more specifically, for assistance from you.

> *What are your beliefs about assisted dying? Is it ever morally right for a physician to help a patient to die? Could you ever assist one of your patients to die? What physical conditions would a patient need to have to receive aid-in-dying? Have you established your own guidelines?*

LEGAL AND PROFESSIONAL CONSIDERATIONS

Although physician-assistance occurs widely and discovery and censure is extremely rare, there are still risks that you need to consider. If you're discovered, you risk the possibility of arrest and prosecution, censure by state medical boards, loss of medical license, and the effects of the publicity that could result from such official action.

Although only one physician has lost his medical license in recent years as a result of aiding in the death of an incurably ill patient, other physicians who are less vocal in their actions still take a risk. Beyond the legal risks, however, there is also a potential for medical malpractice suits if, for example, you fail to involve those closest to the patient in the decision process, or if you do not take into account the possibility for failure and the further harm that could result from providing a less than effective prescription to assist in a patient's death. Such risks for lawsuit might also exist if it can be shown that the provision of assistance was inappropriate given the patient's medical condition, prognosis, and psychological state, or if the request was fulfilled "too early" in the dying process or was motivated by other than medical factors.

> *Have I given full thought to the possibility that criminal charges could be brought against me if my assistance is discovered? Have I considered what the effect of such legal action could be on my professional career? Have I fully studied the feasibility that civil action for wrongful death could be initiated by significant others if they've not been included in the decision process?*

DETERMINE WHO QUALIFIES FOR HELP

Next, you should think about the conditions under which you might consider assisting a patient to end his life. You might decide that one should be helped to die only if their condition is terminal and untreatable, and they have no apparent "quality of life" as they define it. Or you may feel that there needs to be the presence of intolerable and irreversible physical pain or suffering, and that no one should be helped to die simply because of the fear of future pain and suffering.

> *Should assistance-in-dying be reserved only for those in the late stage of a terminal illness? Should help also be available before the onset of an intolerable end-stage condition? Should help be provided earlier in a terminal illness where there is little or no self-defined quality of life? Could an incurably ill patient with an irreversible and intolerable condition qualify for your help? Should a patient who is incurably or terminally ill be helped before the likely onset of a condition that could render them unable to help themselves to die later on? What are the minimum circumstances where it might be appropriate for you to help?*

THE REQUEST AS AN OPPORTUNITY FOR TALK

As a physician charged with providing medical care for your patients, it is not up to you to open the dialogue about assisted dying. Nevertheless, it is quite appropriate to discuss the likely course of the patient's illness and to initiate an open conversation, asking specifically about his thoughts, hopes, fears, and concerns about death and dying. It is critical at this point to *listen* closely to what your patient has to say. In this way, if your patient tells you that he does not wish to continue living under certain conditions, you can better assess what your patient means exactly and get a clearer picture of your patient's understanding, concerns, and desires.

Early discussion about *all* end-of-life options, therefore, can increase your own knowledge of the patient's motives and desires and better enable you to respond to her medical complaints. For example, some patients feel that because they have cancer they're going to die no matter what. They may believe there's no use in further treatment, not realizing that in a substantial number of cases there may well be a real opportunity for cure or long-term remission. Others may want assistance in dying because they've witnessed or had some experience they wish to avoid. Just knowing the patient's concerns, and the source of her motives, can enable you to explain to her realistically whether her fears are justified and how you might handle such a situation if it were to arise.

For this reason, any attempt by a patient to talk about her dying should be met with honesty. This especially is the case with the topic of assisted dying. For example, your patient may ask for your help when you don't feel that all quality of life is gone. In that case you need to be willing to express your reservations and describe the conditions under which you might feel that your assistance could be justified. To not talk of such matters until the end-stage of a terminal condition can close off other medical options, rush the final decision-making process, and even halt open communication between you and your patient. Therefore, by testing the waters early, the patient should be seen as performing a service that can do much to improve communcation and make you better aware of her real complaints and concerns.

The best time to think about all available options is before you have to decide, before you're faced with a crisis decision, especially if the decision being considered is to help a patient to end his life. Open discussion early on can reduce later misunderstandings, last-minute requests, and hasty assistance rooted in a feeling of medical duty instead of a mutual understanding of the concerns of both you and your patient. Open dialogue also can do much to ease a patient's stress and reduce emotional discomfort.

> *Have you allowed your patient the opportunity to discuss his fears and concerns about his medical condition and about death and dying? Have you ignored your patient's attempt to open the dialogue about assisted dying? In requesting your assistance, could your patient be seeking assurance that you will do all you can to provide comfort care? Could your patient's attempt to talk about the topic be his way of expressing dissatisfaction with the current course of treatment?*

Any responsibility of such magnitude—for life and death itself—needs to be based on a partnership between you and your patient that is rooted in openness and equality of decision making. Your patient must know not only what is best for him, but also for you. Both of you need to feel that this is the right decision, given all other medical options. By discussing it, you can determine both the need for your involvement and whether it is something with which you feel absolutely comfortable.

Two important steps. Use the occasion of the patient's request to set up a special appointment, if necessary, to talk with your patient in more detail about her probable plight, and make her more comfortable, knowledgeable, and accepting of it. This should be seen as the first step in providing aid-in-dying.

The second step is for the patient's significant others to be brought into the process. This may be difficult for a patient to do alone. If so, the reasons for this hesitancy need to be explored. As the patient's physician, you can help facilitate this discussion. With your patient's permission, you might talk with all parties, separately and together, and alert them to the patient's medical status, impending death, and the various ways that she is considering to handle the dying process (e.g., narcotics, antidepressants, DNR orders, physician-assisted dying, etc.). This can help significant others to look more realistically at the patient's dying process. Friends and family also need the opportunity to think about this, ask questions, raise fears and concerns, and come to grips with their own ideas about death. Knowing this, you might suggest that someone else best suited for the job—such as the patient, significant other, family member, minister, counselor, etc.—can facilitate such a meeting for all parties. It's conceivable that your own involvement might take several meetings with different people in attendance, depending on their attitudes and feelings on the subject.

If aid-in-dying is being readily discussed, this is the time for you to describe your own criteria for assisting, what requirements are necessary to be met, and what role you would actually play in the final process.

Have you included the patient's family or significant others in any discussions about this issue? Have you made your position on physician-assisted dying absolutely clear during any discussion? Have you described the minimum conditions under which you would even consider helping a patient in this manner?

Are You Talking the Same Language?

Full and open dialogue also can enable you to avoid problems of misunderstanding that may be based on cultural, ethnic, linguistic, religious, or educational differences. What your patient is asking for, and what you are hearing, may be two different things. A patient who asks you for "help in dying" may not be asking for a lethal prescription. Instead, she may only be seeking the reassurance that you will continue providing the best quality care for her until the end. Similarly, patients may assume that you will help them die if you say that you will "not let them suffer."

Make absolutely certain that both of you understand what the other is saying. If your patient has a different cultural or linguistic background than your own, you should secure the services of another person—a patient's family member or close friend—who is knowledgeable about the patient's culture or language who can act as an "interpreter."

Is your patient of a different cultural, ethnic, linguistic, religious, or educational background than your own? Might this difference create

the possibility for miscommunication? Does your patient fully under-
stand her medical condition, prognosis, and course of treatment?

Do you see the patient's situation through his or her eyes? Can you
get a sense of what your patient is feeling? Do you and your patient
mean the same thing when you talk about such things as physician-
assisted dying, being there for your patient, or doing all that is required
to ease suffering?

Obtain All the Facts

Open discussion might lead you to realize that your patient is un-
happy with the course of his medical treatment, is discouraged
about the direction the illness is taking in spite of active treatment,
or has physical conditions that might be better treated through different or further medical intervention. Inadequate pain relief or
side effects from medications might be easily resolved or at least
addressed prior to your involvement in the patient's death.

After your patient requests aid-in-dying, you should explore
his motives in detail, discuss the current course of treatment, and
then open a dialogue about other factors that might be influencing
his request for aid-in-dying, such as emotional, familial, social, and
economic concerns.

Be certain of your patient's medical condition. Aid-in-dying is
warranted only under certain conditions. Although these have yet
to be codified, some ethicists have argued that a patient's condition
at a minimum must be "incurable, and associated with severe, un-
relenting, intolerable suffering." (My own criteria are presented at
the end of this chapter.) Ultimately, you need to be certain that
this case meets your own personal guidelines. First, carefully review your patient's medical and treatment history and become
as familiar as you can with all the medical facts in this case. Second, treat to alleviate pain and suffering, and assess other options, including the possibility of a referral to other specialists or
hospice care.

At this point, to protect yourself and the patient, you'd be wise to seek a consulting opinion from a specialist whose skills and opinions you trust. If you feel it is necessary, you might also request further diagnostic work for the patient.

If the patient refuses further treatment either to address the particular disease or to alleviate associated distress, you must decide if you can provide aid-in-dying to the patient under these conditions. Your patient needs to know all the options and what you believe is best under the circumstances. Ultimately, the patient needs to be the one to make the final decision. If you don't feel that the patient's choice is acceptable, you must decide what your relationship to the patient should be, and whether a change of physicians might be better.

Has a terminal or irreversible prognosis been confirmed? Have you sought a confirming diagnosis or second opinion in this case? Is your patient's suffering intractable and intolerable? How do you define this?

Have you explored all possible pain- and symptom-control measures? Have you consulted with a specialist about pain or symptom control in this case?

Is your patient refusing further treatment options? In your opinion, is this refusal informed and rational? Could further treatments improve the patient's quality of life? Would you require further treatment before agreeing to assist in his death? Have you described your own requirements for assisting the patient in dying?

Consider a psychiatric referral. If you are considering assisting in a patient's death, you should also explore the patient's psychological state and emotional well-being. Some requests from patients for physician-assistance stem from depression or other emotional sources. It is critical that you do not help anyone who is clearly depressed or in any way unable to make a well-reasoned decision.

In terminal illness some depression is normal. It is often transient and needs no intervention, but in certain cases it can affect judgment if left untreated. Furthermore, it is not uncommon for depression to result from the use of various medications, or even during and shortly following chemotherapy treatments. If you have any doubts about the person's emotional state, seek a consultation with the patient's caregiver, partner, or significant other and, if you believe it is warranted, don't hesitate to recommend a second opinion or independent assessment of the patient's psychological state.

The purpose of a psychological or psychiatric exam is to see if the patient's judgment is *significantly* impaired. Because of the difficulty you might have in getting a patient to accept a counseling referral, you need to approach the patient with a comfortable and positive attitude. The patient needs to know that you, as his physician, can benefit from such an evaluation and be better able to treat his problems as well as respond to his request for assistance in dying.

> *Can you assess the rationality of your patient's decision to die? Might this decision result partly from depression? Might depression be a result of the current course of his medical treatment or be a result of side effects of medications he is receiving? Have you referred the patient for a psychological or psychiatric assessment? Have you talked with a mental health professional about the features of this case?*

If the patient is unable to travel and is presently obtaining treatment in a hospital, receiving (residential or at-home) hospice care, or in a convalescent-care facility, you also might consider talking with the social worker on the case or asking the patient to agree to a visit and assessment by a psychiatric social worker or other mental-health professional. Without necessarily discussing the patient's request for aid-in-dying with this professional, you might request her opinion as to the possible presence of treatable depression or other condition that might in some way significantly impair the patient's judgment.

Similarly, a patient may decide to die due to the emotional exhaustion that is often involved in fighting a terminal or incurable illness. Perhaps there is a way for you, as the medical professional, to provide a temporary or even permanent respite from treatment to alleviate this emotional stress. In certain situations you might also consider recommending that your patient seek private counseling or join a group for emotional support.

Under all circumstances it is important that you, as a patient's physician, do not act as the sole judge of competency and rationality unless you feel absolutely certain that you know the patient well enough to make this decision and that you personally feel the patient's request is rational and appropriate.

Has the patient obtained counseling or emotional support? Have you investigated support groups for patients in your area? Have you asked your patient to obtain a psychological assessment as a condition for your assistance in his death? Have you talked with a social worker or others who are knowledgeable of factors that might be influencing the patient's request for aid-in-dying?

ASSESS THE PATIENT'S MOTIVES

Before you agree to help this patient die, be as cognizant as you can of the motives that are driving the request. Discuss, in as detailed a manner as you can, the patient's physical, emotional, and social reasons for requesting your help, especially if your relationship with this patient has not afforded you with an up-close knowledge of her family life and social or economic conditions.

Financial concerns. In this regard, it is critical that you be absolutely certain that your patient is not basing this request primarily on financial need, the cost of medical care, or lack of medical insurance. Death should not be seen by a patient as a way to reduce their financial burden on others or because they fear the consequences of future economic difficulties. On the other hand, many who are suffering intolerably with little quality of life—who may not want to be a financial burden to their families—can also make rational choices to forego expensive treatment or further care that is prolonging the dying process.

This is a delicate issue. As the patient's physician, however, it's up to you to determine the patient's dominant motive for wanting to die and to be certain that financial concerns are only secondary. Moreover, it is again necessary to be certain that the patient's request doesn't result from an underlying depression or the need for counseling and emotional support.

> *Has your patient expressed to you any financial concerns that may be influencing his request for aid-in-dying? Have you asked your patient if he has any financial concerns? Does your patient have an adequate level of health insurance to cover either the remainder of end-of-life treatment or any other treatment options that might be effective for alleviating suffering? If not, have you talked with your patient about whether the request for your help and any financial considerations might be linked? Have you referred your patient to social workers or benefit coordinators to discuss other sources for payment of health-care services?*

Family pressures. It is also important that you assure yourself that the person asking for your help in dying has freely arrived at this decision and has not been unduly influenced by others who may have their own motives for supporting his death. These might be economic factors or others such as exhaustion over caregiving activities or other pressures in the household in which the patient may reside.

> *Whose idea is this? Can someone else be influencing your patient's decision? Does the primary caregiver have adequate respite to reduce possible burnout? Are you knowledgeable of possible options or can you refer your patient to a social worker to discuss them in more detail? Might your patient be seeking aid-in-dying to please another or because he might be a financial, emotional, or caregiving burden to others?*

Emotional exhaustion. Another reason for discussing a patient's motives in asking for aid-in-dying is to uncover how well the patient is dealing with the often time-consuming and emotionally exhausting work of being ill. This work includes such things as arranging transportation for medical treatment, waiting in long lines for treatment or prescriptions, and filling out forms to obtain government or insurance benefits that could alleviate financial stress and the resulting emotional distress.

As the physician, become better informed with what is involved in being a patient and see if there might be some way that you can act on your patient's behalf or find other local resources that can be called upon to help in this manner.

Might your patient be emotionally exhausted from the daily work that is involved in being ill? Might your effort as the patient's physician be better spent obtaining information on available resources or providing referrals for a patient advocate who can help your patient in a number of ways?

Finally, if you are not the primary health-care provider or have not been the patient's physician for very long, look more deeply into the reasons why you were asked to aid in the patient's death. The first person to ask, of course, is the patient, but you might also explore the patient's medical and personal history and even contact the patient's former physician to fill in any missing details.

Why have you been asked to serve as the patient's physician? What was the patient's relationship with her former physician? Did the patient ask her former physician for aid-in-dying? Might the patient's former physician know personal or social factors of which you should be aware?

DETERMINE THE ENDURING NATURE OF THE REQUEST

It is crucial that your patient's request be explicit and persistent. Create for yourself a minimum waiting period between the time your patient asks for your help and the time you fulfill this request. You might also decide to adjust the length of this waiting period for patients in different terminal or incurable categories.

You may decide that a patient in an end-state terminal condition, who is facing intolerable and irreversible pain or suffering, should be assisted quite quickly, perhaps within a couple of days. By contrast, you may determine that a patient who is earlier in the dying process and whose suffering is more treatable, but who still lacks quality of life, should wait a substantially longer period, perhaps several weeks or months. Your patient may need your guidance about timing, and both of you should understand each other's perspectives.

> *How many times and over what period has your patient requested your help? Do you feel confident that your patient's decision to die is sincere and consistent? Might your patient be looking for feedback as to whether you think it's time for her to die? Again, could she be seeking assurance that your assistance may not be necessary and that you will do all you can to provide comfort care?*

Document your patient's requests confidentially and separately from her medical records. You might consider having these requests put into writing—and perhaps even witnessed—on at least one occasion. Study your patient's request, how often is it made, whether it is consistent, and if there is any hesitancy. If you notice any inconsistency or hesitation, discuss your observations with your patient, explore the source of any hesitancy and, if necessary, talk to anyone else who knows the situation.

EXAMINE YOUR OWN MOTIVES

If you are seriously considering assisting in your patient's death, think clearly about your reasons for agreeing to do so. A wide range of beliefs and feelings may surface and could play a role in your decision.

First, confirm that you're thinking of assisting your patient out of compassion toward her situation, because you're medically certain that this situation will continue to get worse, and because you believe this to be a proper form of compassionate care that you can provide some patients who are irreversibly ill.

Second, consider whether you're thinking of assisting because *you* believe your patient has no quality of life, because *you* would not want to live under similar circumstances, or possibly because your patient's requests have worn down your opposition to helping. In combination with the former, none of these latter motives necessarily are wrong in themselves, but it's important to ask yourself:

- Have I clearly assessed my own motives?

- Are my own reasons good enough?

- Do I really want to help the patient in this manner?

- Would I feel comfortable doing so?

If you don't want to help, don't! Trust and follow your feelings. Otherwise you may be later burdened by your decision. Furthermore, if you don't believe in assisting the patient in dying, but still consider the request to have validity, you might refer the patient to another physician.

Do you see your "duty" as a physician to provide aid-in-dying as an option during terminal care? Do you view your patient's request for your assistance as an emotional burden? Do you look upon such an action favorably, with grave reservations, or with cautious hesitation? Are you comfortable with the idea of helping this patient die?

In addition, you also should look closely at your relationship with the patient, and do *not* provide assistance in dying if you have any friendship or familial connections with this person, or if aid-in-dying is being requested by a friend or colleague to whom you feel any obligation to comply. This moves the act of assisting from the physician-patient relationship to a more private realm, and may make it too difficult for you to follow your own established guidelines.

What motives do you have for agreeing to assist this patient? Do you feel pressured in any way by this patient to provide assistance in dying? With the medical situation being equal, would you help another patient in the same way? At some future time might you resent or regret helping this patient die? Are you absolutely certain that this is the best course of action given the patient's medical condition and prognosis?

The decision for assisted-suicide must always rest with the one who is dying and never be in the hands of another. This includes a family member *or* a physician. Similarly, the decision to help, though mutually discussed, must be yours alone.

What Will It Mean to Help

Critical in any discussion with your patient about helping her to die is that both of you know exactly what role each of you will take. If you agree to help, specify clearly to your patient what this means to you. Some physicians tell their patients that they will "do all that is necessary" or that they "won't let them suffer," but mean only that they will provide adequate pain relief or emotional support. If this is what you mean to say, make this known clearly and early in your discussions so your patient is never under the wrong impression. Know your limits, explain them, and stick to them.

Failure to specify exactly what you will and will *not* do may lead a patient to assume too much, and this can have serious consequences if he waits too long to seek other medical sources of assistance. The patient and his significant others may feel themselves forced to take matters into their own hands and may have to use less-than-adequate means. At that point, family members and friends often become more involved out of obligation or a sense of duty, and the potential for failure increases.

If you agree to assist your patient, however, specify the nature of the help you'll provide and whether it will include only a prescription for lethal drugs, the possibility of IV administration of lethal medications, or the addition of your presence at the death to ensure its ease and success.

Discussions with your patient should include the possibility of a self-enacted death, accomplished without your help. If this is agreed upon, you should ask the patient if she has read materials about the best methods for ending her own life. You should ask the patient about her feelings on this subject and also explore your own. Ultimately, in assessing your own role, you need to look at whether your direct intervention might be warranted due to the patient's medical condition and possible inability to accomplish this act alone without your help.

If you agree to help, do you and your patient understand each other clearly about the type of help you'll provide? Have you given thought to how you might assist in your patient's death? Have you given careful thought to the methods to be used under the medical circumstances?

Will you be assisting the patient indirectly by providing prescription drugs? If so, have you taken into account the nature of your patient's condition? Are you confident that the prescription provided will work? Are you certain of the patient's ability to carry out the instructions? Will the patient be able to swallow, keep down, and absorb these drugs if provided orally?

Would you be willing to be more directly involved by administering an IV injection of a lethal substance? Under what conditions might you find this to be necessary and appropriate?

To reduce the potential for deeper involvement by others than you or your patient desire, discuss the patient's plans for his death. One sure way for family or friends to become more involved is by selecting the wrong drugs for this purpose or by failing to take into account the patient's ability to complete this act alone. Help reduce the possibility of failure by doing your own homework and clearly considering the methods to be used in light of their side effects and the patient's specific condition. Discuss the possibility of failure; it happens. Then discuss alternative methods, how they might be used, and whether you'll be available on call as a backup.

Have you been informed of the patient's plan and are you confident that the method you both have selected will fit with that plan and be successful? Will this method work within the time limits provided by the plan?

Would you be willing to be on-call to intervene in an emergency if the prescription you've provided fails to work? In the case of failure, will you be available for further assistance, if necessary? What might this emergency assistance entail? If you do not wish to become more involved, should it become necessary, do you have a backup plan? Do you have another physician you can call under these circumstances?

If you decide to be present at the death to assist actively, you need to feel absolutely comfortable with the setting and with any others who might also be present. This is another reason why it's important to be informed of the overall plan for this event. Again, when you discuss "active" assistance, both you and your patient need to know in detail what this will mean. All others who may be present also need to be informed in advance of what will likely occur, so they can be emotionally prepared. If you feel uneasy with your possible role, think again about assisting and reconsider the extent of your involvement.

> *Will your direct involvement and presence be necessary? Is your patient physically unable to perform this act alone? In envisioning the possibility of your patient's failure in completing the act alone, do you view your further involvement as ethical or unethical?*
>
> *If you agree to be present, do you know who else will be there? Are you comfortable with the idea of these others being present? Have you discussed in detail what role each person may play?*
>
> *Have you discussed the possibility of failure, and what additional methods of assisting are acceptable or unacceptable to you? Are you certain that others who may be present know what these methods will be? Are you certain that each person who will be there is comfortable with these methods?*

THINK ABOUT THE POSSIBLE EFFECTS ON YOU

Before finally deciding to help your patient, think hard about how this may affect you emotionally. Consider how you may feel the next week or month, and if you might feel guilt for helping your patient in this way rather than in some other manner. You also may experience a form of grief that you may not have experienced previously in the deaths of other patients. Have the professional resources available that you might need later on. Also, consider how your involvement might affect your relationship with other patients who are also going through the dying process.

·   ·   ·

Until laws are changed, assisted dying will continue to be a secret act. Nevertheless, we can learn from others' experiences. By thinking through topics and questions like the ones in this chapter, you can develop your own guidelines that can be your anchor and can provide you assurance that you've given the matter the depth of thought it requires.

Only after you answer these types of questions can you realistically decide whether the patient who requests—or whom you believe needs—your help qualifies by your own guidelines for your possible assistance. Similarly, only after exploring your own feelings can you determine exactly how much help you might be willing to provide.

Suggested Guidelines for Assisting

Ask yourself if the patient you are thinking of assisting:

- Is terminally ill or suffers from an incurable and irreversible condition, which, in your professional judgment, will continue to worsen or result in death in a reasonable period of time

- Is experiencing severe, intractable, and irreversible physiological suffering, which has little prospect for relief, drastically reduces quality of life, and is found by the person to be unacceptable and intolerable

- Has received a confirming diagnosis and prognosis from a second physician, who is a specialist in the area of the patient's illness and who has reviewed the medical records and seen the patient

- Is a mentally competent adult, who is able to make a well-reasoned decision and whose judgment is not significantly impaired by depression or other psychological condition

- Is not experiencing severe emotional distress, and is not being influenced in his request by economic hardship or other social factors

- Has explored all reasons for wanting to die and is certain that economic concerns are not a major reason for this decision

- Is not seeking aid-in-dying as a result of receiving less-than-adequate medical care

- Has exhausted practical and acceptable treatment options and understands the consequences of refusing further treatment

- Has made this choice based on well-informed facts of diagnosis, prognosis, alternatives, and likely outcomes, which are fully understood

- Has expressed—explicitly and without hesitation—the desire to die on repeated occasions over a period of at least several days if experiencing an end-stage terminal illness, or perhaps several weeks in other cases

- Has explored hospice care as an option and is receiving palliative care and maximum pain relief

- Has made this decision freely, without coercion, suggestions, or influence from others

- Has informed all family members or others with whom a close personal relationship exists or has reasonable justification for not doing so

- Has attempted to reach emotional closure with those with whom a close personal relationship exists or has reasonable justification for not doing so

- Has discussed in advance with all who will be involved what it will mean for a physician to "assist," what exactly may be involved in the process, and has obtained their agreement

As one who is considering assisting a patient in their death, you:

- Need to be assured that this person has met the just-listed requirements

- Should be certain that you and your patient completely understand one another and are in total agreement as to what is involved in your decision to assist him in dying

- Need to assess your motives for agreeing to help this person die

- Should be certain that your motives for agreeing to assist are based on compassion, altruism, shared decision making, and your belief in a professional conduct for caring for the sick

- Should have an established relationship with this patient, and in some way be emotionally invested in her well-being

- Should discuss in detail your own concerns and be certain that you've reached full agreement and understanding with your patient

- Should know what an agreement to assist entails and have discussed these details with your patient

- Should be physically and emotionally capable of performing the agreed upon act of assistance

- Need to be fully informed of any changes in your patient's physical condition and psychological status prior to providing assistance and be able to verify this status to determine better the rationality of your patient's decision to die

Appendix 1

QUESTIONS AND RESPONSES

In my presentations the same general questions are asked again and again, regardless of the setting and the audience. I offer those questions here and provide some of the responses that I have often given. Most of these questions require each of us to draw our own conclusions. As a result I have no "answers," only comments.

Is assisted dying the same as suicide?

Suicide ends a life that could continue, and implies irrationality rooted in an identifiable mental condition that may be treatable with proper therapy and medications. By contrast, an assisted death is one where all involved have seriously considered the questions and guidelines in this book, including physical, social, emotional, and economic factors, spiritual and ethical issues, and the emotional impact of this action on others. It ends the life of the patient who has gone through this process, whose hope for continued living and cure is gone, and who is faced with the alternative of suffering until inevitable death.

Is assisted dying the same as killing?

Killing takes a human life against the will and without the consent of a person who wants to continue living, and has the primary intention of doing harm. Assisted dying, by contrast, is a compassionate act voluntarily requested by a patient who is destined to die and wants to die to relieve her suffering. As such, it should be carried out only after open dialogue with one's physician and significant others, assessment of all other options, opportunities for counseling, and serious reflection.

Is assisted dying rational?

Some argue that all self-intended death, regardless of circumstances, is irrational, and this includes requests for assisted death in the case of a terminal illness. Studies of suicides stress that in nearly every case, even in suicides by the terminally ill, the individual suffered from a definable psychiatric disorder. In rebuttal, it is easy to interpret a deceased patient's prior statements of "hopelessness" as an indicator of depression, forgetting that terminal illness indeed *is* "hopeless" by definition. In addition, there are other serious problems with this rationality argument, not the least of which are methodological. As my own study has shown, nearly all assisted deaths are *never* documented as suicides, but as natural deaths. Discovered suicides and assisted deaths are two very distinct populations. Many suicidologists never see suicide as rational because those who contemplate and engage in rational suicide make certain they're never seen by suicidologists. Instead, they are an invisible population that makes every effort to remain so.

Doesn't pain control eliminate the need for assisted dying?

Physical pain is only one of many conditions that lead the terminally ill to make the decision to die. Physical suffering and quality of life involve several other factors that can rationally influence this decision. Moreover, while most terminal metastatic cancer pain can be controlled, there is still a substantial amount of pain that can't be controlled without a pharmacologically induced sleep that socially approximates death.

Is assisted dying a sin?

This is a theological question that is answered in varying ways by different religions and religious denominations. Some equate requesting and receiving aid-in-dying, regardless of the presence of intolerable suffering and terminal illness, as an act of suicide; they also equate providing assistance the same as killing. Others define requesting and providing assistance as justifiable and merciful.

Although suicide is not prohibited in either the Old or New Testament, religious views on it are not static but have changed over time. Current Catholic Church theology, for example, argues that suicide is a sin and considered "a rejection of God's sovereignty and loving plan." Nevertheless, "at times there are psychological factors that can diminish responsibility or even completely remove it." In this way the verdict of insanity almost always ensures a Christian burial. This is a modern change that softens a position held since the Council of Braga in 563.

The first Christian declaration against suicide was made by St. Augustine in his *City of God* in the early fifth century, and it was officially declared a sin in A.D. 452 by the Council of Arles, which reaffirmed Roman slave clauses prohibiting suicide by servants. Some writers suggest this change was prompted by the volume of deliberate acts of martyrdom in the early church, which amounted to about one hundred thousand deaths. Martyrdom was seen as erasing all sin and ensuring a quick passage to heaven, and suicide following baptism was seen as a logical way to avoid sin. There are numerous reports, for example, of mobs of early Christians demanding death sentences at the hands of the Romans, and this form of "assisted death" was so extensive that Clement, bishop of Alexandria, condemned deliberate martyrdom, not because he saw suicide as a sin, but "because the martyr tempted the pagan to commit the act of murder." Also common were deaths resulting from ascetic self-penance.

The Church's elaboration of suicide as a sin came in the thirteenth century with the *Summa Theologica* of Thomas Aquinas, in which he proposed that "life is a gift made to man by God" and, therefore, if only God gave life, then only God could take it away. This view has been officially applied to both murder and suicide.

Would legalized aid in dying be better than the current practice?

The drawbacks of the current practice are obvious. Patients who are suffering are at the mercy of physicians who may not be willing to take risks, and these physicians either refuse to help or often respond in professionally "safe" ways by providing commonly pre-scribed—but less-than-adequate—means to die. In either case, the unintended result can be unwanted involvement by significant oth-ers who, without access to proper drugs are forced to go to great ex-tremes to ensure a loved one's last request to die. This is usually done without counseling and full assessment and discussion of al-ternatives, and can seriously magnify the loss felt by survivors while increasing the legal risks. Assisted death in its current form doesn't provide the safeguards that legislation could require. To protect themselves legally, physicians often avoid talking in-depth with pa-tients or patients' significant others about the decision to die and may fail to seek consulting medical opinions or request evaluations by mental-health professionals. The current system, therefore, does nothing to ensure that all other options are explored, that those re-questing this action have the opportunity to receive counseling, that those who are assisted qualify for it, and those most in need have the option of receiving it.

Would legalization damage the physician-patient relationship?

Evidence suggests that such relationships are currently not always positive. In fact, opponents of legal assisted death point to these problems to explain away public demand for legal change, and argue that the answer is more compassionate care, not assisted death. They further argue that some physicians may find it easier to help patients die than to respond to their therapeutic needs, point-ing to research that shows that physicians are seldom comfortable, intimate, and competent in the management of terminal suffering, and that they frequently fail to respond to the needs of dying pa-tients, but instead often feel an antipathy toward the dying that may arise from their own anxieties about death and feelings of failure about their inability to cure these patients. As a result, physicians may emotionally withdraw from the dying and minimize and under-treat their pain.

This relationship can only improve if assisted death is seen as an extraordinary act that requires extensive dialogue, and is legal-ized with guidelines, safeguards, and a model of clinical practice that opens up this currently private relationship to professional input and scrutiny. It must increase—rather than decrease—the accountability of physicians for (I) meeting the needs of dying patients; (2) communicating with patients and their significant others about their end-of-life concerns; and (3) addressing issues of relentless pain, suffering, and possible depression.

Would legalization undermine public trust in physicians?

Some opponents believe that physician aid-in-dying would undermine public trust in medicine's dedication to preserving the life and health of patients, and that physicians may be more reluctant to invest their energy and time serving patients whom they believe would benefit more from a quick and easy death. In rebuttal, I would argue that one of the reasons behind the public demand for legal change in assisted dying is both patients' desire for more control and the *existing* lack of trust in the ability of physicians to relieve their suffering. If assisted dying were legally available as an extraordinary option under strict rules, and patients knew that if they were suffering their issues of pain and dignity would be addressed, then public fear of the dying process might lessen and trust in physicians might consequently increase.

Wouldn't legalized assisted dying lead to abuse?

Just the opposite. Legal change with strict controls would reduce the current problems of inappropriate aid-in-dying by physicians and significant others, and ensure quality of care for the dying. It could do so by opening up the decision process and requiring documentation and supporting evidence in the case of each death, and also including strong clinical guidelines for physicians to use in determining when to assist a patient to die and criminal penalties for any violation.

What is the difference between assisted dying and euthanasia?

Assisted dying is a model that includes both what has been called physician-assisted "suicide" and voluntary active euthanasia. It suggests a difference in the degree of involvement and behavior. Physician-assisted dying entails making lethal means available to the patient to be used at a time of the patient's own choosing. By con-

trast, voluntary active euthanasia entails the physician taking an active role in carrying out the patient's request, and usually involves
intravenous delivery of a lethal substance. Physician-assisted dying
is seen to be far easier emotionally for the physician than euthanasia as she does not have to cause a death directly; she merely supplies the means for the patient's personal use. My own study of
non-physician-assisted dying bears out this claim; those less directly involved have fewer difficulties overall accepting their actions.
Supporters of physician-assisted dying say that it carries the added
benefit of allowing the patient to determine the time of death and
provides the opportunity for the patient to change his mind up to
the last moment. I'd argue that this possibility similarly exists in cases
of voluntary active euthanasia and may even enable a physician to
discuss topics of motives and options with the patient one last time.

How might the rights of patients to an assisted death be ensured?

Since both the request and provision of aid-in-dying must be voluntary, a list of physicians could be maintained by local patients'
rights groups, the patients' rights advocate in the area, or even by
hospital or hospice social workers. Beyond this, I foresee this role
being taken over by nonprofit organizations like Seattle's Compassion in Dying, or local Hemlock Society chapters or similar organizations that could provide referrals to physicians and counselors
willing to work with patients who potentially qualify to receive aid.
These groups would *not* provide aid-in-dying but would ensure that
patients could be placed in contact with physicians who are not
morally opposed to assisted dying "under every circumstance." In
this way, a patient could begin the qualifying process, but would
not be guaranteed assistance. Such a physician would still be required to follow strict clinical guidelines, such as seeking a consulting opinion from a specialist in the patient's disease and working
with an ethics committee. I do not favor assisted-suicide specialists
or "underground" physician-aid-in-dying. Instead, I believe that
the person best able to determine the validity of a patient's request
is the patient's own physician, who has provided care over time.
This assumes, however, that this physician is adequately trained in
pain control and palliative care. As this is seldom the case, I would

argue that the consulting physician should have these credentials or hospice experience.

How would the disadvantaged be protected?

I would argue that assisted death be considered as an extraordinary act, and that the involvement of hospital social workers, counselors, and hospice could do much to eliminate this threat of abuse. Legal provision should also be made to restrain physicians or anyone else from proposing it as an option to patients. While opponents claim that legalizing assisted dying should not even be considered until we have universal health care, this denies the fact that (1) many patients are currently suffering; (2) plans for universal coverage have been proposed without solution since the early 1970s; (3) both "passive" and active euthanasia in the form of withdrawal or withholding of life-sustaining treatment and "double effect" are widespread and occur without similar concern; and (4) assisted dying is widely practiced without any present controls or guidelines. Any legislation allowing for assisted dying should also require private and public insurers to guarantee payment for other possible options such as hospice and in-home nursing care as well as for end-of-life counseling for the patient and significant others. In the absence of this possibility, other approaches might include tying legislation to increased public funding for community-based residential and home hospice programs or even the drastic act of prohibiting private or public insurers from paying any associated costs of assisted death except for counseling services.

The assumption here is that these populations, for economic reasons, would feel the psychological pressure to choose death over the high cost of end-of-life medical care. This economic argument hasn't been borne out in studies of other behaviors, such as the relationship between income and family size, and it most certainly hasn't yet been shown to exist in end-of-life decision making. It's not as if people would be faced with only the choice of relentless suffering or assisted death. And it's not as if economics is the only factor individuals and families take into consideration in making decisions. Nevertheless, rationing of health care, futility of care, and health care costs are issues that are only now being addressed, and the debate will continue for several years. I envision that assisted death and termination of care will unavoidably be at the center of these issues.

What about surrogate decision making?

I have serious problems with surrogate authority to make *any* termination-of-care or assisted-death decisions without written intent for those no longer competent. Current laws in most states allow withdrawal or withholding of treatment from such patients, in the absence of knowledge of prior intention, at the request of legal surrogates. This implies a current willingness to "allow" patients to die in ways that are *not* voluntary. This can especially be seen in neonatal futility cases involving infants with severe life-threatening abnormalities, which place hospitals—even Catholic hospitals—and physicians in conflict with surrogates desiring continued care for their family members. I am troubled by the entire panorama of this practice and believe that standards need to be established for all futility and end-of-care cases. Moreover, consistency in all surrogacy decisions is necessary whether we're talking about "only allowing"—or actively helping—a patient to die. To place assisted dying in a special category in terms of surrogacy ignores the fact that "allowing to die" and "helping to die" have the same result.

One way out of this dilemma is to err on the side of caution, with assisted-dying legislation excluding the possibility for surrogate decisions—without prior documented indication of desire—until *all* surrogate end-of-life decisions can be resolved in a consistent manner by a special commission. Furthermore, I believe that all such surrogate decisions, regardless of prior documented indication of desire, need to be subject to automatic review by hospital ethics committees. All of this may seem a step backward given current practices in terms of "allowing to die" but, as I've said, perhaps these current practices need to be revisited.

Wouldn't legalized assisted dying lead to involuntary euthanasia?

Much of the opposition to legalized assisted dying is based on the fear that voluntary requests for aid-in-dying would soon move to these surrogate decisions and then to involuntary euthanasia of in-competent patients whom physicians or others felt no longer had any quality of life. As I described earlier, the surrogacy argument seems to bear some weight as court decisions from Quinlan to Cruzan have upheld the request of surrogates to withhold or with-draw life-sustaining treatments when these patients made their atti-tudes known prior to loss of competence. This is the basis of current "living will" provisions. In essence, the courts might even-tually see no difference between "allowing to die" and easing suf-fering by "helping to die" more quickly. In terms of moving to nonvoluntary euthanasia, opponents of assisted death point to both the Netherlands and Nazi Germany as examples to be avoided. These arguments, however, ignore the facts.

In the Netherlands qualified patients can request and receive ei-ther lethal prescriptions or direct euthanasia (lethal injections). Government studies have found that one thousand patients a year are "euthanized" without such a request. What is lost in this argu-ment is that the Dutch make no distinction between passive and ac-tive euthanasia, and that many of these "life-terminating acts without explicit request" (LAWER) result from withholding or withdrawing life-sustaining treatment—a practice that is wide-spread in America. Moreover, many other deaths involved prior discussions between patients and physicians. These LAWER cases have come to public attention only because the Dutch have created a system that allows qualified patients to request and receive assis-tance, and requires physicians to report them. Also ignored is the fact that nonvoluntary euthanasia is quite common in American hospitals but goes unreported as it's often sheltered under the wider umbrella of "double effect," even though in some cases it's obvious that the intention of massive pain relief has indeed been to end life, not just pain. Furthermore, in my own research I uncovered in-stances of physicians also providing family or partners with lethal medications to be used for one who was dying, but who was no longer competent due to AIDS dementia or end-of-life sedation in cancer cases. Although these are all anecdotal reports, they suggest that the slippery slope already exists. Legal controls can do much to make this slope explicit and bring abuses to light.

Opponents of assisted death, who cite the abuses in official programs for euthanasia in Nazi Germany, seem to forget that these were designed from above with the intention from the very beginning of gradually creating a system of genocide rooted in the concept of racial purity. This was *never* voluntary or based on freedom of choice. The true slippery slope in Nazi Germany was the loss of civil liberty and freedoms. By contrast, the current call for legalizing physician-assisted dying is rooted in the concept of freedom of choice for the individual. Totally restricting choice and enforcing a public health model that protects individuals from harming themselves—even in the case of terminal illness—is more dangerous to civil liberty than an approach that provides guarantees of freedom under strict guidelines.

Will legalization mean that physicians will have a duty to assist patients to die?

Some ethicists have argued that what will begin as a right of patients to request aid-in-dying from their physicians under specified conditions will soon become a duty of the physicians. I would counter this by saying that autonomy works for both patients and doctors, and that physicians should never be required to provide such assistance, just as they are not now required to perform other surgical procedures they are morally opposed to, such as abortions. The right to receive, and therefore to perform, abortions has not resulted in such a medical "duty." Very few physicians currently perform abortions, and special clinics and family-planning centers have had to be established to fill this need without, I should add, the strict controls and counseling requirements that I'd recommend in cases of assisted death.

Won't this lead to suicide centers?

At first glance, this would appear inevitable if most physicians refused to provide assistance to dying patients, and with the largest percentage of private hospitals being associated with the Catholic Church. Recent studies, however, show that up to a third of physicians in some areas already admit having provided assistance, and the number appears to be much higher among practitioners treating cancer or AIDS. These same studies have found that as many as half or all physicians say they would be willing to provide aid-in-dying in certain cases if laws were changed. Given these numbers, I doubt there would be a shortage of physicians who'd be willing to help their patients die. Unless confidentiality was guaranteed, however, strict reporting requirements might substantially reduce this number, as not all physicians might be willing to practice under close legal and public scrutiny.

This should not be a problem if at-home hospice programs, critical-care units in hospitals, and skilled nursing facilities agreed to provide aid-in-dying as an extraordinary option when their own efforts at pain control and palliative care failed to relieve suffering. Unlike outpatient abortion clinics I can't envision outpatient "death clinics" that would meet requirements for involvement by primary-care physicians and ethics committees. Instead, I'd suspect that the dying would prefer the current model of privacy in regard to the practice of assisted death: if possible, dying at home while surrounded by loving partners, family members, or friends.

Does assisted dying violate medical tradition?

There is no such thing as a linear medical "tradition" that has been handed down over thousands of years. Each new generation of physicians has reinterpreted this ethos for themselves, influenced by social conditions and technological changes. These shifts especially can be seen in the treatment of the dying. For example, Hippocrates, in *The Arts*, wrote that the physician was to "refuse to treat" those who are overwhelmed by their diseases, realizing that in such cases medicine is powerless. In ancient medicine and until the time of Bacon and Newton, the care of the dying and the hopelessly ill was not considered to be part of a physician's obligation. Indeed, to do so was felt to be immoral. Similarly, physicians who believed a case was hopeless routinely suggested suicide, and often supplied the lethal drugs with which to accomplish it.

Earlier in this century, the ethos of medicine moved swiftly in the direction of prolonging life as a result of advances in medical technology. This technological ability to keep patients alive, even against their will or when they're in persistent vegetative states, has led to numerous court cases and legislation over the past twenty years on behalf of patients' rights. In addition, these legal actions have been followed in the past few years by reversals in hospital policies of just a decade ago regarding the use of cardiopulmonary resuscitation. As a result, do-not-resuscitate (DNR) orders by physicians are becoming commonplace. And though physicians cannot legally "help patients to die," they can—and frequently do—"allow patients to die," even mentally incompetent patients, by withholding and withdrawing life-sustaining treatments, including artificial nutrition and hydration. These various changes clearly show that the ethos of medicine is not something that has remained the same even during the past fifty years. Now the question to be asked is whether the ethos will change further to recognize that more harm may be done by favoring a slow and agonizing death for a patient than by following a patient's desire to alleviate suffering quickly and gently with assistance from a physician.

How is assisted death compatible with biomedical ethics?

The four principles of biomedical ethics include beneficence, nonmaleficence, autonomy, and justice. Beneficence can be understood as the opportunity for a patient to be released from suffering. Nonmaleficence, to do no harm, can be interpreted as doing less harm by not prolonging unnecessary suffering. Autonomy can be seen by respecting the rights, desires, individuality, and personhood of the patient, with final authority for all decisions resting with this person. And justice can reside in equality of care for all terminally ill with availability for both hospice care and aid-in-dying.

Appendix 2

IMPLEMENTING
ASSISTED DYING:
A Brief Proposal

By the end of the next decade, after significant debate and court rulings, assisted dying will undoubtedly be implemented in some jurisdictions as an option in certain cases of irreversible suffering and terminal illness. It will likely include both assistance by lethal prescription and injection. Depending on legislation and court rulings, it eventually may be available to fully competent patients as well as to those who began the decision process and completed advance directives but who are no longer competent at the time of administration. The nature and scope of this practice, of course, will depend on legislation, court rulings, and establishment of clear policies regarding all end-of-life decisions.

Ultimately, implementation will have to balance the needs of patients, families, physicians, and the larger medical community, while safeguarding all parties from wrongful actions. I do not foresee this practice will ever be legally available to terminal or incurably ill patients simply upon request. Instead, I believe it will be reserved for extraordinary cases that fail to respond to efforts at palliative care. Moreover, it should be provided in a way that promotes an ideal of medical intervention that carefully looks at each case and balances a patient's suffering with the principles of beneficence, nonmaleficence, autonomy, and justice.

In light of this, I would make several recommendations for change. First, I would propose that strict guidelines be implemented that parallel those I've specified throughout this book, and notably those in Chapter Eight. Briefly, these would establish criteria for determining which patients should qualify to receive assistance as well as safeguards and guidelines for clinical practice to protect both patients and health-care providers. These would ensure that a patient's suffering is irreversible, that available options for care have been attempted, the patient's motives have been fully explored, depression has been excluded, counseling opportunities have been provided, and issues of rationality and social and family dynamics have been addressed.

Second, I would recommend that changes be made in existing homicide statutes to include provisions with criminal penalties for both assisting in a death and for mercy killing. In this way, laws covering assisted death would be enforceable if the statutory guidelines and safeguards were bypassed. Similarly, mercy killing statutes could cover cases of *nonvoluntary* active euthanasia, where issues of patient competence were involved or where a significant other acts on her own, without a final written request from the patient, and carries out that person's earlier verbally expressed desire to die. In cases where motivation is proven to be altruistic and disinterested, penalties might well be nominal or nonexistent.

Third, I would call for creation of appointed or ad-hoc ethics committees at regional hospitals or through such entities as local medical associations or hospices, that would be charged with overseeing the practice of assisted dying. These committees would receive and review in-depth reports from physicians on each case, advise physicians on difficult cases (in terms of clinical procedures and guidelines, standards of care, and qualification of patients), assess final reports from physicians, and pass on their findings to state medical licensing boards or other governing bodies for data collection purposes. Ethics committees might include such individuals as a local hospice medical director, hospital and hospice social workers and nursing personnel, and others to ensure a balanced perspective. Each case, however, should be handled confidentially to protect patients, significant others, and physicians. This team approach ensures that both the decision-making and assisted-dying process is opened to scrutiny. In addition, these committees could oversee continuing medical education efforts locally on issues involving pain control and end-of-life care.

Fourth, the patient requesting aid-in-dying from his primary-care physician would be immediately referred either to hospice or to a consulting physician trained in hospice care. This would also begin the psycho-social assessment process where the patient would be interviewed about her decision. This takes the responsibility out of the hands of the primary-care physician, ensures that coercion has not occurred, and ascertains that such a decision did not originate at the suggestion of the patient's physician—an act that should be considered a criminal offense. In the case of patients who are hospitalized, this investigative function could be carried out by the hospital social worker, patient advocate, or someone in a similar category. Again, patients in the community might be seen by a hospice social worker or someone similarly charged with performing mental-health assessments but trained in counseling the terminally ill.

In conclusion, a team approach to implementation ensures that a patient has received the best quality of pain management and comfort care available, and that physicians do not have to decide alone, but can share the decision-making responsibilities with other professionals such as nurses, counselors, and social workers. In this way, assisted dying can be transformed from a private act that involves only a patient and physician to one where the full circumstances of a patient's situation is brought into the equation. In fact, hospice itself, with its psycho-social-spiritual emphasis on total caregiving, and the opportunities it provides for emotional counseling and respite for caregivers, makes it a natural entity to provide assisted dying as an extraordinary option for those under its care.

RESOURCES

Suicide Prevention

For information on suicide prevention services in your area look under *suicide prevention, crisis intervention, community services* or *hotline* in your local phone directory.

Suicide Information Hotline
(403) 245-3900

American Association
of Suicidology
4201 Connecticut Ave., NW,
Suite 310
Washington, D.C. 20008
(202) 237-2280

Survivors of Suicide
PO Box 1393
Dayton, OH 45401-1393
(513) 223-4777

D/ART Depression Awareness,
Recovery, and Treatment.
(800) 421-4211

BOOKS ON SUICIDE AND MENTAL HEALTH

Cronkite, Kathy. *On the Edge of Darkness: Conversations about Conquering Depression.* New York: Doubleday, 1994.

Torrey, E. Fuller. *Surviving Schizophrenia: A Manual for Families, Consumers, and Providers.* New York: Harper Perennial, 1995.

Grollman, Earl A. *Suicide: Prevention, Intervention, and Post-Intervention.* Boston: Beacon, 1988.

Mueser, Kim T., and Susan Gingerich. *Coping with Schizophrenia: A Guide for Families.* Oakland, CA: New Harbinger, 1994.

Assisted Dying

For general information on assisted dying, local support group services, counseling, ethics consultation, and education, contact one of the following organizations.

Compassion in Dying
PO Box 75295
Seattle, WA 98125-0295
(206) 624-2775

ERGO!—Euthanasia Research
and Guidance Organization
24829 Norris Lane
Junction City, OR 97448-9559
(503) 998-3285
Internet: ergo@efn.org
World Wide Web Mosaic:
http://www.islandnet.com/
~deathnet

Hemlock Society of Northern
California
870 Market St., Suite 563
San Francisco, CA 94102
(415) 398-9297

Hemlock Society U.S.A.
PO Box 11830
Eugene, OR 97440-4030
(800) 247-7421

Life and Death Consultations
PO Box 570
Mill Valley, CA 94942
(415) 381-4257

Right to Die Society of Canada
PO Box 39018
Victoria, BC V8V 4X8
Canada
(604) 380-1112
Internet: World Wide Web:
rights@islandnet.com

LITERATURE ON METHODS OF ASSISTED DYING

Humphry, Derek. *Final Exit.* New York: Dell, 1993. The original *New York Times* best-seller on how to end your life, which includes a list of lethal drugs. Available in bookstores or mail order through ERGO! Call or E-mail for current price and information.

Humphry, Derek. *Self-deliverance from an end-stage terminal illness by use of the plastic bag.* Junction City, OR: ERGO!, 1993. A four-page foldout with step-by-step information in self-asphyxiation, available only from ERGO! for $5.

Hemlock Society U.S.A. *Drug Dosage Table.* Los Angeles: Hemlock, 1984. The original $3 four-page foldout list of lethal drugs that was the predecessor to *Final Exit.*

Docker, C. G., and C. K. Smith. *Departing Drugs,* 1993. Claimed by its authors to be "the most authoritative guide to humane suicide" methods ever written, this sixty-eight-page booklet is only available to members of right-to-die societies with *proof of membership* for a *minimum of three months* (i.e., mailing labels, membership cards, or personal correspondence).

Docker, C. G., and C. K. Smith. *Beyond Final Exit: New Research in Self-Deliverance for the Terminally Ill,* 1995. This new guide to additional information is also available in the Unites States, Canada, and Great Britain from the same sources but has no membership requirements for purchase. Call the organizations that sell *Departing Drugs* for prices and information.

USA:
Cheryl Smith
PO Box 2422
Eugene, OR 97402
(503) 686-1330
($12)

CANADA:
Right to Die Society of Canada
PO Box 39018 Victoria, BC
V8V 4X8 Canada
(604) 380-1112
email: World Wide Web:
rights@islandnet.com

GREAT BRITAIN:
Voluntary Euthanasia
Society of Scotland
17 Hart Street
Edinburgh EH1 3RN

Scotland
031-556-4404

GERMANY:
Deutsche Gesellschaft für Humanes Sterben
(DGHS)—German Association for Humane Dying
Lange Gasse 2–4
Postfach 1105 29
86030 Augsburg
Germany
0821-502-350
The German-language version, *Selbsterlösung Durch Medikamente,* is available from DGHS, with a twelve-month membership requirement.

BOOKS ON ASSISTED DYING AND EUTHANASIA

Battin, Margaret Pabst. *The Least Worst Death: Essays in Bioethics at the End of Life.* New York: Oxford University Press, 1994.

Burnell, George M. *Final Choices: To Live or to Die in an End of Medical Technology.* New York: Plenum Press, 1993.

Colt, George Howe. *The Enigma of Suicide.* New York: Simon & Schuster, 1991.

Dworkin, Ronald. *Life's Dominion: An Argument about Abortion, Euthanasia, and Individual Freedom.* New York: Alfred A. Knopf, 1993.

Nuland, Sherwin B. *How We Die: Reflections on Life's Final Chapter.* New York: Alfred A. Knopf, 1994.

Quill, Timothy E. *Death and Dignity: Making Choices and Taking Charge.* New York: W. W. Norton, 1993.

Rachels, James. *The End of Life: Euthanasia and Mortality.* New York: Oxford University Press, 1986.

Shavelson, Lonny. *A Chosen Death: The Dying Confront Assisted Suicide.* New York: Simon & Schuster, 1995.

Singer, Peter. *Rethinking Life and Death: The Collapse of Our Traditional Ethics.* New York: St. Martin's Press, 1994.

Walter, James J., and Thomas A. Shannon., eds. *Quality of Life: The New Medical Dilemma.* Mahwah, NJ: Paulist Press, 1990.

Illness and Caregiving

For information on resources for caregivers in your area contact the social services department at your local hospital, or look under the *community services* section of your phone directory.

HOSPICE

Hospice Education Institute
(Hospice Link)
5 Essex Square, PO Box 713
Essex, CT 06426
(800) 331-1620
Connecticut
(203) 767-1620

National Association for Home Care
519 C Street, N.E.
Washington, DC 20002
(202) 547-7424

National Hospice Organization
1901 Moore St., Suite 901
Arlington, VA 22209
(703) 243-5900

BOOKS ON HOSPICE

Stoddard, S. *The Hospice Movement: A Better Way of Caring for the Dying,* updated and expanded. New York: Vintage, 1992.

Zimmerman, J.A. *Hospice: Complete Care for the Terminally Ill.* Baltimore: Urban & Schwartzberg, 1986.

Disease Information and Support Services

AIDS and Cancer Research
Foundation Hotline
(800) 373-4572

Alzheimer's Disease Information
(800) 621-0379

American Self-Help Clearing-
house (support-group
information) (201) 625-7101

Elder Care Locator
(800) 677-1116

Leukemia Society of America
(800) 955-4LSA

National AIDS Network
(800) 342-2437

National Alliance of Breast
Cancer Organizations
(212) 719-0154

National Cancer Center
(800) 4-CANCER

National Coalition of Cancer
Survivorship
(301) 650-8868

Patient Advocates for Advanced
Cancer Treatment
(prostate cancer information)
(616) 453-1477

Social Security and Medicare
Eligibility Information
(800) 772-1213

Y-Me Breast Cancer Support
Organization
(800) 221-2141

Books on Pain Control

Cowles, J. *Pain Relief: How to Say No to Acute, Chronic and Cancer Pain.*
New York: Master Media, 1993.

Johanson, G. A. *Symptom Relief in Terminal Care.* Sonoma County Academic Foundation for Excellence in Medicine, 1992. Available for $35,
plus $3 for shipping and handling. Write SCAF at 3324 Chanate Rd.,
Santa Rosa, CA 95404, or call (707) 527-6223.

Lang, S. S., and R. B. Patt. *You Don't Have to Suffer: A Complete Guide to
Relieving Cancer Pain for Patients and Their Family.* New York: Oxford University Press, 1994.

Books on Caregiving

Baulch, E. M. *Extended Health Care at Home: A Complete and Practical
Guide.* Berkeley: Celestial Arts, 1989.

Callanan, M., and P. Kelley. *Final Gifts: Understanding the Special Awareness, Needs, and Communication of the Dying.* New York: Bantam, 1992.

Detlefs, D., R. Myers, and J. R. Treanor. *1996 Mercer Guide to Social Security and Medicare.* New York: Mercer, 1995.

Duda, D. *Coming Home: A Guide to Dying at Home with Dignity.* Santa Fe: Aurora, 1987.

Lustbader, W., and N. R. Hooyman. *Taking Care of Aging Family Members: A Practical Guide.* New York: Free Press, 1994.

Matthews, J. *Beat the Nursing Home Trap: A Consumer's Guide to Choosing and Financing Long-Term Care.* Berkeley, CA: Nolo Press, 1993.

Oshiro, C., and H. Snyder. *Medicare/Medigap: How to Cut Through Red Tape and Get Complete Medical Coverage.* New York: Consumer Reports, 1994.

Rob, C., with J. Reynolds. *The Caregiver's Guide: Helping Elderly Relations Cope with Health and Safety Problems.* Boston: Houghton Mifflin, 1991.

Books on Healing, Inspiration, and Complementary Medicine

Achtenberg, J., B. Dossey, and L. Kolkmeier. *Rituals of Healing: Using Imagery for Health and Wellness.* New York: Bantam, 1994.

Barasch, M. I. *The Healing Path: The Soul Approach to Illness.* New York: Jeremy P. Tarcher/Putnam, 1993.

Beisser, A. *A Graceful Passage: Notes on the Freedom to Live or Die.* New York: Doubleday, 1990.

Benjamin, H. H., and R. Trubo. *From Victim to Victor.* Los Angeles: Jeremy P. Tarcher, 1987.

Borysenko J., and M. Borysenko. *The Power of the Mind to Heal: Renewing Body, Mind, and Spirit.* Santa Monica, CA: Hay House, 1994.

Chopra, D. *Ageless Body, Timeless Mind.* New York: Harmony, 1993.

De Vita, V. T., S. Hellman, and S. A. Rosenberg, eds. *Cancer: Principles and Practice of Oncology.* Philadephia: Lippincott, 1989.

Dossey, L. *Healing Words: The Power of Prayer and the Practice of Medicine.* New York: Harper, 1993.

Ferrucci, P. *Inevitable Grace.* Los Angeles: Jeremy P. Tarcher, 1990.

Frank, A. *At the Will of the Body.* Boston: Houghton Mifflin, 1991.

Frankl, V. E. *Man's Search for Meaning: An Introduction to Logotherapy.* New York: Simon & Schuster, 1984.

Hanh, T. N. *Peace Is Every Step: The Path of Mindfulness in Everyday Life.* New York: Bantam, 1991.

Hirshberg, C., and M. I. Barasch. *Remarkable Recovery: What Extraordinary Healings Tell Us About Getting Well and Staying Well.* New York: Riverhead, 1995.

Horowitz, L. *Taking Charge of Your Medical Fate.* New York: Random House, 1988.

Jampolsky, J. *Love Is Letting Go of Fear.* Berkeley: CA: Celestial Arts, 1979.

Kornfield, J. *A Path with Heart: A Guide Through the Perils and Promises of Spiritual Life.* New York: Bantam, 1993.

Lerner, M. *Choices in Healing: Integrating the Best of Conventional and Complementary Approaches to Cancer.* Cambridge, MA: MIT Press, 1994.

Levine, S. *Meetings at the Edge.* New York: Anchor, 1982.

———.*Who Dies?* New York: Anchor, 1982.

Love, S. *Dr. Susan Love's Breast Book.* Menlo Park, NJ: Addison-Wesley, 1990.

Melzack, R., and P. Wall. *The Challenge of Pain.* New York: Penguin, 1988.

Morra, M., and E. Potts. *Choices: A Cancer Sourcebook.* New York: Avon, 1994.

Naparsteck, B. *Staying Well with Guided Imagery.* New York: Warner Books, 1994.

Pelletier, K. R. *Sound Body, Sound Mind: A New Model for Lifelong Health.* New York: Simon & Schuster, 1994.

Siegel, B. *Love, Medicine & Miracles: Lessons Learned About Self-Healing from a Surgeon's Experience with Exceptional Patients.* New York: Harper Perennial, 1990.

Zinn, J. K. *Full Catastrophe Living: Using the Power of Your Body and Mind to Face Stress, Pain, and Illness.* New York: Delacorte Press, 1990.

Grief and Bereavement

For bereavement services in your area look under *crisis intervention,* or *community services* in your local phone directory. Suicide prevention centers also frequently provide bereavement counseling and outreach.

Accord
1941 Bishop Lane, Suite 202
Louisville, KY 40218
(800) 346-3087

The Compassionate Friends
PO Box 3696
Oak Brook, IL 60522
(708) 990-0010

BOOKS ON GRIEF AND BEREAVEMENT

Akner, L. F., with Whitney, C. *How to Survive the Loss of a Parent: A Guide for Adults.* New York: William Morrow, 1993.

Caine, L. *Widow.* New York: Bantam, 1981.

Froman, P. K. *After You Say Goodbye: When Someone You Love Dies of AIDS.* San Francisco: Chronicle, 1992.

Hunter, R. L. *Helping When It Hurts.* Minneapolis: Fortress Press, 1985.

Kalish, R. *Death, Grief, and Caring Relationships.* Pacific Grove, CA: Brooks/Cole, 1985.

Moffet, M. J. *In the Midst of Winter: Selections from the Literature of Mourning.* New York: Vintage, 1982.

Neeld, E. H. *Seven Choices: Taking the Steps to New Life After Losing Someone You Love.* New York: Delta, 1990.

Parkes, C. M. *Bereavement.* Madison, CT: International Universities Press, 1972.

Raphael, B. *The Anatomy of Bereavement.* New York: Basic Books, 1986.

Staudacher, C. *Men & Grief: A Guide for Men.* Oakland, CA: New Harbinger, 1991.

Storr, A. *Solitude.* New York: Ballantine, 1988.

Tatelbaum, J. *The Courage to Grieve.* New York: Harper & Row, 1980.

Vale, E. *A Personal Guide to Living with Loss.* New York: John Wiley & Sons, 1982.

Viorst, Judith. *Necessary Losses.* New York: Simon & Schuster, 1986.

Worden, W. *Grief Counseling and Grief Therapy.* New York: Springer, 1982.

BOOKS ON DEATH AND DYING

Anderson, P. *Affairs in Order.* New York: Macmillan, 1991.

Carlsen, L. *Caring for Your Own Dead.* Upper Access Publishers, 1987.

Eadie, B. *Embraced by the Light.* Placerville, CA: Goldleaf Press, 1993.

Kübler-Ross, E. *Living with Death and Dying.* New York: Macmillan, 1981.

———. *On Death and Dying.* New York: Macmillan, 1969.

———. *Questions and Answers on Death and Dying.* New York: Macmillan, 1974.

Levine, S. *Healing into Life and Death.* New York: Doubleday, 1989.

———. *Who Dies?* New York: Anchor/Doubleday, 1989.

Morse, M., and P. Perry. *Transformed by the Light.* New York: Vintage, 1992.

Ring, K. *Heading Toward Omega: In Search of the Meaning of the Near-Death Experience.* New York: William Morrow, 1985.

Rinpoche, S. *The Tibetan Book of Living and Dying.* HarperSanFrancisco, 1992.

NOTES

INTRODUCTION

xviii   ... *a three-year-research project:* I began my research in mid-1991 by word of mouth in the San Francisco Bay area, initially interviewing contacts made through the local Hemlock Society chapter and with the help of several health-care professionals in hospice and terminal care. I used preliminary interviews to focus my research and refine my questions and then expanded my project by announcing it at Hemlock Society events, at presentations before medical groups, and then by publishing a call for interviews in the Hemlock Society of Northern California's newsletter, *Northern California Update.* In some cases, Hemlock Society members in the region as well as my own support group members took it upon themselves to act as intermediaries and took the project into other cancer, AIDS, and grief support groups, and to the streets. Some informed me of an event worthy of study and then agreed to ask the individual involved to contact me.

In 1992, I put out my first call for national interviews by publishing project announcements in several issues of the National Hemlock Society's *Hemlock Quarterly,* which went to more than 50,000 members. I was soon rewarded with phone calls and letters that became too numerous to respond to with full interviews.

I made my first research trip to Great Britain and Europe in 1992 and followed up by conducting interviews across Great Britain in 1993, with additional visits to Great Britain and Germany in 1994. While I worked mostly alone, in Great Britain I received warm support and assistance from the Voluntary Euthanasia Society (VES) in London and the Voluntary Euthanasia Society of Scotland (VESS) in Edinburgh. Both of these organizations were also helpful by announcing my project in their own newsletters.

In most instances, I used initial telephone calls to screen potential interviewees and to then set up a time for longer interviews either by phone or in person. Whenever possible, I met with my interviewees in person, with cases often involving both telephone and in-person contacts. Where multiple parties were involved I conducted interviews separately. In all cases, I used a "natural history" approach and allowed each person to first tell me his or her story. I then followed up with a set of open-ended questions covering: relationships among the parties involved, the decision-making process, discussions prior to the assisted death, alternatives considered, motives for dying and for helping, expectations about the experience, methods of assisted death, type and source of drugs, the nature and setting of the death, the "official" cause of death, knowledge among friends and family about the actual cause of death, and both the initial and delayed effects of participation.

These interviews, numbering 160, lasted anywhere from under an hour to as long as seven hours, over multiple meetings. Where possible, interviews were tape-recorded.

To protect my sources, I immediately applied pseudonyms to each case and erased all tape-recordings after transcription. At the end of the project, I also destroyed all written records bearing names, phone numbers, return addresses, or other indicators of identity. In nearly every case, except where I personally knew participants, I offered to conduct interviews in public locations or in the homes of third parties. In the case of interviews conducted in the Bay Area, I often used my own home or office locations. Regardless of my guarantees of privacy, many of my interviewees willingly took me into their lives. One man even supplied me with several hours of videotape that showed interviews with his partner over a two-year period up to and including the day of his partner's death. Whenever possible, I also interviewed other parties involved in these deaths.

I then used a qualitative approach to data analysis, involving a form of content analysis, allowing me to create categories and cross-index my findings. Due to the nature of this book, it has made little sense to conduct quantitative analysis on the data at this time. Although my respondents were self-selected and obtained mostly by contacts from right-to-die groups, fewer than half were members of such organizations. And many who were members joined only *after* they had assisted in the deaths of partners, family members, or friends. I am convinced that my research subjects are representative and that their reports typify the experience of assisted death in the United States, Great Britain, and Canada.

xviii   . . . *interviews with 160 participants in some 140 assisted deaths:* These figures do not include cases where the individual details were lacking or could not be accurately described. Nor do they include the substantiated case of one woman who claimed being present at some thirty assisted deaths, of which she directly assisted in twenty. It further does not include cases where initial inteviews could not be completed. And only in a small number of cases did I feel comfortable in mixing business with research or turning crisis calls or visits to the Hemlock office into interviews. Nevertheless, what I've been told over the years has obviously made its way into this book.

Of the total number of deaths studied, only 15 were officially listed as suicides. The others were covered up by families and friends, often with the support of physicians who—sometimes willingly, other times hesitantly—agreed to sign death certificates claiming "natural" causes. In this regard, only five interviewees were ever questioned by officials about possible involvement in an assisted death. Three of these were "confessions" immediately after the death. For example, I interviewed a California man only after he was exonerated by a Michigan jury on charges of helping his wife die by use of a plastic bag. Similarly, a man from Texas and I discussed his case only after he completed his two-year probation there for assisting in his mother's death. In a third case, that of a man from Connecticut, his subsequent "full confession" in a magazine article two years after my interview resulted in his trial and conviction. In the two remaining cases, both involving older women, coroners asked them if they had in any way assisted in their husbands' deaths. After gentle prodding, but adamant denials, no other questions were asked.

Chapter 1. DEATH AND DISCONTENT

5 ... *as many as a third of all doctors have assisted:* See B. J. Ward and P. A. Tate, "Attitudes Among NHS Doctors to Requests for Euthanasia," *British Medical Journal,* 308 (1994): 1332–34; H. Kuhse and P. Singer, "Doctors' Practices and Attitudes Regarding Voluntary Euthanasia," *Medical Journal of Australia,* 148 (1988): 623–27; P. Baume and E. O'Malley, "Euthanasia: Attitudes and Practices of Medical Practitioners," *Medical Journal of Australia,* 161 (July 18, 1994): 137–64; and L. R. Slome, *Physicians' Attitudes Toward Assisted Suicide in Acquired Immunodeficiency Syndrome,* doctoral dissertation (California School of Professional Psychology, 1990).

5 ... *often with the unwitting help of doctors:* In slightly more than half of my sample, the drugs an individual used (either entirely or in combination with other means) to end his or her life were provided by physicians to the patient or to the patient's significant other for purposes of symptom management.

5 ... *suffering from a range of terminal and irreversible conditions:* This has become obvious to me from my own work with the dying, from the cases in my study, and is also apparent in looking at the list of "patients" that Dr. Jack Kevorkian has assisted over the past several years. For a list of the first twenty cases involving Kevorkian see: J. M. Hoefler, *Deathright: Culture, Medicine, Politics, and the Right to Die* (Boulder, CO: Crestview Press, 1994).

5 ... *studies from New York City have found:* This study, by Dr. Peter Marzuk of Cornell University Medical College in conjunction with the Office of the Chief Medical Examiner of New York City, was first reported in 1988. See, for

example, P. Marzuk, et al., "Increased Risk of Suicide in Persons with AIDS," *Journal of the American Medical Association*, 259 (1988): 1333–37.

5 ... *most assisted deaths go undiscovered:* See, for example, P. Cotten, "Rational Suicide: No Longer 'Crazy'?" *Journal of the American Medical Association*, 270 (1993): 797.

8 ... *whether there have been real statistical gains:* For an excellent brief discussion of this debate see M. Lerner, *Choices in Healing: Integrating the Best of Conventional and Complementary Approaches to Cancer*, (Cambridge, MA: MIT Press, 1994): 47–55.

9 *"These interventions are provided":* Raffin, T. "Withholding and Withdrwing Life Support." *Hospital Practice*, March 15, 1991: 133–55.

9 ... *decision concerning Karen Ann Quinlan in 1976:* For a brief discussion of the battle surrounding the Quinlan case, see P. Singer's *Rethinking Life and Death: The Collapse of Our Traditional Ethics.* (New York: St. Martin's Press, 1994).

10 P. Ariès, *The Hour of Our Death.* (New York: Vintage, 1982): 586–88.

Chapter 2. Guidelines for Self-Exploration

16 *"Cancer pain is widely under-treated":* Quoting a report from the Memorial Sloan-Kettering Cancer Center, a California Medical Association position paper on end-of-life care stated that "about two cancer patients per thousand will have an abusive pattern of analgesic use" (*Care at the End of Life.* San Francisco: California Medical Association, 1993).

16 *"it can be effectively controlled":* Researchers have also found that pain control for those with advanced cancer not only increases comfort but may improve chances for recovery by improving appetite and nutrition. In some instances, however, patients have also been to blame when, for cultural or psychological reasons, they refused pain medications in the belief that putting up with pain is sometimes viewed as an admirable trait. For an excellent discussion of pain-control issues, see J. Cowles, *Pain Relief: How to Say No to Acute, Chronic and Cancer Pain.* (New York: MasterMedia, 1993).

18 ... *analyzed euthanasia in the Netherlands:* P. J. Van der Maas, J. J. M. van Delden, and L. Pijnenborg. "Euthanasia and Other Medical Decisions Concerning the End of Life: An Investigation Performed Upon Request of the Commission of Inquiry into the Medical Practice Concerning Euthanasia." (*Health Policy Monographs*, vol. 2. Amsterdam: Elsevier, 1992).

34 ... *your presence is burdensome:* This concern over "being a burden" is not at all a rare phenomenon. For example, a 1992 national opinion survey, conducted on behalf of *The Boston Globe* and the Harvard School of Public Health found that nearly half of those who would consider alternatives to end their lives claimed that their motivation for doing so was based on this concern. See R. J.

Blendon, U. Szalay, and R. A. Knox, "Should Physicians Aid Their Patients in Dying?" *Journal of the American Medical Association*, 267(19): 2658–62.

Chapter 4. Preparing for the Final Decision

82   *"We all have the right to kill ourselves":* This comment was made by Kathi Hamlon, of the International Anti-Euthanasia Task Force, on San Francisco KQED's program *Face to Face* in June 1994.

84   *An earlier book:* According to Humphry in a personal discussion, "*Let Me Die Before I Wake* has sold more than 150,000 copies since 1981 and was crucial in providing financial support to the Hemlock Society during its first several years of operation." It was early limited access to this book and to similar information that made membership in Hemlock so appealing.

84   Drug Dosage Table: Derek Humphry has informed me that this fold-out reprint, which first sold for $2, "brought in a steady $2,000 a month to Hemlock in the first two years" after it was printed.

85   *. . . they'll be sent lists of . . . drugs:* Many believe the Hemlock Society is a source for much more than information. Calls come in daily from people not only seeking "how to" information but looking for drugs. Many—including some members—assume that perks of membership also include the "magic pill," referrals to physicians who will help them, or even access to Hemlock "hit squads" who'll come to their home to "do it." One anonymous caller to the San Francisco office, for example, explained that "a physician friend back east" had come through and mailed him thirty Seconals, but "the package came apart in the mail and only eighteen were left intact." He got enraged when he was told that the office didn't provide drugs, and said, "What am I supposed to do now? You were my last chance; I can't get out of bed anymore." A similar caller once responded with a mixture of disappointment and anger, saying, "If you can't help, then what good is my membership anyway?"

88   *The case of "Diane":* T. Quill, "Death and Dignity: A Case of Individualized Decision-Making," *The New England Journal of Medicine*, 324 (1991): 691–94.

93   *. . . 23 percent "were likely to grant":* See the doctoral dissertation by L. R. Slome, *Physicians' Attitudes Toward Assisted Suicide in Acquired Immunodeficiency Syndrome* (California School of Professional Psychology, 1990).

93   *. . . nearly half had been asked:* An in-depth report of this practice by National Health Service physicians in a section of London was reported by B.J. Ward and P.A. Tate, "Attitudes Among NHS Doctors to Requests for Euthanasia," *British Medical Journal*, 308 (1994): 1332–34.

95   *"The majority of cancer patients":* Gazette Mountain Life, January 4, 1994.

104   *"Roughly half of the barbiturates"*: D. Humphry, *Final Exit* (New York: Carol Publishing, 1991): 84–85.

Chapter 5. WHEN THINGS GO WRONG

138   *"I am not a pillow for hire"*: L. Olszewski, "One Man's Choice," *San Francisco Chronicle*, October 19, 1992.

Chapter 6. RESOLUTION, RITUAL AND THE GOOD DEATH

166   *Two years after telling me:* The article, entitled "Endgame," appeared in the August 1994 issue of *Connecticut* magazine. The reporter was Karon Haller.

180   *"I could have had the usual wake"*: L. Olszewski, "One Man's Choice," *San Francisco Chronicle*, October 19, 1992.

181   *The following Friday evening:* S. Persky, "Preserving Dignity in the Face of Death," *Vancouver Sun*, September 9, 1990.

186   *"family members can often use"*: "Statement of the National Hospice Organization Opposing the Legalization of Euthanasia and Assisted Suicide," Arlington, VA: National Hospice Organization, November 8, 1990.

Chapter 7. DECIDING TO HELP ANOTHER DIE

209   *... numbness to sorrow:* These physical symptoms have been found by various researchers ranging from Colin Murray Parkes to William Worden.

212   *... either three or four distinct phases:* These stages, with subtle differences, have been used by various writers to describe the emotional paths for both grieving and dying processes. Colin Murray Parkes, in his book *Bereavement* (Tavistock, 1972), for example, listed these stages as "numbness, pining, depression, and recovery," while Elisabeth Kübler-Ross, in her book *On Death and Dying* (New York: Macmillan, 1969), has described the stages of dying to include "denial, anger, depression, and acceptance." Her work has similarly been applied to grief. Others have claimed that there are but three stages, but regardless of the number, they should be seen as descriptive and not prescriptive. Knowing that they exist is helpful, but your own grief is special and will follow its own path.

215   In *Grief Counseling:* W. Worden, *Grief Counseling* (New York: Springer, 1982).

Chapter 8. Helping a Patient Die

223 ... *if you're grappling with such a decision:* At the present time, the only place to turn are to articles in medical journals that have appeared over the past few years. Perhaps the best of these is an excellent, well-publicized, article by T. E. Quill, C. K. Cassel, and D. E Meier. "Care of the Hopelessly Ill: Potential Clinical Criteria for Physician-Assisted Suicide," *The New England Journal of Medicine,* 327 (1992): 1380–84. See also F. Miller et al., "Sounding Board: Regulating Physician-Assisted Death," *The New England Journal of Medicine* 119 (July 14, 1994).

223 ... *relationship between a physician and an incurably ill patient:* If studies from the Netherlands are reflective in any way of practices in other countries, then those physicians who assist their patients usually consider several of these factors. For a clear idea of the current state of euthanasia and assisted suicide in the Netherlands, see: P. J. Van der Maas, J. J. M. van Delden, and L. Pijnenborg. "Euthanasia and Other Medical Decisions Concerning the End of Life: An Investigation Performed upon Request of the Commission of Inquiry into the Medical Practice Concerning Euthanasia," *Health Policy Monographs,* Vol. 2. (Amsterdam: Elsevier, 1992); and J. J. M. van Delden, L. Pijnenborg, and P. J. Van der Maas, "The Remmelink Study: Two Years Later," *Hastings Center Report,* 23 (November–December 1993) 6:24. For an excellent discussion, see also P. Singer, *Rethinking Life and Death: The Collapse of Our Traditional Ethics.* (New York: St. Martin's Press, 1994).

227 ... *has lost his medical license:* Only one physician—Dr. Jack Kevorkian—has lost his medical license in recent years as a result of assisting in the death of a patient. This action by medical licensing boards in Michigan and California was probably a result of the risk he posed to the image of the medical profession by his numerous, highly publicized actions, which were not rooted in a typical physician/patient relationship. As a pathologist, who only saw patients for the purpose of ending their lives, Dr. Kevorkian lacked the clinician's ability to provide alternative treatments to keep them alive. Moreover, in helping them die, he did not prescribe lethal doses of medications—the more common method other physicians have used for this purpose. Instead, Dr. Kevorkian has seemed more interested in developing and using innovative and sometimes bizarre technologies for death (i.e., his "suicide" machines for lethal injection, and carbon monoxide canisters for asphyxiation).

Appendix 1. Questions and Answers

247 *Studies of suicide stress:* For an interesting debate on this issue, see: P. Cotton, "Rational Suicide: No Longer 'Crazy'?" *Journal of the American Medical Association,* 270 (August 18, 1993), 7:797; J. Martsberger, "What I Think About

Rational Suicide," *Newslink* (Fall 1992): 6; and D. Mayo, "Rational Suicide Revisited: Can We Find a Common Ground," *Newslink* (Spring 1993): 6–7.

247 . . . *receiving aid-in-dying:* See, for example, G. A. Larue, *Euthanasia and Religion* (Los Angeles: Hemlock Society, 1985).

248 *The first Christian declaration:* For an excellent historical review on Christian attitudes toward suicide and euthanasia, see G. Colt, *The Enigma of Suicide* (New York: Simon & Schuster, 1991).

248 *"because the martyr tempted the pagan":* Eusebius, *The History of the Church from Christ to Constantine,* trans. G. A. Williamson, (New York: New York University Press, 1966); and K. Menninger, *Man Against Himself* (New York: Harvest/Harcourt, Brace & World, 1938).

249 . . . *physicians are seldom comfortable:* S. N. Miles, "Physicians and Their Patients' Suicides," *Journal of the American Medical Association,* 271 (June 8, 1994), 22: 1786–88; "Guidelines on the Termination of Life-Sustaining Treatment and the Care of the Dying," *A Report by the Hastings Center* (Briarcliff Manor, NY: Hastings Center, 1987).

249 . . . *they frequently fail to respond:* For an excellent discussion of the severity of this issue, see: J. Cowles, *Pain Relief: How to Say No to Acute, Chronic, & Cancer Pain!* (New York: MasterMedia, 1993. Also see: "Acute Pain Management: Operative or Medical Procedures and Trauma," *Clinical Practice Guideline* (Washington, D.C.: Agency for Health-Care Policy and Research, February 1992).

250 . . . *patients' desire for more control:* L. Kass, "Neither Love Nor Money: Why Doctors Must Not Kill," *Public Interest,* 94 (1989): 25–46.

254 . . . *lethal prescriptions or direct euthanasia:* P. J. van der Maas, et al., "Euthanasia and Other Medical Decisions Concerning the End of Life," *The Lancet,* 338 (September 14, 1991): 669–74; G. van der Wal, and R.J. Dillmann, "Euthanasia in the Netherlands," *British Medical Journal,* 308 (May 21 1994).

254 . . . *one thousand patients a year meet death:* For a discussion on these practices, see: P. Singer, *Rethinking Life and Death: The Collapse of Our Traditional Ethics* (New York: St. Martin's Press, 1994): 151–56; and M. P. Battin, *The Least Worse Death: Essays in Bioethics at the End of Life* (New York: Oxford University Press, 1994).

255 . . . *genocide rooted in the concept of racial purity:* L. Alexander, "Medical Science Under Dictatorship," *New England Journal of Medicine.* 241 (1949): 39–47; R. J. Lifton, *Nazi Doctors: Medical Killing and the Psychology of Genocide* (New York: Basic Books, 1986).

256 . . . *physicians who believed a case was hopeless:* D. W. Amundsen, "The Physician's Obligation to Prolong Life: A Medical Duty Without Classical Roots," *Hastings Center Report,* 8 (1978), 4:23–31.

257 ... *has led to numerous court cases:* S. Wanzer et al., "The Physician's Responsibility toward Hopelessly Ill Patients: A Second Look," *The New England Journal of Medicine,* 320 (March 30, 1989): 844–49.

257 ... *do-not-resuscitate (DNR) orders by physicians:* Council on Ethical and Judicial Affairs, American Medical Association, "Guidelines for the Appropriate Use of Do-Not-Resuscitate Orders," *Journal of the American Medical Association,* 265 (April 10, 1991): 1868.

ABOUT THE AUTHOR

STEPHEN JAMISON, PH.D., directs Life and Death Consultations, a bioethics education program, and facilitates public workshops in the area of life and death decision making. He is a social psychologist and a leading national spokesperson on assisted dying, and is called upon frequently to discuss this topic. He completed his doctoral studies at the University of California at Davis, where he taught courses in death and dying for several years and was assistant director of the university's Public Service Research Program. Formerly a regional director for the Hemlock Society U.S.A. and president of the Mental Health Association of Marin County, he has served as a research consultant on numerous national projects. Stephen Jamison lives in Mill Valley, California, and has two teenage children. He is currently engaged in research on his next book, *Communities for Living and Dying*.